Salesforce Sales Cloud – An Implementation Handbook

A practical guide from design to deployment for driving success in sales

Kerry Townsend

Salesforce Sales Cloud – An Implementation Handbook

Group Product Manager: Aaron Tanna
Publishing Product Manager: Uzma Sheerin
Associate Project Manager: Deeksha Thakkar
Project Manager: Prajakta Naik
Senior Editor: Esha Banerjee
Technical Editor: Jubit Pincy
Copy Editor: Safis Editing
Proofreader: Esha Banerjee
Indexer: Tejal Soni
Production Designer: Jyoti Kadam
DevRel Marketing Coordinators: Deepak Kumar and Mayank Singh

First published: April 2024

Production reference: 2300724

Published by Packt Publishing Ltd.
Grosvenor House
11 St Paul's Square
Birmingham
B3 1RB, UK

ISBN 978-1-80461-964-3

www.packtpub.com

The opportunity to write this book coincided with a particularly difficult time and required a considerable time investment. I would like to thank my mum for her unwavering support and belief. Without her, I would not be me, this and all my achievements are as much hers as they are mine.

I would also like to thank Paul Battisson, who helped me believe I could achieve this long-term goal of being published and made sure it happened for me.

I would also like to thank Andrew Hart, my technical reviewer whose confidence in me kept me going through the difficult times.

Contributors

About the author

Kerry Townsend is a Salesforce specialist, working with the platform since 2005 – first as a user, then as a solo Admin. She moved over to consulting in 2010, initially at boutiques, as a global systems integrator, and more recently, returning to working for herself. She has refined her skills while delivering a broad range of Salesforce solutions using multiple clouds, predominantly Sales and Marketing Cloud, for small to enterprise-size businesses.

She has 16 Salesforce certifications and has been recognized as a Salesforce MVP since 2018. She is passionate about enabling others and is a Salesforce community conference and Trailblazer community's group leader. She is also a regular speaker at Salesforce conferences across the globe, including Dreamforce.

About the reviewer

Andrew Hart has worked in the CRM space for 25 years, with over 10 years of experience in Salesforce. He has been associated with a wide range of challenging projects across many industries and geographies. He is highly certified in multiple ecosystems and was the 202nd person to achieve the Salesforce Certified Technical Architect credential.

He currently leads the Services team at Own Company, following spells at Salesforce, Oracle, Accenture, and IBM where he was a platform architect, helping the biggest and some of the most complex customers get value from their CRM investments.

He can be contacted at `andrew.hart@btinternet.com`.

I would like to thank my family for their support in everything I do. But mostly I want to thank Kerry for letting me work with her on this book. Spending time with her and pushing ideas back and forth was as valuable to me, as I hope it was to her.

-Andrew Hart

Table of Contents

3

Design and Build: The Core Sales Process   53

4

Design and Build: The Lead Generation Process   97

5

Design and Build: Sales User Productivity   135

Part 2: Preparing to Release

6

Bringing Data into Sales Cloud

7

Getting Sign-Off

8

Executing Testing   217

9

Executing Training   233

10

Deployment Planning   245

Part 3: Beyond the Fundamentals

11

12

13

Common System Integrations   297

14

Extending with the AppExchange   315

Preface

The *Salesforce Sales Cloud – An Implementation Handbook* is a practical guide on how to design and deliver Sales Cloud solutions. Concepts and functionality related to Sales Cloud are presented and explained in the context of the software delivery lifecycle to illustrate when and how solution decisions are made. Tips, pitfalls, and examples are given to provide enough information to make decisions for their use case without being overwhelming. The book is beneficial for those who are new to Sales Cloud and software delivery and also for those want to gain an insight into the different aspects of Sales Cloud.

Your journey in this book will start with how to set yourself and your Sales Cloud implementation up for success by having clear alignment with company goals, being clear on the scope of the required solution, and having detailed, documented, and confirmed processes and requirements. These foundational elements can often be rushed and overlooked because of a desire to get hands-on straight away and start building your Sales Cloud implementation, but this can be the root of many implementation delays or failures.

The book guides you through how to engage with stakeholders, how to gather requirements for the system, describes the out-of-the-box functionality, and goes on to describe how you approach and deliver the build, test, and release phases of your Sales Cloud implementation.

Furthermore, this book covers how to extend your solution beyond the out-of-the-box Sales Cloud functionality. By the end of this book, readers will have the confidence to start their first Sales Cloud implementation. They will understand all the components that are required to deliver a successful solution. They will be able to make choices that are appropriate for their use case.

Who this book is for

If you are a newly appointed or certified Admin, a consultant new to Sales Cloud, or a stakeholder in a Sales Cloud implementation, this book will give you the insights that will set you up for success. Admins, Consultants, or Business Analysts already familiar with the Salesforce Customer 360 platform will learn how and when to design and build Sales Cloud functionality to solve business challenges.

This book is a practical companion that the reader can follow, or dip in and out of, to guide them in building Sales Cloud implementations. It teaches the technology options available so the reader can make appropriate choices for their use case. It is born of the lessons learned and successes earned by an enthusiastic, accidental admin who transitioned into an experienced consultant. As it is written by and for people without a formal technology education, this book distills the lessons learned over projects. It provides pragmatic, practical advice and tools.

What this book covers

Chapter 1, Preparing for Success, outlines the foundations for the success of any Sales Cloud implementation and how you can ensure success on your project.

Chapter 2, Defining the Approach, walks you through the important upfront decisions that define how you approach the delivery of your implementation. It introduces the Salesforce Application Lifecycle and outlines your development methodology, testing, development environment, and change management options, allowing you to shape the delivery of your implementation as you need.

Chapter 3, Design and Build: The Core Sales Process, focuses on how to gather requirements and design a Sales Cloud Solution that enables your organization's core sales process. It starts by introducing some common sales frameworks to give you the language and understanding to be able to collaborate with sales stakeholders. It moves on to how to gather the details required and then we step through the data structure that is available in Sales Cloud and what it is designed for.

Chapter 4, Design and Build: The Lead Generation Process, focuses on the process before the core sales process and how the leads are managed. Again, we review common frameworks, gathering requirements and the capability available in Sales Cloud.

Chapter 5, Design and Build: Sales User Productivity, explains all the Sales Cloud functionality that is available to increase your sales team's productivity so you can select what is appropriate for your use case.

Chapter 6, Bringing Data into Sales Cloud, guides you through how you load data into Sales Cloud and how you go about planning your implementation data migration.

Chapter 7, Getting Sign-Off, explains why sign-off checkpoints play a critical role in a successful implementation and ensuring you take your stakeholders with you.

Chapter 8, Executing Testing, builds on the testing planning that was discussed in *Chapter 2, Defining the Approach*. It walks you through the practical considerations so you can feel confident in executing testing.

Chapter 9, Executing Training, also builds on the training planning that was discussed in *Chapter 2, Defining the Approach*. It provides you with practical considerations so you can feel confident in executing pre-go-live user training.

Chapter 10, Deployment Planning, explores how to approach deploying the functionality that you have built for your stakeholders in a way that minimizes the disruption to them.

Chapter 11, Territory Management, reviews the capability Sales Cloud has for modeling more complex people structures.

Chapter 12, Modeling Additional Processes with Sales Cloud, shows you how you can go further with the standard functionality or extend it to capture information and support processes that are bespoke to your organization.

Chapter 13, Common System Integrations, explores the types of systems that are commonly integrated with Sales Cloud and reviews the considerations and ways these can be approached.

Chapter 14, Extending with the AppExchange, guides you through how you can deliver system requirements by adding third-party applications that tightly integrate with Sales Cloud. We start by considering the paradigm of *buy vs build* and then, we move on to how you can approach gathering information and selecting an appropriate tool.

To get the most out of this book

A good working knowledge of your organization's sales process and the organization's goals for the Salesforce Customer 360 platform will help you get the most out of this book.

All the guidance in this book assumes that your Edition of Salesforce is either Enterprise or above (Performance or Unlimited). Essentials and Professional Edition do not have all the capabilities in Sales Cloud. To carry out any prototyping or development, you will need to have access to a Sandbox, Developer org or Trailhead org with System Administrator permissions, Modify All Data, and Customize Application.

Suggestions will be made on what tools you need in the *Supporting tools and information* section of each chapter however always considering use the tools available in your organization first. This will make it easier to collaborate with colleague, including senior stakeholders.

Download hi-resolution images

Some of the images in this title are presented for contextual purposes, and the readability of the graphic is not crucial to the discussion. If you wish to view these images in greater detail you can download them from our free graphic bundle: `https://packt.link/gbp/9781804619643`.

Conventions used

There are a number of text conventions used throughout this book.

Bold: Indicates a new term, an important word, or words that you see onscreen. For instance, words in menus or dialog boxes appear in **bold**. Here is an example: "To enable Territory Management, enter Territory Settings in the **Quick Find** search or go to **Setup** > **Feature Settings** > **Sales** > **Territories** > **Territory Settings**."

> **Tips or important notes**
> Appear like this.

Get in touch

Feedback from our readers is always welcome.

General feedback: If you have questions about any aspect of this book, email us at customercare@packtpub.com and mention the book title in the subject of your message.

Errata: Although we have taken every care to ensure the accuracy of our content, mistakes do happen. If you have found a mistake in this book, we would be grateful if you would report this to us. Please visit www.packtpub.com/support/errata and fill in the form.

Piracy: If you come across any illegal copies of our works in any form on the internet, we would be grateful if you would provide us with the location address or website name. Please contact us at copyright@packtpub.com with a link to the material.

If you are interested in becoming an author: If there is a topic that you have expertise in and you are interested in either writing or contributing to a book, please visit authors.packtpub.com.

Share Your Thoughts

Once you've read *Salesforce Sales Cloud - An Implementation Handbook*, we'd love to hear your thoughts! Scan the QR code below to go straight to the Amazon review page for this book and share your feedback.

https://packt.link/r/1-804-61964-7

Your review is important to us and the tech community and will help us make sure we're delivering excellent quality content.

Download a free PDF copy of this book

Thanks for purchasing this book!

Do you like to read on the go but are unable to carry your print books everywhere?

Is your eBook purchase not compatible with the device of your choice?

Don't worry, now with every Packt book you get a DRM-free PDF version of that book at no cost.

Read anywhere, any place, on any device. Search, copy, and paste code from your favorite technical books directly into your application.

The perks don't stop there, you can get exclusive access to discounts, newsletters, and great free content in your inbox daily

Follow these simple steps to get the benefits:

1. Scan the QR code or visit the link below

https://packt.link/free-ebook/9781804619643

2. Submit your proof of purchase
3. That's it! We'll send your free PDF and other benefits to your email directly

Part 1:
Building the Fundamentals

In this section, we will cover the following chapters.

- *Chapter 1, Preparing for Success*
- *Chapter 2, Defining the Approach*
- *Chapter 3, Design and Build: The Core Sales Process*
- *Chapter 4, Design and Build: The Lead Generation Process*
- *Chapter 5, Design and Build: Sales User Productivity*

1
Preparing for Success

There are many factors that influence the success of a Sales Cloud implementation. In this book, we will explore all the essentials of a typical Sales Cloud delivery project. At the beginning, there are a lot of hopes, dreams, and promises. Your implementation will be considered a success if these are delivered by the end. It is likely that some things will change and some unexpected things will come up during the course of your implementation. The aim is to stay true to the core reasons for the project's inception. One of the key ways of staying on course is defining what success looks like at the start. Being able to revisit the shared vision means focus stays on what matters. This is the best way to realize success.

We start this chapter by exploring some of the common challenges commercial teams experience that lead to the purchase of Sales Cloud and how the tool addresses them. This will help you understand the challenges your sales stakeholders face and the capabilities you might focus on to solve them. We move on to learning the importance of ensuring your implementation and technology goals are aligned with your company strategy and values. Once Sales Cloud is implemented, you want to show that it adds value and to do this, you need a plan from the start. We also learn how user adoption plays an essential part in success, what prevents it, and how to avoid these issues from the start.

Finally, we explore how to define what is and isn't included in an implementation by defining the project scope and how managing this keeps you on course to deliver the original vision.

All of these factors have an overall impact on implementation success. Understanding them and keeping them in mind throughout the implementation allows you to set yourself up for success.

In this chapter, we're going to cover the following main topics:

- Common sales challenges
- Alignment with company strategy and values
- The importance of adoption
- Defining the scope of your implementation

Supporting tools and information

To get the most from this chapter, it would be useful to have a working knowledge of your organization's strategy and values and understand the goals and the business case for the purchase of Sales Cloud.

The information you discover and define relating to the content of this chapter, such as defining implementation goals and scope, can be captured in standard business tools such as word processing and spreadsheet tools. Where your organization has project management tools, you may start to capture the overall implementation vision using these.

Common sales challenges

The role and expectations of the teams that generate sales, also known as the commercial function, are continually evolving. While there is always an expectation to deliver increases in revenue year on year, ways of working and customers' expectations also change. Technology and macro social and economic factors are also having a big impact. Customers are looking for personalized one-to-one relationships and are more intentional about how they spend their money, meaning sales teams have to be able to demonstrate value.

The 2020 pandemic forced many sales teams to rapidly find alternative ways of working. It took away the majority of in-person interactions, forcing organizations to quickly try and find ways to connect to customers online. Those who already had the working practices and technology had an advantage. Salespeople who built relationships in person at meetings and events needed to adopt a different approach. While the overwhelming desire in society has been to get back to in-person interactions and activities, there are some aspects of the new ways of working that people appreciate and want to continue with. For some people, working from home had benefits such as less time and money spent on commuting and more time spent with family or on leisure activities. Some people made big life changes by moving to new homes with office space and more rural locations. Equally, some organizations realized that they could conduct business without having to spend so much time and money on travel.

This enforced a global shift to working from home that proved that it was possible, although there are differences in opinion with regard to productivity. For some workers, it has meant they don't want to go back. For sales, this means they have to be prepared to build relationships with people both in person and remotely. So, organizations have been able to do this really well, which has raised the bar further for those who are just starting their journey.

Another significant disruptor is generative **artificial intelligence (AI)**. Following the impact of ChatGPT, we are seeing all organizations talking about how they might incorporate artificial intelligence into their ways of working to gain competitive advantage. Although this dominates conversations, most organizations are still at the early stages of understanding the potential and the implications and deciding where to incorporate it. There are questions to answer and decisions to be made to ensure that organizations receive the benefits without unintended consequences or bias.

Salesforce has announced several exciting AI features in recent months, and I am sure there will be many more. As it is early in their release, they are not widely adopted at this point. Those who are more mature in their AI journey will start to explore the benefits of these. Most organizations are still considering what these technological advancements mean for them. To capitalize on the benefits of AI, it is essential to have a volume of accurate, relevant, connected data that AI can learn from. In this book, we will not be focusing on the new AI tools as they are rapidly evolving, but we will focus on how you can implement Sales Cloud with an appropriate data model and quality data so you can connect it to other data sources and layer appropriate AI tools over the top when your organization is ready to adopt those at scale.

Next, we will explore some of the sales function-specific challenges that sales teams and leaders experience. This is not an exhaustive list but will give you an understanding of the types of challenges you might hear about.

Managing the sales pipeline

Pipeline management is the activity of managing the detailed steps in the sales process; understanding what has happened and what needs to happen next to move the deal to a close. The sales pipeline shows the status of a prospective deal at a given time. By inspecting the pipeline, a sales leader can see how many deals have been made by each salesperson and what their values are. They should also be able to see what prospect stakeholders are involved, what activities and meetings have taken place and what emails have been sent, and what the next steps are.

In addition to seeing where the pipeline is at any given time, leaders also want to know how it has changed compared to last week or last month. This allows them to take action if any negative trends are seen, such as the pipeline reducing in value or the close dates of deals being pushed out.

It is common for sales leaders to want more visibility on what is happening in the pipeline and for it to be up-to-date and accurate at any given time. Sales Cloud enables this by providing the functionality to record activities and the people involved, as well as offering a Pipeline Inspection view that gives a summary and comparison of what has changed, which we will learn about in *Chapter 3 – Design and Build: The Core Sales Process*. Integrations with other business tools also streamline the logging of activities, which will we look at in *swsw, Common System Integrations*.

Forecasting accuracy

Forecasting is the process of predicting value or the number of sales that will be achieved at a given point in time, usually by month or quarter. This number becomes a commitment to the business in terms of how much revenue will be generated, which also has an impact on the business in planning spending commitments. For example, organizations plan what they can spend on marketing or if they can hire additional people depending on the revenue forecast. Failure to achieve the revenue predicted means that cuts need to be made or plans need to be downgraded. This also had wider implications when the organization is publicly traded or when the business has been backed by investment.

Forecasting is a fundamental and essential part of business planning. The accuracy of the forecast impacts the whole organization.

Sales Cloud has both specific Forecasting functionalities and Report and Dashboard functionalities for further analysis. It also enables the setup and enforcement of a consistent sales process so that data is consistently recorded by all. The forecasting functionality has features to allow leaders to view different people's forecasts and quickly drill into the records. This allows leaders to see exactly what makes up the forecast and make manual adjustments based on their judgment so that they are confident in the forecast they commit to. We learn about *Analyzing and visualizing data – Reports and Dashboards* in *Chapter 5*.

Increasing sales productivity

All organizations welcome improvements in productivity. It would be unusual to find a commercial leader who wouldn't want their teams to be more effective. Productivity can be increased by automating tasks such as logging data and notifying colleagues or providing them with relevant information, making it easier for team members to collaborate.

Sales Cloud offers many ways to increase productivity. Creating a single source of truth for commercial dates means Users know that they are working with and making decisions on the most up-to-date data. Stream and automate the logging of activities such as calls, emails, and meetings, automate the creation of records and notifications, and capture who is collaborating together on sales deals and in organizations to increase efficiency. We learn about setting up an appropriate data model and recording Opportunity and Account Teams in *Chapter 3, Design and Build: The Core Sales Process*. We review all the ways you can create a great user experience, including automation, in *Chapter 5, Design and Build: Sales User Productivity*.

Achieving sales and marketing alignment

Another common challenge that so many organizations face is creating alignment between sales and marketing. This refers to the role that marketing has in generating sales prospects, what determines that they have shown enough interest to a salesperson to take over, and how that handover is carried out.

Sales Cloud can assist with this as the sales prospects, Leads, resulting sales deals, and Opportunities can be tracked in one system. This means that it is possible to track a prospect all the way through its lifecycle. Ownership can be tracked and changed to capture the handover, as well as rules and guidance that support the way of working to successfully transition a prospect. With this reporting functionality, managers can assess the performance of the process. We learn about lead generation in *Chapter 4, Design and Build: The Lead Generation Process*.

Selling to buying groups

The buying group is the group of people who influence whether an organization makes a purchase. Particularly in a business-to-business setting or when there's a purchase of a significant value, there can be a number of people involved in assessing the suitability or approving a purchase. For this reason, salespeople have to be able to successfully engage with multiple people.

Sales Cloud provides the functionality to be able to capture every person a salesperson interacts with and specify the role they have in the buying unit. Having this documented makes it easier to see the overall picture, create a plan, and gain the support of others. We learn about Contacts and Opportunity Contact Roles in *Chapter 3 – Design and Build: The Core Sales Process*.

Enabling sales teams

Enabling sales teams with the knowledge, tools, and materials they need to service prospects and achieve their targets is another challenge organizations look to solve. Sales Cloud with a level of customization for specific needs will provide the tooling. In *Chapter 2, Defining the Approach*, we learn about the importance of the role that Change Management has in ensuring Users are prepared to use Sales Cloud. In *Chapter 5 – Design and Build: Sales User Productivity*, we learn about functionalities such as Sales Path and In-App Guidance and provide users with guidance on what they need to do right when they need to do it.

The examples given here are just a few of the examples of how Sales Cloud provides solutions for common sales challenges. In the next section, we will explore why it is important that you understand how your Sales Cloud implementation aligns with and enables your company strategy and values.

Alignment with company strategy and values

In this section, we will explore why it is important to not only focus on the details of your Sales Cloud implementation but also to ensure that your delivery and solution align with your company strategy, goals, and values. Ultimately, you want your Salesforce strategy to align with your company strategy; the former should enable the latter. This sounds quite obvious, but when the implementation team gets into the details, it can be easy for the focus to deviate. In some cases, it is also possible that the Sales Cloud implementation team doesn't have visibility of how what they're building contributes to delivering the company strategy. This can easily happen if the implementation is being delivered by an external supplier. When your Salesforce strategy aligns with your organization's strategy, you can expect that Sales Cloud will help you achieve your goals sooner and you will be able to demonstrate how it is doing that.

The first step in developing alignment is to understand your company's strategies, goals, and values. For example, your organization might have a goal of reducing operational costs or it might have transparency or collaboration as a value. Once these are understood, the next step is to determine how the Sales Cloud implementation supports these. For example, you might be looking to reduce the time, the number of steps, or the number of clicks required to complete a process to gain operational efficiency, you might implement an open data-sharing model to ensure transparency across the organization, or you might deliver collaboration functionalities in early releases to show commitment to them.

It is highly likely that the benefits expected by the Sales Cloud implementation are aligned with business goals, or else the purchase would not have been approved in the first place. During the implementation, it is essential not to lose sight of what we promised, as this is how success will be judged.

It is worth remembering that companies are made up of people, and companies only achieve their goals when people work together. While diversity of thought can be a strategic advantage, it is also essential that people pull in the same direction to achieve company goals.

Achieving business alignment

To achieve business alignment internally, Salesforce uses a process called **V2MOM**, which stands for **Vision, Value, Methods, Obstacles, and Measures**. Everyone in the organization completes a V2MOM, which aligns so that every person understands how their actions contribute to the overall goal. Salesforce provides information on why and how to create a V2MOM on their public learning platform, Trailhead. You can find links to this information in the *Further reading* section.

To achieve a successful implementation, everyone on the project, and the stakeholders, should understand what the implementation is trying to achieve and how their role contributes.

There are a number of steps that can be taken to help achieve this: communicate the goals of the implementation regularly to all stakeholders, bring stakeholders on the journey by including them in defining requirements and requesting feedback, and train and support users so they both understand the value and can perform the tasks asked of them. We explore how you can do these in subsequent chapters in this book, starting in *Chapter 2 – Defining the Approach*.

To ensure the focus throughout an implementation is on the overall goals, it is common to have regular **steering committee meetings** to keep track of progress, make decisions, connect to the business, access additional budget, and get commitment from other areas of the business. Depending on the scale of the implementation, these meetings happen weekly or monthly and include senior members of the organization, typically the executive sponsor and senior members of the implementation team.

These meetings ensure that any issues or decisions can be identified early and appropriate actions can be taken. One of the benefits of having a clear vision is that it makes prioritization easier. It is worth noting that some stakeholders may be personally invested in the success of the implementation, as it either has an impact on their role or their reputation.

For example, if your organization prides itself on transparency, then you will probably find your data model will be quite open, allowing people to view most records. If your client confidentiality is core to your business, you are likely to have a private model with restrictions on who can see what data. If collaboration is important, the functionality to enable it must be delivered in early releases to show commitment to it.

> **Salesforce Strategy Designer Certification**
>
> Salesforce understands that the success of its solutions is dependent on how they contribute to an organization's overall success. Salesforce provides services to clients to help them achieve alignment using strategy design tools and techniques. To help organizations achieve this, they have developed a curriculum and certification to teach and validate an understanding of strategy design. This certification is called Salesforce Strategy Designer. You can find details of the certification on Trailhead along with resources to learn about this topic. There are links to these resources in the *Further reading* session.

In the next section, we explore the concept of adoption and its role in a successful Sales Cloud implementation.

The importance of adoption

In this section, we explore what we mean by adoption and why it is important for the success of your Sales Cloud implementation. First, let's explore what we mean by adoption.

What is adoption?

In the context of a business application, adoption is a measure of whether Users are logging in and using a system, such as Sales Cloud. There are a number of metrics to measure this, the simplest being the percentage of people who have access and are logging in on a regular basis, (i.e., daily, weekly, or monthly). Another approach is to measure activities in the system, for example, record creation or processes completed. In a sales context, this might be the number of companies and people entered (Accounts and Contacts) or calls, meetings, and emails logged (Events and Tasks). These can be tracked as the overall totals to show the overall usage of the system; however, these can also be used as a measure of individual adoption and performance. It can be common to measure the number of meetings booked as a measure of individual performance and future sales performance. The trade on this type of metric can be used to determine how well the system is being adopted, how easy it is for people to perform the tasks asked, and if the implementation of the system is realizing the benefits promised.

It is at the organization's discretion which measures it uses. The measures and the focus that is put on these will determine Users' behaviors. A mix of these measures can be used to determine if the system is a living breathing asset to the organization that people want to use or if it is simply ornamental.

In addition to usage, you can also consider adoption as the proportion of the capability you are using. Sales Cloud has a lot of functionalities, which increase with every release. Increasing the functionalities used is another way to derive additional value.

To get the maximum value, consider Salesforce as an additional member of the team. As you would with any team member, regularly review its performance to see if it can take on additional responsibilities and deliver more value. A natural interval to review performance would be helpful but around the time of the new functionality releases. This is a really good time to review what is being released to see if there is a new update that addresses requested system improvements or allows a new process and Users to be brought onto the platform. Salesforce provides a lot of content about its releases in multiple formats. This included Release Notes, Release Readiness webinars, and a Release Readiness Collaboration Group on Trailhead. You can find links to these resources in the *Further reading* section.

Salesforce releases

Salesforce releases functionalities three times per year. They are the winter, spring, and summer releases, and they happen in September, February, and June, respectively. There is no Fall release. Releases are rolled out over a weekend by Salesforce, so you do not need to be involved or schedule the release. It is worth noting that this happens in the maintenance window that Salesforce specifies. You can't influence or delay these. Where changes are carried out that might have an impact on your setup, Salesforce will communicate these in advance. You can review changes of this type in **Setup** > **Release** Updates. For updates that might have an impact, it is typical for Salesforce to make these available for you to turn on when you choose before mandating the update. The month before each release, Salesforce upgrades sandboxes to allow you to test that you will not see any impact and also test any new functionalities so you can use them in your Production Org as soon as they become available. It is important to know when the release window is and factor that into when you release your functionality so one doesn't impact the other. We explore planning your deployment in *Chapter 10, Deployment Planning*.

Now that we understand what adoption is, we will learn why it is important.

Why is adoption important for Sales Cloud success?

Adoption is important because it takes every member of the sales team to deliver sales objectives and targets. The benefits that systems such as Sales Cloud offer can only be realized if they are used consistently by all those who deliver the processes they are designed to enable.

If a small group, or even just one person, doesn't see the value in using it, doesn't know how to use it, or just doesn't want to use it, it means that for some, the data or activities are not complete. Worse, they might revert to a spreadsheet or other system to perform their tasks, sometimes referred to as a shadow system. This means a system such as Sales Cloud isn't truly the source of truth for a type of data. Users might start to question the information the system holds and decide they would prefer to work in an alternative way of their choosing too.

To get the full benefits from a centralized system, such as a complete and accurate view of customers, an improved customer experience, greater efficiency, and greater collaboration, the data needs to be complete and accurate, and everyone has to be engaged and play their part.

As we learned in the section *Alignment with company strategy and values,* the success of your implementation and Sales Cloud overall depends on how well what you deliver aligns with what and how a company plans to achieve its goals.

In the next section, we learn what gets in the way of adoption and what you can do to prevent these things from happening.

Barriers to adoption

We have established that adoption is an essential component in achieving **return on investment (ROI)**. However, in real-world implementation, there are a number of situations that can arise that create barriers to adoption. The following are some scenarios to watch out for and suggestions on how to mitigate them:

- **Not engaging with users during the design and build**: This means that Users' voices and needs are not heard during the time they can influence the build. This introduces the risk that the system may not deliver what Users need. It also means that Users feel no attachment or ownership of the system and may decide it is not for them. To avoid this, have User representation present in requirement-gathering sessions and sessions for going over what has been built so feedback can be incorporated.

- **Not enough supporting and training users**: This means Users are not provided with enough of the training they need to understand what is expected of them and how to do it. To avoid this, engage with your training team if you have one and develop a plan for training that is appropriate for your users. We explore the role and options for training in *Chapters 2 and 8.*

- **Leadership not engaged with the system**: This means that Users are not seeing their leaders also adopt the system, and they may possibly request that information be provided outside of Sales Cloud. To avoid this, ensure that senior leaders lead by example. Examples include running regular sales and pipeline meetings with Sales Cloud on the screen, asking deal owners to talk about the next steps and check that information is up to date, and adopting the philosophy *"If it isn't in Salesforce it doesn't exist".*

- **Not measuring Adoption**: This means that the level of adoption is not known, so high adoption is not being celebrated and low adoption is not being addressed. To avoid this, track some adoption metrics such as those that we stated in *What is adoption*. If lower levels of adoption are observed, then the root causes can be identified by talking to users and understanding their issues or barriers; and then creating a plan to address them. That might include additional training or system changes.

- **Not having an ongoing maintenance and improvement plan**: This means that there is no one to listen to Users' issues or change the system as processes evolve and new ways of working come about. It also means new functionality is not being used to ensure RIO year on year. To avoid this, someone should be identified to own and administer Sales Cloud. As a minimum, they or your IT teams should support Users with their day-to-day issues, including troubleshooting login problems and reporting issues. They should capture User requests, review the new functionalities in each release, and make recommendations to leaders when updates would be beneficial.

These barriers usually arise because the value of the activities and the impact of not doing them are not appreciated. The scenarios explored here are not an exhaustive list, but they do occur relatively frequently. We don't cover day-to-day administration and maintenance in this book, but it is important to understand that the implementation is the start of the journey.

In the next section, we consider how your individual approach to an implementation can have a positive impact on the outcome.

What is your approach?

As the leader or a member of the implementation team, you can influence how successful it is; no matter what your role, you can make a real impact. It is important to remember that all Sales Cloud implementations are about providing a system that helps people serve the needs of other people. How you approach your role in the implementation will influence the outcome. The following are some suggestions on approaches you can adopt that will have a positive impact.

- **Collaboration**: Embrace and encourage collaboration with all stakeholders, as encouraging diverse points of view results in a solution that serves a wider audience. It is important to bring Users on the journey, and the later important information is discovered, the more complicated and expensive it is to incorporate.

- **Empathy**: Put yourself in the position of the stakeholders you are serving. Most people come to work to do a good job, so when they share their challenges, it is important to listen and try to find solutions, as this is more likely to result in a solution that internal stakeholders will use. It also builds cooperation and trust.

- **Build trust**: Build trust with your internal stakeholders by being sure to do what you say you are going to do, listen and understand their requirements, and then play back the functionalities that deliver them. Building trust from the start provides a strong foundation, which is beneficial if more difficult conversations or decisions are necessary later in the implementation.

- **Become an internal salesperson**: Part of your role will be to persuade, and effectively sell, the functionality you are building to business stakeholders. You can learn from the information that sales stakeholders are providing about selling and apply it when selling the Sales Cloud implementation to them. For example, this could be the format they use to communicate, the language they use, and how they handle objections.

In *Chapter 2 – Defining the Approach*, we will learn how you define the approach to your implementation, which includes aspects such as selecting a development methodology and exploring Change Management and training. Many of the topics in that chapter expand on what we have learned in this one.

In this final section, we will explore another essential component: scope.

Defining the scope of your implementation

In this section, we will consider what we mean by scope, why it is important to clearly define at the very beginning of your Sales Cloud implementation project, and the importance of managing this throughout the life of the project. Let's start by understanding what we mean by scope.

What is scope?

The scope of work defines what is included and, ideally, you would also state what isn't. Defining the scope of work is a very important step in defining a piece of work, like a project, that will be carried out. Having a documented scope makes it easier for those working on the project to understand what they should and should be working on, it sets boundaries. This helps with overall alignment with the company goals which we talked about in the *Aligning company strategy and values* section.

It is common to get key stakeholders to sign off. In *Chapter 7, Getting Sign-off*, we look at getting formal sign-off as a method of confirming that stakeholders understand and agree to what is and isn't in scope. Sign-off is also involved for scope changes, in the form of change requests.

Defining the scope

Defining the scope of your Sales Cloud implementation project is an essential first step. This typically happens during the Sales Cloud purchasing process or directly after the decision to purchase Sales Cloud. This early definition means allowing for the hopes and aspirations of the sales process to be captured.

The scope will typically include the business functions business processes, and the teams. For example, sales and marketing, the sales and lead generation process, and US and European sales teams. It matters less how it is written, and more that the stakeholders affected understand what it means. If your organization has a standardized way of defining project scopes you should follow that format. Wherever possible you should aim to avoid ambiguity or areas for interpretation. Although not always included it can be very valuable to include what isn't going to be included. This might include data from specific systems, automating complex processes that are carried out infrequently, or certain groups of Users. Explicitly stating these means that anyone who wasn't expecting these exclusions can raise their concerns earlier so the reasoning can be explained or they can be brought into scope.

Now we will learn about the role of managing scope in delivering a successful implementation.

Managing scope

Throughout the duration of the implementation, it is important to manage the scope of the work. During the life of an implementation, things change; for example, business conditions or team members change. Also, Stakeholders' expectations can easily expand to features, functions, and capabilities that are not in the original plan. This often happens as people become more familiar with Sales Cloud capabilities and imagine how they can help them. It is also common for those working on the implementation to want to add extras they think will help Users and improve the end solution, even though they are outside the gathered requirements.

Deviating from the original scope is known as **scope creep**. This leads to increases in costs, as these are spent on delivery functionalities but not on what was agreed or what the business expected.

In practice, managing scope means listening to the requests that come in from stakeholders, but before agreeing to deliver them, comparing them to the original scope to ensure actioning them is an appropriate use of resources. Where requirements are in scope, they can be actioned. Where they aren't, or where it is unclear, it should be communicated to the requester that they might not be in scope but will be captured and assessed. The requests and requirements should be logged in a backlog and brought to the attention of an individual or team of business stakeholders who can assess them in terms of business importance. This assessment might be carried out by a steering committee, which we introduced in the *Alignment with company strategy and values* section, or a Product Owner, who we will describe in more detail in the next chapter, *Chapter 2, Defining the Approach*. Where it is agreed that a change should happen, the scope should be changed, and the change should be signed off by the relevant stakeholders. If there are any external suppliers involved, this sort of change may require a contractual change, even if there is not an increase in effort or cost.

In summary, defining and managing the scope of your Sales Cloud implementation is an essential part of securing success. Even if you are not responsible for the overall scope of the implementation, you can still play an important part in ensuring that what is delivered is within the agreed scope.

Summary

At the beginning of this chapter, we started by exploring how the expectations of sales have changed, some of the common challenges sales leaders and teams face, and how Sales Cloud can help solve these. We moved on to learn about the importance of aligning your Salesforce strategy, goals, and values with your company's and how failure to do this can prevent you from being able to demonstrate overall implementation success.

We went on to define what is meant by adoption when it comes to business applications and how Users' willingness to use the system determines if they succeed or fail. We also explored some of the common barriers to adoption and how to address them.

Finally, we learned about scope and the importance of clearly defining this at the beginning of an implementation and then managing it throughout to ensure your implementation doesn't deviate too far from the original expectation. We learned that scope creep can be a reason why implementations run over time and budget expectations and result in you not delivering the original benefits promised.

In the next chapter, we will learn about the decisions you need to make and define how you approach your implementation. This includes your implementation delivery methodology, what environments you use, how you test what you've built, and how you prepare your Users to adopt the system.

Further reading

Trailhead:

- *What is Trailhead?*:

  https://www.salesforce.com/blog/what-is-trailhead/

V2MOM:

- *Organizational Alignment (V2MOM)*:

  https://trailhead.salesforce.com/content/learn/modules/manage_
  the_sfdc_organizational_alignment_v2mom

Salesforce Strategy Designer:

- *Trailhead: Salesforce Strategy Designer: About the exam*:

  https://trailhead.salesforce.com/en/credentials/strategydesigner

Adoption:

- *Adoption Metrics – Trailhead*:

  https://trailhead.salesforce.com/content/learn/modules/user-
  adoption-metrics/measure-salesforce-usage

Preparing for a Salesforce Release:

- *Release Notes*:

  https://help.salesforce.com/s/articleView?id=release-notes.
  salesforce_release_notes.htm&language=en_US&release=248&type=5

- *Release Readiness webinars*:

  ```
  https://www.salesforce.com/plus/experience/release_readiness_live
  ```

- *Release Readiness Collaboration Group on Trailhead*:

  ```
  https://trailhead.salesforce.com/trailblazer-community/
  groups/0F9300000001okuCAA?tab=discussion&sort=LAST_MODIFIED_
  DATE_DESC#
  ```

Alignment with Company Strategy:

- *Trailhead: Alignment as a strategic craft*:

  ```
  https://trailhead.salesforce.com/content/learn/modules/alignment-
  as-a-strategic-craft
  ```

2

Defining the Approach

Sales Cloud and the Salesforce Customer 360 platform have a lot of capabilities and can seem quite complex. It can be daunting to work out how to approach the customizations you need to implement, from ideation through to successful deployment to the end users. Some changes to the platform can also be very simple, so it is easy to dive right in and only realize the consequences later.

In this chapter, we'll start by learning about Salesforce's **application life cycle management** (**ALM**) to give you a framework you can use to think about the stages of your implementation. With this understanding, we'll explore the topics you need to understand and make decisions about at the start of your implementation before any building work is carried out. We'll look at the characteristics of two commonly used development methodologies, Agile and Waterfall, and how these are applied in practice. We'll also learn about the environments Salesforce provides to develop and test changes and Sandboxes, as well as when to use them.

By the end of this chapter, you will understand the key areas that you need to be aware of as you approach Sales Cloud implementation. You will understand the native tools that Salesforce provides to develop your solution, as well as how you can approach your testing and training to ensure quality and adoption. We'll cover the latter two in greater detail in later chapters.

In this chapter, we're going to cover the following main topics:

- Salesforce ALM
- Salesforce environment strategy and DevOps tools
- Developing a testing approach
- Change management and training

Supporting tools and information

To complete this chapter, you'll need to have knowledge of the development methodology and the tools that are used to support it. You must also know what your Salesforce edition is and how to use Sandboxes.

Salesforce ALM

ALM describes how the life cycle of a business application such as Sales Cloud is managed – that is, how an idea or requirement gets defined, built, tested, and delivered. It is a combination of people, processes, and tooling. Having a structured approach to delivering your Sales Cloud solution provides predictability and repeatability in a way that enables teams to work together to deliver appropriate high-quality solutions. The following diagram shows the ALM. This diagram is based on the Salesforce ALM process document on Trailhead but we have expanded it beyond deploying the solution:

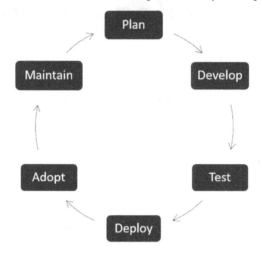

Figure 2.1 – The ALM process

Figure 2.1 shows the key stages of the life cycle at a high level. Within each stage, there are several other well-understood activities and actions. Although testing is listed as a separate stage in the preceding diagram, we will discuss why it can be beneficial to incorporate testing into the build stage in the *Developing a testing approach* section.

The following table shows what activities relate to which stage and who is typically responsible for them. Although the stages of the ALM are in chronological order, the foundational activities that support them often begin while earlier stages are in progress. An example is change management. Although the purpose of this is to secure adoption, which is the fifth stage, actions related to change management start from the planning stage and run in parallel to the other stages. This is because people need time and information to accept a change. So, if it was only started when everything else was finished, it would add notable and unnecessary time to an implementation:

Plan		Develop	
Activity	**Typical Owner**	**Activity**	**Typical Owner**
High Level Requirement Gathering	Functional Lead/ Business Owner	Detailed Requirement Gathering	Functional and Technical Lead
Scope	Project Lead/ Business Owner	Architecture Design	Technical Lead
Development Methodology	Technical Lead	Solution Design	Functional Lead
Environment Strategy	Technical Lead	Build	Configurators/ Developers
Testing Approach	Technical Lead		
Change Management Approach	Project Lead/ Functional Lead		
Identifying Project Team	Project Lead		
Test		**Deploy**	
Activity	**Typical Owner**	**Activity**	**Typical Owner**
Functional Testing	Testers	Release Planning	Project Lead
Non-functional Testing	Testers	Build Release Package	Developers
		Release	Developers
Adopt		**Maintain**	
Activity	**Typical Owner**	**Activity**	**Typical Owner**
Change Management	Project Lead/ Functional Lead	Support	Business Owner
Training	Functional Lead	Ongoing Training	Business Owner
Gathering Feedback	Business Owner/ Functional Lead	Governance	Business Owner/Project

Table 2.1 – ALM activities by stage and owner

Table 2.1 shows that there are several activities at each stage and that some types of activities occur in more than one stage.

> **Discovery stage**
>
> As indicated by the activities listed, there are a lot of things that need to be defined in the Planning stage. In addition to the stages that we have described in the ALM, you may also hear reference to a Discovery stage or phase. Different organizations use slightly different terms. However, a **discovery stage** or phase usually refers to a stage at the very beginning where time is spent understanding the current situation and technology, desired situation, and technology, and then proposing a plan of how to get from one to another.
>
> This type of stage is particularly important if the work is being carried out by an external organization as the estimated cost of the project is based on their understanding of the current situation. As an external organization, there is a limit to how well they can understand the current systems in advance unless they have the opportunity to review them. A discovery phase allows for a detailed understanding to be gathered so that a plan and any effort estimates are as accurate as possible. This reduces the risk of unforeseen issues later in the implementation that can increase time and cost.

For the remainder of this chapter, we'll focus on the functions of the planning stage that we didn't cover in *Chapter 1*, *Preparing for Success*. In subsequent chapters, we'll learn how to execute this planning for the development, testing, deployment, and initial adoption. We won't cover the ongoing maintenance of Sales Cloud in this book.

In *Chapters 3 – Design and Build: The Core Sales Process*, *4 – Design and Build: The Lead Generation Process*, and *5 – Design and Build: Sales User Productivity*, we'll explore how to gather detailed requirements and design and build solutions with the Sales Cloud capabilities. This is broken down into three chapters, each focusing on a key area: the core sales process, the lead generation process, and sales productivity. A single implementation might include all of these or each one might be a project in its own right.

In the next section, we will look at development options on the Salesforce Customer 360 platform.

Low-code and pro-code development

One of the key benefits of the Salesforce platform is its blend of low-code configuration and customization tools and pro-code tooling to allow you to extend beyond the platform's out-of-the-box capabilities. **Low code** refers to point-and-click development, also known as declarative development, and is the method of customizing and configuring the platform without writing code. **Pro code** refers to customization that involves writing code such as Apex and Lightning Web Components (JavaScript, HTML, and CSS) to customize the platform.

It is an established best practice to use the standard functionality first, then low-code methods of customization whenever possible before building code-based solutions. The benefit of this approach is that Salesforce supports and maintains standard functionality and low-code methods. So, when updates are released, which occurs three times a year, you can expect that it will have no or minimal impact on functionality. They also enhance these capabilities giving existing capability users additional benefits. Building pro-code solutions rather than using standard and low-code tools requires additional effort, as well as ongoing support, maintenance, and regression testing against releases, and potentially limits access to new platform functionality.

At the start of an implementation, it is common to agree on some design and build principles so that everyone involved in the delivery takes a consistent approach. Adopting the best practice of low code before pro code is usually one of the agreed principles. Some organizations don't have pro-code developers in-house, so they will have no one to maintain pro-code solutions unless they arrange a managed service contract. For this reason, some organizations implement a process where any requirement that needs a pro-code solution needs to be reviewed and approved before it can be built so that there is no avoidable code.

> **Note**
>
> Sometimes, organizations that have technical pro-code people in-house choose to self-implement. These are people who can be highly skilled in software development but not familiar with the Salesforce Customer 360 platform and its standard and low-code functionality. These implementations often have additional fields or code where standard or low-code functionality could have been used.
>
> Over time, these implementations have a higher cost of ownership as they require people with technical skills to maintain and extend them. The in-house people who implement them go back to their full-time workload and try to avoid being pulled back for support tasks. As the requirements for the platform grow, some of the initial setup needs to be refactored to use the standard and low-code functionality so that the organization can use newly released functionality. If you are self-implementing the information in this book, this should help you avoid some of these issues.

Development methodologies

The two most commonly used development methodologies are the Agile framework and Waterfall. Both methodologies are used across the software industry. In practice, organizations apply elements of one or both to suit their particular needs.

In the following two sections, we will explore these methodologies in more detail and then consider what happens when the two combine to form a hybrid approach.

Agile

Most Sales Cloud implementation projects use an Agile way of working. An **Agile** methodology is an approach to project management that is based on the Agile Manifesto. It promotes collaboration and delivers smaller packages of work. Different process frameworks give teams principles and structure on how they work together. The Scrum framework, or an interpretation of it, is commonly used on Sales Cloud projects.

> **The Agile Manifesto and Scrum framework**
>
> The Agile Manifesto, crafted in 2001 by a group of software developers seeking more effective approaches to software development, encapsulates a set of guiding principles for agile methodologies. It emphasizes individuals and interactions over processes and tools, working software over comprehensive documentation, customer collaboration over contract negotiation, and responding to change over following a plan. These values promote flexibility, adaptability, and customer satisfaction in software development projects. There are 12 guiding principles that you can read at `https://agilemanifesto.Org/principles.html`.

Within Scrum, Stories are used to specify small packages of work, which are accepted into Sprints, or timeboxed periods of work. Members of the sprint team have a daily Scrum or standup, which is a short (15-minute) meeting where they describe what they have done since the last standup, what they will do before the next standup, and anything that is blocking their progress. Teams are self-organizing and the standup forms part of their commitment to each other. The process of Sprint Planning defines and refines the stories and determines the scope of the Sprints. It shows working software very early on, in comparison to Waterfall. A **Product Owner** is part of the Scum team to represent the business by providing clarification on what is required for developers. A deep dive into Agile is beyond the scope of this book, but many resources on Agile are available both for software development in general as well as for delivering Salesforce projects.

Agile can be a good choice for developing solutions for complex requirements that need cross-functional involvement. It provides the framework for a solution to evolve as the requirements need to get a good solution. It can be challenging when the scope (time and cost) is tightly defined. Agile works when the business can work with a **minimal viable product** (**MVP**). An MVP is a release of the solution that provides a working solution but with minimal features. It is not appropriate if the solution being delivered needs to be delivered in one go – for example, if it is required to replace an existing system from the first release.

It is a myth that Agile doesn't require documentation; rather, the methodology favors face-to-face communication over documentation. Pure Agile is better suited to internal delivery teams than delivery by external providers due to the tight scope required by the latter. In this case, it is usually a hybrid Agile approach.

Agile working practices can be a new concept for many organizations and their leadership teams. Getting the full benefit of Agile usually requires an organizational mind shift. If your organization has not already adopted Agile ways of working, then you may benefit from engaging with an Agile specialist who can help your organization with the organizational change required.

Waterfall

Waterfall is a more traditional project management approach and works well when all the requirements are fully known and defined at the start of the project. Each of the stages is clearly defined, then completed, and signed off before the next is started. It can also be the most appropriate approach to develop solutions for regulated industries when it is not appropriate to deliver a solution in phases, such as a solution in the medical or financial space. Waterfall is how most non-software projects are run (for example, construction), and as such, it is an approach that most people are familiar with and gravitate toward. It offers a lot of implied certainty up front, with clear milestones and estimations of cost. This makes it very comfortable for businesses to understand and want to adopt. Here are some other characteristics of Waterfall:

- Clearly defined, detailed requirements.

- Detailed documentation at each stage.

- One big release, which means deployment can come with high pressure.

- Longer **time To value** (TTV) as functionality is only released at the very end. TTV is a measure of how long it takes for stakeholders to get value from software.

- Users don't get hands-on with the system until it is delivered.

- It's harder to make changes as you move closer to the end of the project.

The Waterfall approach is not particularly well suited for fast-changing businesses or some types of software development. This is because it can be a long time before any new functionality is delivered, by which time the requirement may have changed or the technology could be out of date. This will only increase with the acceleration that we're seeing with AI.

However, some aspects of the Waterfall approach are very attractive to businesses, including having a clearly defined scope and a specified end date.

If you already have a prebuilt system or a system that has a critical set of capabilities and needs to work end to end, then a Waterfall approach may be more appropriate for your delivery.

A hybrid approach

It is very common to see an organization adopt a hybrid of these two methodologies, particularly for business application development. When an organization develops software as part of its core business or is very large and requires a lot of business application development, it will typically have engineering software leadership that will define and refine the methodology and tools used. They will most likely have an in-house team that can build strong relationships and get the most out of a methodology such as Agile. The business will understand that the nature of Agile means change happens during the development cycle.

Hybrid Agile is a much harder concept to adopt for organizations that are using traditional project methodologies to deliver their products or services. It is also difficult to work with full Agile when the application development is outsourced to an external party as a clear scope, requirements, time scale, and costs are typically part of the contractual agreement. In these instances, a hybrid approach becomes more common, whereby the definition of the requirements and scoping is done in detail up front, before being split into a logical set of timeboxes to allow for incremental delivery in phases and a quicker time to value.

> **In practice**
> The methodology that an organization uses in practice is defined by the technology leaders. If an organization doesn't need to have this capability in-house, it will adopt the approach followed by its development partner.

Now that we've learned about the overall development life cycle that you would expect to follow for your Sales Cloud implementation and two of the methodologies that you could adopt, we will explore some of the practical tools available.

Salesforce environment strategy and DevOps tools

In this section, we will look at the development environments and tools that Salesforce provides to support the ALM of both low-code and pro-code development. Salesforce provides two types of environments: **Sandboxes** and **Scratch Orgs**. They provide these so there is no reason to carry out customization and development in your Production Org, which is considered a bad practice.

We will start by exploring the Salesforce Sandbox development environments.

Salesforce development environments – Sandboxes

In this section, we will explore the Sandbox development environments that are available for your Sales Cloud development. We'll review Scratch Orgs in the *Salesforce DX (SFDX)* section. It is bad practice to make certain types of changes directly in your production Sales Cloud environment. Although many Sales Cloud changes seem quick and easy, they can harm Users and integrations if they are not appropriately planned and tested. Sandboxes are created from your Production Org. They replicate the setup, known as metadata, from your Production Org so that you can make changes and test against your exact setup before deploying them into the Production Org.

Different types of Sandboxes are designed to be used for different purposes. Sandboxes can be created from your Production Org by going to **Setup** > **Sandboxes**. *Table 2.2* shows the Sandboxes that are available to you. The versions are differentiated by their storage limit and refresh interval. This table shows the different versions:

Sandbox Edition	Storage	Refresh Rate	Copied
Developer	Data storage: 200 MB File storage: 200 MB	1 day	Metadata
Developer pro	Data storage: 1 GB File storage: 1 GB	1 day	Metadata
Partial copy	Data storage: 5 GB File storage: Same as production	5 days	Metadata Sample data
Full copy	Data storage: Same as production File storage: Same as production	28 days	Metadata Full data copy

Table 2.2 – Sandbox comparison table

As you can see, there are four types of Sandboxes. Some of these types are automatically included with the Salesforce Edition you purchase. Salesforce Professional Edition has 10 Developer Edition licenses and the number and editions increase with Enterprise, Unlimited, and Performance. Starter Edition does not have any sandboxes. Check out the *Further reading* section for a link to a web page that shows the quantity and type of Sandboxes that are included with each edition.

> **Developer Sandbox versus Developer Org**
>
> Because the naming is so similar, it can be easy to get confused between a Developer Sandbox and a Developer Org. A **Developer Sandbox** is, as we described in this section, created from a Production Org, and includes the metadata setup of the related Production Org. A **Developer Org** is a Salesforce environment that anyone can sign up for to learn about the platform. It is completely independent of any Production Org and has limited customization. Developer Orgs have tight limits in terms of the number of Users and data storage, but they do have more features enabled than you might have in the packages you have purchased. These are not to be used for commercial purposes. It is not possible to move anything that is developed in a Developer Org into a Production Org using Change Sets. The latter type of environment is great for independent learning and building anything that you want to keep completely separate. This environment is limited and is not provided for commercial use.

Next, we will review how you can use these environments during your Sales Cloud implementation.

Implementation environment strategy

As a guiding rule, each Sandbox should be created for a specific purpose, either build work or a type of testing or training. We will talk about testing in more detail in the *Developing a testing approach* section. Ideally, each member of the build team should have a Sandbox of their own. This approach means that each person can make changes and unit test what they have built without experiencing test failures based on changes that others have made.

The idea is to have a Sandbox environment for each type of functional testing being carried out for the implementation, along with environments for configurators and developers.

This is what it might look like with the type of Sandbox you would use:

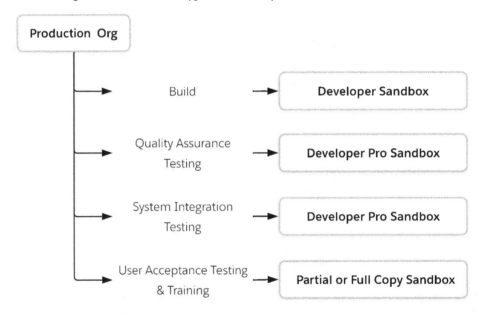

Figure 2.2 – A typical Sandbox environment strategy

As shown in *Figure 2.2*, your environment strategy is closely related to your test strategy. In practice, the Sandboxes you use will depend on several factors, as well as your test strategy, which includes the scale of your implementation, how many people you have working on it, and the skills they have. It will also depend on your budget. A full-copy Sandbox is great for user acceptance testing and user training, but it has an additional cost. So, it might not be an option. We'll explore this further in the *The impact of deployment methodology and environment strategy on testing* section.

Now that we have understood the Sandboxes that are available for development work, we will learn more about the tools that Salesforce provides for more customization and metadata, from one environment to another.

Salesforce native life cycle management tools

Salesforce provides tools to move metadata between the Production Org and its Sandbox environments. We will look at these in order of their complexity, starting with Change Sets.

Change Sets

Up until recently, **Change Sets** were the only low-code method of deploying metadata changes between Salesforce environments. In December 2022, Salesforce released DevOps Center as an alternative, something we will review in the *DevOps Center* section.

Change Sets offer a point-and-click method of selecting components that have been customized in a Sandbox Org and moving them to either another Sandbox or the Production Org. Change Sets are created in **Setup** by going **Setup** > **Environments** > **Change Sets** and then either **Inbound Change Sets** for changes that are coming from a different Org or **Outbound Change Sets** to package changes to go to another Org.

To create an `Outbound Change Set`, click **New**; you will be prompted to enter a name and description. Be as descriptive as possible in the description so that colleagues can also understand what the Change Sets include. Then, click **Save**. From the **Change Set Components** section click **Add**. Once you've done that, select **Component Type** from the pulldown menu and then check the box next to the component you want to add. After, click **Add to Change Set**. If there are components that are dependent on that one, click on **View/Add Dependencies**. This displays components that have a direct dependency, not child dependencies, so you might want to click on this button multiple times. If the component has a visibility or edit permission element, such as fields, you will want to make sure that you add the profile or permission set so that the intended Users can view or edit in the target Org. Once all the components are added, you can click **Upload** and select the Org you want to move the Change Set to. Once a Change Set has been uploaded, new components can't be added to it. If you need to make an edit to it, you can clone it.

To release a Change Set into an Org, click **Inbound Change Set**. You will have three options: **Validate**, **Deploy**, and **Delete**. Validating a Change Set carries out all the checks in the Org but doesn't release the metadata. This is an important check to carry out as it will reveal if you have included all the dependent components required. You should always carry out this check first. Once it has been validated, you can deploy it, which updates the metadata in the Org.

For a Change Set to be uploaded to a different Org, an inbound connection to the target Org has to be set up. To do this, log into the Org that will receive the Change Set, go to **Setup** > **Environments** > **Deploy** > **Deployment Settings**, and click on the Org you want to be able to accept changes from. Click **Edit**, select **Allow Inbound Changes**, and then click **Save**.

Change Sets are only available in Production and Sandbox Orgs; you will not be able to look at how these work in a Developer Org.

The benefit of Change Sets is that they require very little setup – you only need to create the initial connection. They are also easy to understand so they can easily be used by everyone. The other options we will require Users to understand some DevOps concepts and, in some cases, code.

Change Set limitations

Change Sets do have some limitations. The only options to work around these limitations are to either make the changes manually or to use an alternative deployment method.

Some limitations are as follows:

- They don't show which components have been changed which means the developer needs to remember what they have changed and add it to the Change Set.
- Standard fields and Objects can't be selected, which means that things such as field visibility, help text, and picklist values can't be updated via Change Sets.
- A Change Set can only be uploaded to one Org.
- Page Layouts from Managed Packages can be selected, which means changes to those Page Layouts can't be deployed via that method. We'll explore Packages in more detail in the *Managed and Unmanaged Packages* section.
- Destructive changes, such as deleting fields, are not possible via Change Sets.
- No rollback option is available; once deployed, there isn't an option to undo it.

This is not a comprehensive list of limitations but some of the ones you should be aware of if you are planning to use Change Sets during your implementation. Next, we will look at the latest metadata migration tool Salesforce has released.

DevOps Center

DevOps Center became **generally available (GA)** in Dec 2022. Before this release, Change Sets were the only declarative tools that Salesforce provided to move metadata, and the tool was predominantly used by admins. SFDX, which we will explore in the next section, was primarily used by Salesforce developers. One of the aims of DevOps Center, like all DevOps solutions, is to increase collaboration between low-code and pro-code developers, as well as enable Salesforce metadata to be stored in a source code repository.

DevOps is relatively new in terms of its development and is updated regularly, so you will want to review the capability and assess if it meets your needs at the onset of your implementation. To compare this against your requirements, we'll cover how you can identify commercially available DevOps in the *Commercially available DevOps tools* section.

DevOps Center is available if you have the Professional, Enterprise, Performance, or Unlimited edition of Sales Cloud. If you have specific data residency requirements, you will want to confirm that this functionality is compatible. It is worth noting that DevOps Center can't be installed in a Sandbox. If the Org that has DevOps Center is refreshed, all the data will be lost. You can install DevOps Center in a Scratch Org.

SFDX

SFDX stands for **Salesforce Developer Experience**. It is a set of tools for developers that aims to provide a better experience than tools that have traditionally been available on the platform. It is based on the following tools and principles:

- Source-driven development
- Salesforce **command-line interface (CLI)**
- Scratch Orgs
- Open and standard developer experience
- Reimagined packaging

One of the aims was to allow pro-code developers to use industry-standard tooling. For example, the development of the CLI and plugin means that developers can use VS Code, an industry-wide code editor, to write Apex and **Lightning Web Components (LWCs)**.

In the *Salesforce development environments – sandboxes* section, we learned about Sandboxes. We also referenced that there is another type of developer environment, Scratch Orgs. Scratch Orgs are intended to be used with a source-driven development approach and a **version control system (VCS)**. This is where the metadata that defines the setup in an Org is stored in a version-controlled code repository such as GitHub, rather than the Production Org being the only place where this is captured.

Scratch Orgs are temporary Orgs with a very short life; the default is 7 days with a maximum of 30 days. The metadata that defines the setup of the org is pulled from the source control system each time the Scratch is created. When a pro-code developer works with these, they create the Org and set things up with the latest setup, build and unit test the functionality they need to, submit this to the version control system, and then delete the Scratch Org and spin up a new one of their next assigned piece of functionality.

The main focus of this book is building solutions with the low-code options first, so we are not going to deep dive into tooling for pro-code solutions. If you are already familiar with these tools, you may want to use them to deploy functionality between orgs or set up more automated deployment approaches.

If you aren't already familiar with some of these types of tools, either from the Salesforce platform or other technologies, Salesforce provides a lot of information on how to get started. They are linked in the *Further reading* section.

If you have requirements that require a code solution, and your organization doesn't have experience building and deploying pro-code solutions on the Salesforce Customer 360 platform, it may be best for you to engage with an external organization or a freelance consultant. While there is a lot of information and resources available on how to write code with Apex and LWCs, it introduces risk to learning while delivering a critical implementation. Working with someone or people who have experience reduces risk in your implementation and provides an opportunity for knowledge transfer. In particular, deployments are usually time-critical and high-pressure, so you wouldn't want any concerns with your deployment tooling.

What is DevOps?

DevOps is an abbreviation for Software Development and IT Operations. It is a set of philosophies, both cultural and practical, that aims to increase collaboration and automation and reduce time to delivery. It includes both general working practices and specific technology concepts.

DevOps is both a broad and deep topic that is typically the domain of software developers and is a career discipline in itself. When you carry out any customization in Sales Cloud or on the Salesforce Customer 360 platform, it is important to have an understanding that these philosophies and concepts exist so that you can determine if you should be applying them. In this book, we will review the high-level concepts and terminology so that you have enough information to start researching and have meaningful conversations with people inside and outside your organization that can help you learn more. You may already be very experienced in this discipline, in which case, you can move on to the next section.

DevOps has several principles. The following principles are particularly applicable to Sales Cloud and Salesforce Customer 360 platform implementations:

- **Collaboration:** This is a key component of DevOps. One of the overall aims is to increase cooperation and break down silos between software development teams and those that support it in production. It encourages sharing feedback and working as a single team.

- **Automation**: This is a fundamental part of DevOps. Automating the process of transferring metadata between environments means that more time can be spent building features, reducing human errors, and increasing productivity.

- **Version control**: This is a system that records changes to a file or set of files over time so that specific versions can be recalled later. It enables multiple people to work simultaneously on a project, managing and merging changes from different contributors efficiently to avoid conflicts and preserve the project's history.

- **Continuous integration (CI):** This is a software development practice where developers frequently merge their code changes into a central repository, ideally multiple times a day. This process is automated to build and test code every time a change is made, helping to catch and reduce bugs early in the development cycle.

- **Continuous delivery (CD)**: This is an extension of CI that aims to automate the software delivery process to ensure that code can be safely deployed to production at any time. By automatically building, testing, and preparing code for release, CD minimizes the manual steps required for deployment, enabling faster and more reliable delivery of updates to users.

In the following section, we will consider the commercially available DevOps tools.

Commercially available DevOps tools

In addition to the tools that Salesforce provides, several companies provide DevOps tooling. These commercially available tools are usually feature-rich and go beyond the capabilities of the free Salesforce tools. This includes functionality such as comparing the differences between Orgs and allowing deployments to be rolled back.

You can find many of the commercially available tools on AppExchange or the internet by searching for the term "DevOps." We'll learn more about using AppExchange in *wssw – Extending with the AppExchange*.

Now that you understand the environments that Salesforce provides for development on the platform, next, you'll learn how to develop a testing approach for your Sales Cloud implementation.

Developing a testing approach

Testing is the third stage of the Salesforce ALM. In this section, we'll review the planning that is required to set up your testing approach. In *Chapter 8, Executing Testing*, we'll expand on the content in the section and look at the specifics of the functional testing phases that we'll introduce in this section. We'll also consider the practical aspects of testing. We'll start with a foundational understanding of why testing is important.

Why is testing important?

Testing is part of any quality assurance process, which aims to prevent defects and errors in software solutions. Testing confirms that the functionality that's built delivers the requirements specified and will be an important part of your implementation delivery. This ensures that the solution delivers on stakeholders' expectations and that it can be trusted. A solution that has errors and defects will quickly be mistrusted and abandoned by users. Trust in a system is harder to gain once it has been lost than it is to establish from the start, and this is why developing a thorough testing approach is key.

When to test

The time and cost required to fix an error or defect increase the further along it is discovered in the development life cycle, with the highest cost being when the functionality is in Production. For this reason, the aim is to identify and resolve defects as early as possible in the development life cycle. This can sometimes be referred to as a **shift left** mentality or shift left testing. An example is where testing is carried out in parallel with development. There is even a testing methodology where test cases are created first and code is developed to pass the test cases. The different approaches have pros and cons.

Quality assurance and testing is itself a discipline and profession. They are both broad and deep topics that we will cover in enough detail for you to understand their importance and role in your Sales Cloud implementation. However, this is not a comprehensive guide on this topic. If you are responsible for testing for your implementation, you may want to explore this topic in more detail.

It is worth noting that how a project approaches testing will depend on the organization's approach, scale, and maturity in the software development life cycle. While the aim should always be to identify and resolve defects as early as possible, the approaches available can be restricted by time and budget. If you work in a regulated industry, your organization will likely have a more stringent approach to quality assurance than those that don't.

Testing low code versus pro code

One of the key benefits of the Salesforce platform is its declarative, low-code tools. The declarative approach makes some changes, such as adding fields, really simple and almost trivial. With this quick pace of change, it is easy to get swept along and forget that any testing is required. In this example, the field itself is only one element. It needs to be on the correct page layouts, be visible and editable by the right Users, and be checked to ensure that if it is a required field or has validation, existing processes do not break. These other elements can be easily overlooked but have significant security and integration implications. No system-enforced process requires declarative changes to be tested. However, as the capability of the low-code tools increases, as seen with the automation capability of Flows, there is a move to introduce testing options. Now, you have options to debug your Flows and for some types of Flows, you can also create and save tests, although this is not required to activate a Flow.

On the other hand, for pro-code solutions such as Apex classes, Salesforce mandates that a level of unit testing is required. For any Apex code to be deployed to a production environment of Sales Cloud or Salesforce, it must have a unit test exercising it. The overall test code coverage in a Salesforce production environment is a measure that is calculated. It is the percentage of lines of code in the Org that are exercised by unit tests. A production Org must have an aggregated test code coverage of at least 75% (or ideally above) for new code to be deployed. Every Apex class and trigger must have at least 1% test code coverage. In addition to unit testing the code in the production Org, Salesforce runs unit tests for planned releases to identify potential issues. This is known as the Hammer. This book focuses on the low-code tools before extending with pro-code tools, but it is important to be aware of this, especially if you are implementing Sales Cloud in an existing Org.

The impact of deployment methodology and environment strategy on testing

In the previous sections, we explored common development methodologies and the environment strategy that's used for Sales Cloud projects. The approach taken here has an impact on how testing can be incorporated into the development life cycle. Let's explore how each has an impact:

- **Development methodology**: Agile and Waterfall require different testing skills. The difference between working with an Agile, rather than Waterfall, methodology is that the focus is on face-to-face communication rather than extensive documentation. This means there is less documentation for testers to work from. Documentation is required. Agile can be harder for testers as there is a need to continuously adapt. Testers on Agile projects fulfill a range of roles, including attending sprint planning, estimating tests, writing test cases, and attending reviews.

- **Environment strategy and management**: Not having dedicated environments for testing or delays in setting up environments can harm the testing progress. Testing in the same org as development is very challenging, and not recommended, as functionality, the UI, and data continually change.

When starting, the choices of how you approach your implementation are all interdependent. These details must be worked through so that the elements of the project support each other.

In the next section, we'll explore the types of testing that might be included in Sales Cloud implementations.

Types of testing

In this section, we'll review the terms and types of testing that are most commonly used in Salesforce projects to give you the language to use when you talk about testing. You may find that other terms are also used across the software testing industry.

The following are the areas of testing you should be aware of:

- **Functional testing**: This is a type of testing that is used to confirm that software performs the function specified in the requirement.

- **Non-functional testing**: This is a type of testing that verifies factors that impact the end-user experience, such as performance, page load times, and security.

- **Unit testing (functional)**: This is carried out by the person developing the functionality. Its purpose is to confirm that the functionality works as expected. Unit tests should be carried out to confirm that the functionality that's been built performs the expected actions.

- **Quality assurance testing (functional)**: This is carried out by an individual or a team, other than the person who developed the functionality. Its purpose is to independently confirm that what has been built performs as the requirements specify.

- **Regression testing (functional)**: This is carried out by an individual or a team who is familiar with the organization's existing Sales Cloud capability. The purpose is to test the performance of the existing system capability to confirm that the new functionality doesn't harm it. Tools are available to automate regression testing so that it can be carried out for every new release.

- **System integration testing (functional)**: This is carried out by an individual or a team who is familiar with Sales Cloud and the other system(s) that make up the end-to-end solution. The purpose is to confirm that the end-to-end tasks can be performed across system domains.

- **Smoke or sanity testing (functional)**: This is carried out by members of the deployment team and selected business users. The purpose is to verify that a software deployment has been executed correctly and that the environment is ready for the next actions. It is also known as build verification testing.

- **User acceptance testing (functional)**: This is carried out by the future Users of the system who have specified the system requirements. It is usually only a selected subset of the Users rather than all of them. The purpose is to confirm that the solution implemented meets the User's expectations of the requirements. They not only test functionality but also usability, security, and performance. It can reveal differences between the solutions and the requirements, as well as the documented requirements and the User's expectations. This is typically the last phase of functional testing and reveals the most about Users' attitudes to what has been built and any gaps in the user stories.

- **Performance testing (non-functional)**: This is carried out by an individual or a team. Salesforce recommends incorporating performance testing early in your development cycle when you have a large number of Users, a large volume of records, or when you are handling B2C scale applications. Any performance testing on the Salesforce platform must be pre-arranged with Salesforce using the process defined in Performance Assistant.

- **Security testing (non-functional)**: This is carried out by someone or a team of security vulnerability experts who are independent of the build team.

- **Penetration testing**: This is also referred to as **pentesting**. It is carried out by an individual or a team. Its purpose is to attack a system to expose any vulnerabilities.

- **Manual testing**: This is tested by people going through manual steps. This is the most common type of testing on Sales Cloud implementations.

- **Automated testing**: This is executed via predefined scripts, usually by test automation tools that are **graphical user interface (GUI)**-based. It is important to note that test automation tools should never hold production data.

- **Exploratory testing**: This type of testing has no scripts. Time spent on this is time-boxed. Testers are tasked with seeing if they can push or even break the system. After the allocated time has passed, testers discuss and raise issues.

- **Negative testing**: Negative tests test scenarios when the system should not work to confirm that is the case.

This is a list of terms that are commonly used on Sales Cloud implementation projects. Testing is both a broad and deep topic and will be covered in enough detail for you to understand its importance and its role in Sales Cloud implementation. If you are responsible for testing for your implementation, you may want to explore each of these topics in more detail.

In the next section, we will compare the different levels of documentation you can expect to see relating to testing.

Test strategy versus test plan versus test cases

In this section, we will get to know the artifacts that provide structure and consistency to your testing approach. These documents or artifacts capture the why, what, and how of testing. There are three levels of testing documentation: test strategy, test plans, and test cases. Here, the test strategy provides an overarching view of testing, and test cases provide the detail required for execution. We'll start by exploring the content and role of the test strategy.

Test strategy

A **test strategy** is a high-level document that summarizes what and why software testing is carried out in an organization. It provides a framework that is platform and technology-agnostic. Each implementation project should use this framework to define a testing plan for their implementation that is tailored to the platform, technologies, scale, and complexity they have.

Defining a test strategy before your project starts illustrates that quality is important and provides a reference document throughout the project that all team members can reference. Your strategy states the aims of your testing, the types of testing that will be carried out, the processes that will be followed, and the people and skills that will be needed to deliver testing. It gives you the best opportunity to ensure a consistent approach is taken by all stakeholders.

If your Sales Cloud implementation is the first, or one of only a few, business application development projects that your organization is undertaking, then you might be defining your test strategy and project test plan at the same time. In this case, for simplicity, you might choose to capture this content in a single document. If your organization develops software itself or is at the scale that it carries out many business application customization projects, you would expect to have a test strategy for the organization and a test plan for each project that captures the practical variations for the type of solution being created. If you have a test manager or test team in your organization, you will want to engage with them during the planning phase so that you can understand how your organization delivers testing and benefit from the documentation, processes, and tools already in place.

The test strategy will need to evolve as the organization increases the scale and complexity of the customization projects it undertakes. For example, setting up Sales Cloud for the first time in a greenfield (brand new) org with no system integrations will only require a strategy for testing what is being designed. If integrations are included, then system integration testing will be required. If functionality is being deployed into an existing live org, then regression testing might be appropriate.

> **Greenfield Org**
>
> A greenfield implementation refers to the creation and development of a new project, system, or application in an environment that is entirely new and lacks any prior constraints, limitations, or existing infrastructure. In this context, "greenfield" symbolizes an untouched landscape, implying that the implementation can start with a clean slate, without needing to integrate with or adapt to pre-existing systems or legacy code. This approach allows for greater freedom, flexibility, and creativity in designing and implementing the new solution.

The level of detail you go into for your test strategy will depend on the scale of the transformation the Sales Cloud implementation provides.

You would expect to have the following in your text strategy:

- **Vision**: A statement of your company's testing vision – that is, what the organization is hoping to achieve with testing.
- **Scope**: What the testing strategy covers.
- **Types of testing**: The type of testing the organization expects to be carried out across all technologies.
- **Common testing process**: Any testing-related processes that are independent of the technology being tested and are mandated across the organization – for example, the defect management process.
- **Approach to data**: How and what data should be used for testing. This might include how to generate or anonymize test data.
- **Testing tools**: Testing specific tools that are available and should be used on projects – for example, defect management tools or test automation tools.

The test strategy may also specify any regulations that must be complied with. The test strategy provides guidance on how testing should be approached across an organization so that a consistent approach is taken.

In the next section, we'll drill down into the next level of detail: the test plan.

Test plan

A **test plan** is a document that describes the testing that will be carried out for a specific implementation project. It takes the approach that is defined in the strategy and applies it to the specifics of the platform being implemented and the technologies being used. For large-scale or complex implementations, it can be beneficial to have a test plan per test phase. In *Chapter 8*, *Executing Testing*, we'll explore the functional test phases you would expect to see in a Sales Cloud implementation and provide example content for a test plan for each phase. For simple implementations where there is no integration, it is likely that the same person will carry out the testing and that the solution is built in a greenfield org. In this case, the environment strategy is likely to be simple with just a single test plan.

In a test plan, you would expect to have the following information. This could be in a dedicated section with the name specified here or in a simplified format:

- **Objective**: What the testing should achieve
- **Scope**: What will and will not be tested
- **Schedule**: When it should happen
- **Resources**: Who should be involved
- **Environments**: The Sandboxes or Scratch Orgs that will be used for testing
- **Datasets**: The specification for the data that will be used for testing, including any ammonization needed and required data
- **Defect process**: This will likely be common across all phases and projects.
- **Artifacts**: The document and diagrams that will be created to support or record testing.
- **Sign-off**: Who, when, and what is required to confirm that testing is complete

Table 2.3 shows some examples of how you would expect an organization's test strategy to be translated into content for a Sales Cloud test plan:

Topic	Test Strategy	Test Plan
Scope	All business application customization projects shall include functional testing, with a focus on testing as early in the development process are practically possible. It is expected that all implementations will have a minimum of unit, quality assurance, and user acceptance testing. SI testing must be included where the application integrates with another.	The principle of testing as early as possible in the development process will be adopted for the Sales Cloud implementation project. The earliest phase of testing that can be carried out will be unit testing, which will be carried out immediately after the functionality has been built by the building developer.
Environments	When carrying out business application customization, the aim should be for each developer to have a build environment. Once built and unit tested, functionality is moved to a different environment for each testing phase so that each phase can be carried out independently of the other.	On the Sales Cloud implementation project, each developer will be provided with a Developer Sandbox to carry out build and unit testing. A Developer Pro Sandbox will be created for quality assurance. A Partial Copy Sandbox will be used for user acceptance testing.

Table 2.3 – Examples of test strategy content translated into a test plan

This table provides a couple of examples of how the aims and principles that are defined in the strategy can be translated into specifics for your Sales Cloud implementation project.

Next, we will explore what's included in test cases.

Test cases

The **test case**, or **test script**, details how each test is to be carried out. It contains enough detail for a tester to execute the test. The test case document has areas for the tester to record the outcome of the test and any supporting information. They form a record of the testing that has taken place and the result.

Each user story or requirement has at least one test case, although it is likely to have more than one. The number of test cases per user story or requirement will depend on its complexity. As a general rule, you would expect a test case for every user story's acceptance criteria. For more information about user stories, see the *Capturing user stories* section in *Chapter 3*.

A common template is used to capture test cases. The template will typically include the following content:

- **Test case reference**: A unique reference number that the test can be identified by.

- **The requirement or user story**: The original functionality that was requested.

- **Acceptance criteria**: The conditions the functionality has to meet.

- **Test scenario**: The scenario that the test is replicating.

- **Test steps**: The individual steps the tester needs to perform to complete the test.

- **Actual result**: A description of the actual result observed.

- **Pass/fail**: A statement of whether the functionality achieved the acceptance criteria for a pass or if it failed.

- **Notes**: Any notes for descriptions or screenshots of the things the test observed. This is particularly important for fails where links to records and the step on how to recreate results in a quicker resolution.

- **Status**: The status of the test in terms of the defect resolution process (open, in triage, in fix, ready to retest, change, as designed, passed).

- **Assigned tester**: The person who has carried out the test.

In *Chapter 8 – Executing Testing*, we'll look at how to translate user stories into test cases.

It is common for the test case template to be created in a spreadsheet tool as they are widely available to business users and easy to share. If your organization has a dedicated test team, then you might have access to a dedicated test management tool that may automate testing actions and communication. You should aim to have test cases written and signed off before the test phase begins.

Invest in testing

Testing is not a one-off activity that is only relevant for your initial implementation. Once your customized system is live, there needs to be ongoing testing need to ensure the functionality that's delivered continues to work. Every time the system is changed, there is a possibility that the existing functionality is affected. Your Sales Cloud solution is changed every time Salesforce releases functionality, when you release new functionality, and when an integrated system is changed. In reality, Salesforce releases don't have an impact in the vast majority of cases and when there is a change that is likely to have an impact, they communicate this in advance, but it can happen. For this reason, it is best to view testing as an ongoing investment in the quality of your solution and incorporate testing into your ongoing maintenance.

In the next section, we will explore some more advanced testing concepts that are used in Salesforce implementation and add value once you have mastered the concepts we have already covered.

Beyond the basics

In this section, we'll take a quick look at how to build on your testing foundation to streamline your testing processes. If your organization has experience delivering business application customization projects, they may have already adopted these practices. It is worth checking if these are already carried out in your organization as this will make it easier for you to assess if they are appropriate and apply them.

Automated testing

Automated testing is the process of checking for defects and ensuring that the application functions as expected without manual intervention. It involves using specialized software to run tests on a software application automatically. This method speeds up the testing process, increases coverage and consistency, and allows developers to focus on more complex testing and development tasks. It enhances the quality and reliability of software and facilitates rapid development cycles.

Automated testing is particularly beneficial for regression testing, which is often not otherwise carried out or to a minimum level if it needs to be done manually. It is also an essential component of a DevOps CI/CD setup. It allows testing to be fully integrated into the development process.

To implement automated testing, you will need an automated testing application, Salesforce doesn't provide this, but it is possible to build and save some tests in Flow. Time will also be required to build the tests. You determine when this is carried out, which could be after each feature is built, as a batch once the implementation is live, or somewhere in between. As discussed in the *When to test* section, the earlier testing takes place, the cheaper it is to fix the defects. Top of Form

It is worth noting that Salesforce presents some specific challenges for some automation approaches and tools as records have different IDs between environments and dynamic IDs, which means tests will fail. The Lightning framework means that the elements on the page load at different rates that can result in test failures and functionality such as the Sales console are harder to test against.

Measuring testing performance

As organizations increase the volume of testing they carry out, it is beneficial to measure the performance of testing. It provides an understanding of the quality and reliability of the software, enabling teams to identify areas for improvement and ensure that the product meets the required standards before release. It also provides insights into the efficiency of the development process, helping teams to optimize resource allocation, reduce time to market, and improve overall project management.

You will likely start by tracking the total number of defects reported or the fixed defect percentage (defects fixed/total defects reported) as these indicate the work remaining on an implementation. However, progressing to further metrics such as the rework effort ratio (total effort on rework/ total effort spent) or schedule slippage ((estimated days/ actual days)) x 100) can help to identify if there are areas in the testing process that might need looking at for efficiency improvements.

Test-driven development

Finally, we will briefly consider **test-driven development (TDD)**, which is a development approach that puts testing front and center. It is an Agile test methodology. It is a software development approach where tests are written before any code, guiding the coding process to ensure it meets the predefined tests and requirements. This method emphasizes the creation of small, manageable pieces of code that are continuously tested and refactored, leading to more reliable and cleaner code output.

While TDD is not implemented in its purest form in most Sales Cloud implementation projects, or at least the ones I have seen, the concept of building a test is valuable as Salesforce requires unit tests for all APEX code. These unit tests should be written at the same time or directly after the feature code as the functionality can't be deployed afterward. The practice of leaving writing the test classes to the end of the build can be inefficient as developers have to remember what was built and it can highlight issues that mean code needs to be refactored.

Now that we have considered the planning phase, we need to ensure the quality of the solution we are going to deliver.

Change management and training

In this section, we'll explore what's meant by organizational **change management**. This fits within the adoption phase of the Salesforce ALM. First, we will learn about what is meant by change management. We will explain the role that **training** has within change management, how it prepares your stakeholders, and its role in adoption. Let's start with change management.

What is change management?

Organizational change management is the discipline of taking people and organizations through change. People, and consequently organizations, can find it difficult to embrace change, which can impact the organization's ability to survive and thrive. Due to its importance to business success, there is a lot of academic research on this, and strategies have been developed to increase change management success rates. The types of organizational change have been categorized, the challenges have been understood, and an established set of principles have been developed to smooth the transition.

Organizational change management is a big topic – much bigger than we will be able to cover in detail in this book. Some people specialize in this function and have roles dedicated to it. If you have a person or team that specializes in change management in your organization, you should engage with them and seek their guidance. In this book, we'll learn about the principles and techniques that are typically used concerning Sales Cloud implementation projects.

There are several different models to explain what happens when people go through change. Some models consider the whole process, whereas others focus on specific elements. For example, Kotter's Theory divides change into eight stages and focuses on understanding why and building momentum for change but is less focused on employee feedback. This is well established and can work well, particularly in large companies. In contrast, Maurer's 3 Levels of Resistance and Change model focuses on why change fails and the emotional reaction with levels of I don't get it, I don't like it, I don't like you. You might work with people that are experiencing these emotions. If you experience resistance from stakeholders, it can be helpful to review change management models for strategies.

There are different types of organizational change, including strategic, structural, technology, processes, and people. With a Sales Cloud implementation, it is most likely to be a technology and/or process change. Implementing Sales Cloud is also most likely to be a transformative rather than adaptive or incremental change as it impacts the whole of the Sales functions and may impact other teams if it is part of a larger project implementing multiple systems. If the implementation is replacing an existing system with much the same functionality, then it might be an adaptive change but if the new system is not adding significant improvement, then an opportunity is being missed. Projects where Salesforce, or another technology, is implemented for multiple functions are often referred to as large-scale digital transformation projects.

> **People, process, and technology**
>
> A technology such as Sales Cloud is implemented to solve a business problem, but sometimes, the problem is a people or process problem, or sometimes both. Although the new technology will make some improvements, it might not deliver all the results hoped for if the root cause is something else. It is important to look at this as it is one of the reasons that implementations stall or even fail – there is a process or people problem that needs to be solved first. Sometimes, it is easier for a business to get a technology project started than it is to focus on process improvement. Look out for situations where process change or harmonization is required to realize the benefits of Sales Cloud. This can take time and cause delays. Change management becomes even more important when processes and people change as stakeholders have to come up with an agreed way forward.

Next, we'll look at why change management is important.

Why is change management important?

People can find change difficult and unsettling. There is often an emotional response to change. As a result, people can resist change, preferring what they know. This can be a problem for businesses that need to constantly evolve what they do to grow and stay relevant. Acknowledging the challenges that are associated with changing and having a plan to overcome them provides a business advantage.

This is particularly important for application implementations such as Sales Cloud as they require end-user acceptance and adoption for success. If there is resistance that is not addressed, it can be problematic as resistance can become contagious. One negative voice can gain momentum.

Centralized systems provide more visibility for managers and standardized ways of working. These are seen as benefits for leadership, but they can seem like negatives for team members who have previously enjoyed autonomy. This can be amplified if the transition is from spreadsheets, where team members have had the flexibility to refine how they apply the sales process and the data they record.

Some change management models specifically consider the emotional response to change. In the previous sections, we referenced Maurer's 3 Levels of Resistance and Change model. There is also the Kübler-Ross Change Curve to consider, which is based on the five stages of grief. The five stages of the Kübler-Ross model are **denial**, **anger**, **bargaining**, **depression**, and **acceptance**. These stages represent some strong emotions and the strength of feeling that change creates. You will want to keep this in mind as you plan and work through your Sales Cloud implementation. If you observe resistance, increasing your change management activities can help keep the implementation on track.

Now that we've considered why change management is important, let's look at practical components you can put in place to support your implementation.

What are the principles of change management?

In this section, we will review practical components that you can put in place that are commonly used in Salesforce and Sales Cloud implementation or update programs. The following are components that you can put in place for your implementation:

- **Clear vision**: Define what change is required and why is it necessary. This must be defined in a way that all the stakeholders affected can relate to it. It must have a benefit to them rather than just financial benefits for the business. The question you what to have an answer for each stakeholder group is *What's in it for me?* You will want to continually and consistently communicate this throughout the project.

- **Committed leadership**: Organization leaders have a very important role in delivering change: they set the direction and culture of an organization. They also control what team members focus their time on and how the budget is allocated. You will want an organization leader to be the executive sponsor of your implementation. This is likely to be the person who has championed the purchase of Sales Cloud. You will also need team leaders to free up time for stakeholders to participate in requirement-gathering sessions, testing, and training. If stakeholders have to do this work in addition to their day job, their commitment can be reduced.

- **Champions**: Champions are people who are positive about the change and like to communicate and engage with others. They are also referred to as change agents. They can be powerful advocates that those who have concerns can talk to. There are usually a small number of people from different stakeholder groups. Possible champions are usually people who volunteer to be involved in the project. They don't have to be the most experienced people on the team. Sometimes, a new team member can bring enthusiasm and find the new system easy to use.

- **Stakeholder involvement**: A primary objective of change management is that you bring people on the journey and ensure they feel invested in the outcome. The best results come from involving people in requirements gathering, decision-making, playbacks, and testing. This makes people feel that the change is happening for them and not for them. It can be tempting to progress through the build without involving stakeholders, particularly when timelines are tight, but this can be an error. Stakeholders raise important concerns, and they are more costly to resolve later in the build.

- **Training and support**: Training provides Users of the system with the knowledge and skills they need to be able to use Salesforce Cloud. Not knowing how to use the system can be a reason for low adoption. We will explore how to create a training plan in the *Planning your training* section. Support comes in once Sales Cloud is live and Users need support resolving issues they encounter. Ongoing support and maintenance of the system can be provided via the organization's IT team or a dedicated Salesforce team. Ongoing support is essential for long-term adoption.

- **Celebrate success**: Implementations have multiple phases. There can be highs and lows, particularly as people in the organization might also be having an emotional response. For that reason, it is important to celebrate the successes when they come and regularly communicate them.

- **Communication**: Another important part of taking people with you is regular communication about progress with a focus on successes. These messages should be personalized for the audiences so that it is easy for them to understand *What's in it for me?* This communication helps build excitement and momentum. You will want to ramp this up as the implementation gets closer to deployment. Aim to use your organization's more common channel of communication. If this is a collaboration tool such as Slack, you might want to create a specific channel. You can also share specific content with champions that enables them to share information.

- **Measure and monitor progress**: It can also be beneficial to keep monitoring the attitude toward the implementation and the change. This could be via team leaders, feedback from champions, or formal surveys. Having a benchmark and qualifying any issues makes it possible to make improvements.

- **Encourage feedback**: Creating a project culture that encourages feedback means that any issues get raised early when they are more cost-efficient to resolve.

- **Learn and adapt**: Once you have encouraged feedback, you must act on it; otherwise, the feedback will stop coming. Adapting to feedback shows your audience that their needs matter, which will build trust and good favor. A bank of trust and good favor can be beneficial as there can be times on projects when difficult or unpopular choices need to be made.

Each organization, implementation, and set of stakeholders is different. Your approach must be customized for your particular implementation. Depending on the scale and complexity of the change your implementation presents, you might use a few or all of the strategies mentioned here.

If it isn't in Salesforce, it doesn't exist

If it isn't in Salesforce, it doesn't exist is a common mantra you will hear in organizations that have a strong adoption of Salesforce. This is most effective when it comes from the top. This is where committed leadership is powerful. If leaders are planning to log in and run their teams based on the information in Sales Cloud, then adoption will be a lot higher than if they run their meetings and teams in the old way. If you have leaders who are not interested in how they can use the system to run their team, that is a red flag, and you should investigate ways you can bring them into the project.

In the next section, we will take a detailed look at training and how you create a training plan.

Planning your training

In the *What is change management?* section, we learned that training is an essential component of organizational change. Training provides an opportunity to tell Users, and other impacted stakeholders, the benefits of what is being delivered, as well as provide the knowledge and the skills Users need for the tasks they will be required to carry out in Sales Cloud.

If your organization has a learning and development team, then you will want to engage with them to understand if there is any institutional knowledge, processes, or tools that you can adopt that will accelerate your training development and smooth User transition.

We will start by exploring the different types of training so that you understand the options that are available as you put together a training plan.

Types of training

In this section, we will go through each of the types of training that are commonly used in Salesforce implementations. We have used the terms that are most often used on Salesforce projects, although other terms are used and mean the same thing.

Here are the types and ways of classifying training that you should be aware of:

- **Instructor-led training**: Instructor-led training is a type of training that is delivered by an instructor or a facilitator and is very interactive. This training is synchronous, meaning attendees can get a response before moving on to the next topic. The instructor explains a concept or the steps to perform a task and attendees can ask questions in the session. This type of training takes place at a set time and location and is likely to have a group of attendees who can also learn from the questions asked and examples given by each other.

- **Self-paced training**: Self-paced training is a type of training that individuals take at a time that suits them and they complete at their own pace. This training is asynchronous, meaning attendees can request a response, but it is unlikely to be available before they move on to the next topic.

- **Blended training**: Blended training combines instructor-led and self-paced training to give users options to learn in a way that best suits them. This type of approach means that users get contact time where they can ask their questions but also have resources that they can refer back to refresh their memories at a later time.

Delivery methods

- **In-Person**: In-person or face-to-face training is a type of training where the person delivering the training is in the same room as the attendees receiving the training

- **Virtual**: Virtual or online training is a type of training where attendees or learners participate online

Formats

- **Written**: Written training is a type of training where the content is written out for learners to read and follow the steps

- **Video**: Video training is a type of training where software demos or role plays are recorded so that learners can see how an action is performed rather than reading steps

- **Lecturer**: Lecture-based training is a type of training where the trainer or lecturer provides the content, usually verbally, with little interactivity

- **Hands-on**: Hands-on training is a type of training where attendees use the product or perform the activity they're being trained on

Other training terms that are commonly used on Sales Cloud implementations are as follows:

- **Train the trainer:** Train the trainer is where members of the development team, who are experts in the functionality of the new system train the people who will be creating the training materials for Users or a selected group of superusers.

- **Just-in-time training**: Just-in-time training is a type of training that allows the consumer to learn the skill or information at the point that it is needed. Content is divided into small bite-size chunks that can be taken individually or as part of a program. For example, the trails that are available on Salesforce's Trailhead learning platform. We will cover this more in the *Trailhead* section.

- **Product training**: Product training is a type of training that is available for employees to take at any time to increase or refresh their skills.

- **Onboarding training**: Onboarding training is a type of training that is provided for an organization's new joiners.

- **Office hours**: Office hours are physical or virtual sessions where users can drop in if they have a question about the system. They are usually scheduled at a regular frequency so that users can record their queries and then ask them all at one time.

- **Release notes**: This is a document that accompanies the release of new functionality and gives a written description of what the changes are. Salesforce provides release notes when they release functionality three times a year. It is good practice to provide release notes when you release Sales Cloud functionality. This can be a useful source of information for those who are interested in what has changed. It is particularly useful for those that have a system support role.

Learning and development is a discipline of its own. We will not be going into any more detail about the types of training that can be created. If you have a person or team that is responsible for this in your organization, you should seek their guidance on the tools and approaches to use so that you can ensure consistency with the way your organization creates and delivers training. They may have people who can assist you with your project. A consistent approach benefits your system users and will ensure a higher take-up of training.

Next, we will have a brief look at learning styles.

Learning styles

Learning styles are about the way people learn. It is well understood that people learn in different ways. The psychology of learning is another area where there is a lot of academic research and understanding if you would like to find out more. For your training to be successful, you want to create a plan that suits your audiences' learning styles. The four learning styles, also referred to as the **VARK model**, are as follows:

- **Visual learning**: Information is presented graphically with charts, diagrams, and symbols.

- **Auditory learning**: Learners listen to information. This might be via lectures or in group conversations.

- **Reading and writing**: Information is presented in words in factsheets, books, or presentations. Learners take notes in their own words.

- **Kinesiology learning**: Learners take a physical role. They get hands-on with the system or activity and use their senses.

This book uses the reading and writing style of learning with some visual elements. For Sales Cloud implementations, the biggest audience is Salespeople. In general, but not exclusively, people who are attracted to a job in sales like to communicate with people. They gather information from their customers but asking questions on the phone or in person or even observing what they do. They have not selected a career that has them sitting behind a desk reading text all day. Because of this, it is unlikely that creating and sending a salesperson a 50-page written manual about the new system is going to be a successful approach. However, this might be a valid approach for someone in a detail-focused role that doesn't want interaction. The training that supports your Sales Cloud implementation is about doing; so, it must be as hands-on as possible.

What is a training plan?

In this section, we will get to know the artifacts that provide structure and consistency to your training approach. These documents or artifacts capture the why, what, and how of training. There are two levels of training documentation that we will explore here: a training plan and a learning plan. The **training plan** is the artifact that captures the training approach for your Sales Cloud implementation. A **learning plan** is a document that describes an individual's proposed and completed development.

We'll start by exploring the content and role of the training plan.

Training plan

If your organization has a format or templates that they use to plan training, then familiarize yourself with that process and use it where appropriate as it will be easier to get buy-in from your internal stakeholders. There are lots of different types and formats of training plans, but the content they include is common. The following is a description of the types of content would expect to see in a Sales Cloud training plan:

- **Scope**: A description of what is and is not going to be covered in the training process – for example, the business processes that will be included and which stakeholders will receive training.
- **Objectives**: What the training aims to achieve. Ideally, these objectives will be measurable.
- **Learning outcomes**: The knowledge and skills to be taught. This can be in the form of completed processes.
- **Audience**: The stakeholders or personas that will receive training.
- **Types and methods**: The mix of the types of training and the delivery methods that will be used, as we reviewed in the *Types of training* section.
- **Curriculum and material**: The topics and the supporting materials that will be created.
- **Timeline**: The timeline for designing and delivering the training content.

- **Resources**: The people, their skillsets, and tools that will be needed to create the training content.

- **Content creation**: A description of the training content that will be created.

- **Measures**: The metrics that will be used to determine the success of the training.

- **Deliverables**: The training programs, sessions, and artifacts that will be produced.

In *Chapter 9*, we'll build on these content types and create an example training plan for your Sales Cloud implementation. We will also explore the practicalities of delivering training so that you have everything you need to deliver training.

> **Onboarding training**
>
> In addition to training to support the rollout of an initial implementation or the release of new functionality, there is also a need to provide training for people who are new to the system. Ongoing administration of Sales Cloud is beyond the scope of this book, but you will want to have a plan for how you provide onboarding training for new Users. You will likely be creating materials that can be used for both. Considering this upfront will make it easier to identify small adjustments that can be made to create materials that are appropriate for both applications.

Now that we have explored the types of training and the content that is included in a training plan, we will explore the resources that Salesforce provides to support your end-user training activities.

Salesforce resources

Salesforce understands the role that training and adoption have in achieving successful outcomes. They have created a significant amount of on-demand training content to help end users, administrators, developers, and marketers adopt their products on their learning platform, Trailhead. They also have tools within the Sales Cloud application for you to create customized prompts to help your users under step understand the steps they need to take, called In-App Guidance. We will explore what role these can play as part of your training program.

Trailhead

Salesforce's online learning platform is called Trailhead and is available at `trailhead.salesforce.com`. The platform offers a gamified way to learn where learners are rewarded with badges and points every time they complete a **Trail**. At the time of writing, there are over 1,000 badges available. Each Trail has either a quiz or a hands-on challenge at the end to confirm the learner has understood the content. The hands-on challenges require learners to log into a Salesforce org and complete an activity. Users can create a **Salesforce Playground** org directly from a Trail challenge to complete the tasks.

There's a significant proportion of Trails that are targeted at Salesforce implementors, either Administrator, Developers, or Marketers, but there are Trails for end users. You can find these by using the content filters. There are Trails on Salesforce products, as well as other topics, such as soft skills. Trails vary in duration from 5 minutes to over an hour, offering just-in-time, bite-size learning. In addition to Trails, there are instruction-led projects and **Super Badges**, which require applying knowledge to a scenario to illustrate a depth of understanding.

Access to Trailhead is free. The content of the Trails can be read without any signup. To complete the challenges and get badges, learners need to sign up for a Trailblazer ID, which is also free. Sales Cloud users can use their Sales Cloud login to register for Trailhead. None of the information from the Sales Cloud org is available to Trailhead. Once a learner has a Trailblazer ID, they also have a profile page that shows the badges and points they have earned. Once a learner has earned 100 badges or 50,000 points, they get Ranger status. As learners add a further 100 badges, they become a double, triple, and so on Ranger until they reach 600 badges, at which point they become an All Star Ranger. This type of gamification keeps learners engaged and reaching the next level. As an implementor, if you are not already using Trailhead to learn about Sales Cloud functionality, you should be.

For your end-user training, you may want to check the Trails that are available for end users and see if any of these support your training objectives. If you do identify Trails you would like your end users to complete, can create a **Trailmix**, which lists them together in the order you define. This means that you can point users to one place to complete a series of Trails.

Sales Enablement

Trailhead has been so popular that Salesforce has made a version of the learning platform available for organization purchase: **Sales Enablement**. Organizations can build their own Trails on Sales Enablement and make the content available to their internal people. If you find that your users really like the Trailhead platform, and you don't already have a learning management platform, you might want to explore this.

Next, we will consider the role that the In-App Guidance functionality in Sales Cloud has in your training program.

In-App Guidance

In-App Guidance is another just-in-time learning tool that Salesforce offers, but this time it is directly within your Sales Cloud org. In-App Guidance is a functionality that you can configure within **Setup** that shows prompts and tips for your Users in the Sales Cloud user interface. You can set up single prompts or walk-throughs, which are a series of up to 10 prompts. This allows you to guide users at the time they are performing an activity. This is not only good to reinforce initial training, but also to support consistent use and long-term adoption. You can see a count of how many times the guidance has been viewed and a completion percentage.

The first three walkthroughs are included in your Sales Cloud license. You can add further walkthroughs by purchasing my Trailhead or Sales Cloud enablement licenses. You can set up In-App Guidance by going to **Setup** > **User Engagement** > **In-App Guidance**.

You may want to include In-App Guidance as part of your training strategy. We will explore the options for In-App Guidance in more detail in *Chapter 5 – Design and Build: Sales User Productivity*.

Now that we have reviewed the types of training capabilities Salesforce provides, we will conclude this section on change management and training and wrap up this chapter.

Summary

In this chapter, we started by learning about the Salesforce ALM, which provides a framework for how we develop our Sales Cloud solution. We reviewed the two customization approaches, low code, and pro code, and explored the different delivery methodologies you can follow.

We then went on to learn about the environments Salesforce provides for development and the tools that are available to move the functionality you have built between these environments. With this foundational understanding of the tooling available, we considered how to develop a test plan for our solutions, something we'll build on in *Chapter 8 – Executing Testing*. We'll continue to explore the importance of change management and training in taking your users on the journey with you to ensure overall implementation success. We'll expand on what we have covered in this chapter in *Chapter 9 – Executing Training*.

In the next chapter, we'll take a detailed look at the sales process and the Sales Cloud data model. We'll start by reviewing some of the key concepts of any sales process so that you have the business understanding and language to work with stakeholders. We'll conclude by learning about the Sales Cloud data model so that you can map your requirements to the available data entities.

Further reading

Sandboxes

- *Sandbox Licenses and Storage Limits by Type*:

  ```
  https://help.salesforce.com/s/articleView?id=sf.data_sandbox_
  environments.htm&type=5
  ```

SFDX

- *App Development with Salesforce DX*:

  ```
  https://trailhead.salesforce.com/content/learn/modules/sfdx_
  app_dev/sfdx_app_dev_setup_dx
  ```

Agile

- *Agile Manifesto*:

  https://agilemanifesto.Org/

- *Agile Principles*:

  https://agilemanifesto.org/principles.html

DevOps

- *For more information about the history and principles of DevOps, see*:

  https://www.ibm.com/topics/devops

- *Scale Testing*:

  https://architect.salesforce.com/well-architected/trusted/
  reliable#Scalability

Change management

- *What is Organizational Change? Article Harvard Business School*:

  https://online.hbs.edu/blog/post/organizational-change-management

- *10 Change Management Models*:

  https://whatfix.com/blog/10-change-management-models/

Training

- *Sandbox Licenses and Storage Limits by Type*:

  https://help.salesforce.com/s/articleView?id=sf.data_sandbox_
  environments.htm&type=5

Trailhead

- *What is Trailhead?*:

  https://www.salesforce.com/blog/what-is-trailhead/

3

Design and Build: The Core Sales Process

Designing and building an appropriate, successful solution is dependent on a thorough understanding of the business process you are modeling. In this case, this involves the sales process and any business pains that need to be addressed. It also involves avoiding common pitfalls, such as trying to do everything at once and letting technology dictate the business process.

This chapter gives you the tools you need and the confidence to explore, understand, and document the sales process and associated requirements. First, you will learn about sales frameworks to confirm your foundational knowledge of the sales business process. You will then learn about the full Sales Cloud data model and look at the key Objects for the sales process, including the main considerations and how they are used in practice. You will learn about the Objects that are related to lead generation in the next chapter.

We will also review the data security tools available in the Customer 360 platform. You will learn what tools are available for you to secure your data. It is assumed you already have a fundamental understanding of the Customer 360 platform's security features and have the knowledge or support to make sure your Org is secure. Once we have explored all the available capabilities that support the sales process, we will look at how to approach translating the requirements into a solution design.

It is worth noting that there is no singular perfect design for a set of requirements. Some solutions are just more appropriate for the business needs than others. This is why it is so important to spend time understanding the needs of the business and the system users at the beginning.

In this chapter, we're going to cover the following main topics:

- Understanding your sales (business) process
- Sales Cloud data model and security
- Reports and forecasting
- Accounts and Contacts

- Opportunities, Products, and Price Books

- Activities

- Users, Account and Opportunity Teams

- Translating sales process requirements into a design

Supporting tools and information

For this chapter, you will require a tool to capture system requirements. A spreadsheet application such as Microsoft Excel or Google Sheets is a good way to quickly capture, share, collaborate, and refine requirements.

For your Sales Cloud implementation, you should consider using the tools your organization standardizes as they will be widely understood and accepted. Requirements can be managed in spreadsheets for simple and very small team projects, but specific requirement management or project management tools offer tailored functionality and will help improve collaboration and organization on larger projects with more people involved. These tools often offer traceability through the life cycle, so you can map the requirement to the configuration changes. Some examples are JIRA by Atlassian or the Agile Accelerator, an application built on Salesforce that can be installed from AppExchange.

For this chapter, you will require a tool to document your sales process. In the beginning, this might be a paper and pen, or the digital equivalent. For sharing with stakeholders or adding to a document, a diagram can be created in a presentation tool such as Microsoft PowerPoint or Google Slides. These are often used as these are the tools that people commonly have access to, but for large or detailed diagrams, they can be challenging. Diagramming applications have shapes and functionality, making them easier to use. Lucidchart has a library of Salesforce shapes but not everyone has access to it in their company.

Understanding your sales (business) process

To explore the sales process, we'll start by delving into the common sales frameworks. Understanding the characteristics of these will help you get an initial understanding of your organization's sales needs and narrow down the Sales Cloud functionality you might be using. For example, if your sales are business-to-business, then you will need to capture information about organizations. Being familiar with the terminology and what it means will also help when you talk to business stakeholders about what they need.

Building on this foundation, we will explore methods of gathering information on the steps your organization takes during a sale, the sales process, and who you should involve. This may already be well documented in your organization, in which case is it simply about familiarizing yourself with the documentation and artifacts. Although there may be some documentation, in practice, the details and variations in the ways of working usually reside in people's heads. To deliver a system that people are happy to use, it is essential to understand not just the desired path, but what truly happens in reality. Usually, the best way to do this is to gather information from multiple sources and present it back to stakeholders to confirm that everyone has a shared understanding.

By the end of this chapter, you will understand the type of sales models your organization uses, and then be able to gather detailed information on what happens in practice and document it in a way that is appropriate for your sales audience. In this section, we will explore common sales frameworks, gather information on the sales process, document findings, harmonize the sales process, and overcome objections.

Common sales frameworks

Sales can be both a science and an art. Each organization sells to its customers in a slightly different way. How an organization sells is determined by many factors, including the following:

- Who it sells to – businesses or consumers

- What it sells – for example, physical goods, digital goods, or services

- The place of sale – online, in-store, or over the phone

- Many other factors can be considered here, including the organization's culture. Fortunately for us, some industry-accepted frameworks can be used to categorize such sales approaches.

An important high-level classification captures to whom and how an organization sells – to a business, consumer, or both. The following are the classifications:

- **Business-to-business (B2B) sales**

- **Business-to-consumer (B2C) sales**

- **Business-to-business-to-consumer (B2B2C)**

B2B and B2C are quite self-explanatory. An example of B2B would be Salesforce selling products and services to businesses. B2C would be a music streaming service that a consumer subscribes to.

With B2B2C, an organization's products are delivered by another company. The **Original Equipment Manufacturer** (**OEM**) doesn't have a direct link to the consumer. With the increasing desire of organizations and brands to build relationships with their customers, organizations using this approach are exploring ways they can connect with consumers directly. An example might be a food manufacturer that sells via a retailer but has a loyalty scheme consumers can sign up.

Understanding an organization's customer type provides fundamental information on how a system needs to be designed. For B2B, the data model will be organization-centric, while for B2C, it will be person-centric. Some organizations will require both models. While these categories are widely adopted, it is worth noting that there isn't an industry-standard definition.

For each organization you work with, adopt and adapt to the terminology and classifications they use. Successful sales leaders will have taken common frameworks, or ones they have used before, and adapted them to fit the needs of their current organization.

We will explore some other frameworks and how they can help us approach a Sales Cloud solution design in the next section.

Sales models

A Sales model describes how an organization identifies and engages with customers. Here are some examples of classifications:

- **Inbound sales**: Buyers are attracted by informational content such as blogs and webinars. Buyers make the first approach.
- **Outbound sales**: Salespeople reach out to a high volume of people via emails, calls, and texts to identify potential buyers. Sales make the first approach.
- **Account-based selling**: A targeted approach where sales, marketing, and other functions work together to offer individual accounts a tailored offer.
- **Self-service selling**: The customer completes the purchase without assistance from the seller.
- **Direct selling**: Products are marketed and sold through personal contact rather than a retail environment.

These examples are all quite different. Considering their characteristics, it is possible to start to understand what might be required from a system to support them. For example, Account-based selling requires multiple teams to access and collaborate on Accounts. Direct selling requires a high volume of sellers who most likely access the system from home to log their sales.

In the next section, we will explore the role of sales methodologies.

Sales methodologies

A sales methodology is an approach that typically provides a framework for how information can be gathered and how the likelihood of a sale can be assessed. Some methodologies have been developed by people or organizations and are published or promoted by them.

Here are some examples:

- **BANT**: A qualification framework that stands for Budget, Authority, Need, and Time.
- **Solution selling**: The focus is on providing a custom solution (mix of products and services) based on the buyer's pain points.
- **MEDDIC**: A qualification process that's used for complex enterprise sales. It stands for metrics, economic buyer, decision criteria, decision process, identifying pain, and champion.

Although you might likely find these examples useful, understanding what methodologies your organization uses can give you further insight into what they might need. For example, if they are asked to gather specific information, they will need places in the system to capture it. If they are encouraged to offer custom solutions to buyers, they will need flexibility with guidance and restrictions on what products and services they can put together. If their sales are complex and to enterprises, there will likely be multiple people involved in the sales on both the selling organization and buyer's side.

Sales processes

A sales process is the specific steps an organization takes to complete a sale. An organization might have different variations in its sales process for different types of products and services.

The sales process is usually described by its stages, which denote the status of the deal. Then, within each stage, the information required and the activities to perform are defined. From my experience, a typical sales process has five to six stages.

The **out-of-the-box** (**OOTB**) sales process in Sales Cloud has 10 stages in the Opportunity Stage field. That's nine sales stages, assuming "Closed Won" and "Closed Lost" are subtypes of the Closed stage. They are as follows:

- Prospecting
- Qualification
- Needs Analysis
- Value Proposition
- Id. Decision Makers
- Perception Analysis
- Proposal/Price Quote
- Negotiation/Review
- Closed:
  - Closed Won
  - Closed Lost

Figure 3.1 shows how the stages are visually represented in a component that is displayed at the top of every Opportunity page:

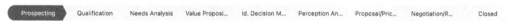

Figure 3.1 – The Opportunity stage visualized on the Opportunity record page

A possible simple sales process might have the stages described in Table 3.1:

Sales Stage	Activities
Qualification	Establish BANT
Company Analysis	Understand more about the organization and the buying group
Proposal	Provide a tailored value proposition
Objection Handling	Respond to buyers' questions and concerns
Close	Either order fulfillment or loss analysis

Table 3.1 – Table showing activities by sales stage

As you can see, the stages of the sales process will be dependent on the sales model and the sales methodology adopted, so understanding these models helps you anticipate the stages your organizations are likely to use. This will help you prepare for conversations with your stakeholders.

> **Tip**
> The criteria a deal needs to meet for each stage must be defined. All deals must be appropriately classified for reporting and forecasting to be meaningful. When you talk to sales leaders, you will need to define this, as well as the stages. This is an essential part of making the process repeatable and predictable.

Next, we will look at how you can gather specific information.

Gathering information on the sales process

In this section, we will explore why it is important to gather detailed information about the process and how it is managed today (the as-is) as well as what it should be in the future (the to-be). We will explore the who and the how of gathering information on the sales process.

Identifying your stakeholders

Sales is a very human process driven by relationships. There are several groups of people who you will want to engage with to understand the sales process. They each perform different activities:

- **Sales leadership** will set the strategy and targets and define the sales process to be followed. They are accountable for the performance of the sales operation and will want to track the key metrics. They are usually numbers-driven and get involved in strategic deals and accounts. *For this group, you will want to focus on what behaviors they want to drive from their team and the metrics and reporting they need.*

- **Sales management** oversees the process on a day-to-day basis. They are responsible for their team's performance and the accuracy of the forecast from their team. They need to support and motivate their team, removing any blockers they might have. *For this group, you will want to focus on the ways they can view their team activities and forecast.*

- **Account executives** have regular interactions with customers, where they seek to understand their challenges and build relationships. They shape and offer solutions by gathering information on customer stakeholders and their needs. They may also be required to generate sources of new business. *For this group, you will want to focus on making it easy to capture the data they need to provide and making it easy to view their customer relationships.*

- **Sales operations** support the sales team to improve efficiency and effectiveness. They enable the sales team by providing tools, training, and resources. They also analyze the data on performance and forecasts to aid decision-making. This allows salespeople to focus on building relationships with customers and meeting their needs. *For this group, you will want to focus on how they can access data and how they can enable their salespeople.*

The titles might have slightly different names and some organizations might have one person performing multiple functions, but all the activities performed need to be known to understand the process. By talking to representatives of all functions, you will get the best understanding of the process.

> **Tips**
>
> Ask the executive sponsors to introduce and position what you are doing so that stakeholders understand that it is important to the organization and its goals.
>
> Ask if individuals will be given time out of their schedules to work with you. You will get limited time and attention as the stakeholders are also trying to deliver their usual workload.
>
> Ask to talk to a range of individuals, high performers whose behavior the organization wants to model, those who are likely to champion the system, and those who are new to the process. They will all have different but valuable perspectives.

Asking good questions

The quality of your final solution will depend on how deeply you, and any other members of the implementation team, understand the users' needs and pain points. The key to getting a good understanding is asking a lot of good questions and listening actively and carefully to the answers. The more you hear and see, the easier it will be to empathize with the people you are delivering for.

When you ask questions, the aim is to understand what they are trying to achieve. You should focus on what is driving the request and not only the request itself. Don't be afraid to ask for further information. You can ask questions such as the following:

- Why would you want to do that?
- What will that help you achieve?
- Why can't you do that now?

Getting past the initial request by asking why can reveal new and significant information. It may reveal that a completely different solution is required.

For example, a good way to open an information-gathering session is to start with some open-ended questions. You may ask, for instance, "Tell me about your sales process" or "How do you take a potential customer through a sales process?" This may encourage participants to converse about the things that are most important to them. Pay attention to what they talk about first and the order in which they talk about topics.

While you are asking questions, listen for outcomes and use these to form requirements. We will talk about documenting requirements in the next section, Information gathering methods.

You may ask questions that you think you already know the answer to or that your participants think you should already know the answer to. In these situations, reassure them that you are asking to confirm your understanding and to hear it from them firsthand.

Questions to ask

The following are some examples of questions to ask stakeholders to gather information. Notice how they are open questions to start a conversation that will lead to targeted questions:

What documentation do you have on the sales process?

Who is involved in the sales process?

Do you have the same stages for every deal?

Do multiple people work on the same deal, and if so, are they from different teams?

What data do you use for forecasting?

How do you forecast?

Is the team mainly office or field-based?

What are the biggest challenges?

Tell me about your sales process…

Sometimes, a person just needs to be heard. This can be because they are worried about the change, or their current experience is poor, and they don't want that to continue. They want the people who are involved in developing the new system to hear their concerns, so when you have time, it is important to listen. Long term, it will help with adoption.

If there is an existing sales management tool in place, people will ask for more of what they have. Try to get to the business need and outcome rather than what they might ask for, which could be an additional field. Delivering essentially the same system but on a different platform will not deliver significantly more return on investment.

Information gathering methods

You have identified who you need to engage with and the type of information they are likely to provide. You have also thought about the questions you need to ask. The next step is to plan how you are going to gather the information. The following are some of the ways we can gather information:

- **Existing documentation**: This is a review of any documents that already exist. These might be documents that have been created for training or documents that are used for configuring an existing system. These are good for understanding how the process is expected to work.

- **Interview**: This is a one-to-one session or one-to-few sessions where you ask questions of individuals. They are good for gathering initial information and finding out how sales leaders have designed the process to work.

- **Workshop**: This is a group session that encourages participation and collaboration. They are good for coming up with new ways of working or setting a shared vision if this is not already defined. They are also good for playing back an initial understanding to identify gaps, disagreements, and details.

- **Observation**: This is where stakeholders are watched while they carry out these day-to-day activities. They are good for validating the information that has been shared. The surface details that people have either forgotten to mention or didn't think were important.

You will likely use a combination of these, if not all, depending on the scale of your implementation, your stakeholders, and their availability.

Tips

Start each information-gathering session with an introduction that includes the objectives and the benefits for the stakeholder group you are working with. Revisit this at every session, even if some participants have seen it before.

Get agreement from the executive sponsor on who and how decisions should be made if stakeholders differ on how something should be done. Document each decision and the reason in a decision log.

Before each workshop, provide attendees with a pack of information that includes the objectives of the workshop, the agenda, what is expected from attendees, and any preparation they may need to do in advance, such as bringing documents or examples with them.

At the beginning of workshops, set ground rules, such as no phones/ laptops, but also let attendees know when there will be breaks so that they can catch up on day-to-day business. Also, ask attendees what they want to achieve from the workshop as this will give you some insights into what is most important to them and their motivation.

Maintain a parking lot document to capture questions that you can't answer in a session or topics that need to be discussed but are not part of the current session's agenda. This helps to stop the session from moving onto topics that do not achieve the session's objectives.

Using the terminology

You will notice that the terminology that's used in Sales Cloud is what you will hear used commonly in sales units. This can be both helpful in conveying the functionality of Sales Cloud and unhelpful if the terms already have existing meanings that differ from the Sales Cloud usage. Often, the words that are used, such as lead, campaign, and quote, have a specific meaning to an organization that infers/implies these items as more than a record in a system. Sometimes, the word that's used in Sales Cloud is not the term the organization commonly uses.

When you are gathering information about an organization's process and business practices, you must clarify what they mean by these commonly used terms. It is also essential that you do the following:

- Adopt the organization's terminology
- Look out for when terminology is being used with different meaning
- Signpost where meanings are different
- Help stakeholders understand and bridge the gap the concepts are different.

Even within an organization, different teams might attribute different meanings to the same terms.

This can lead to confused, extended discussions, and failure to make decisions because stakeholders think they are disagreeing on fundamental principles when they are not. This introduces delays, can introduce negative sentiment, and, if left unresolved, can have an impact on system adoption.

> **A note on the wording**
>
> Throughout this section and the remainder of this book, I will use the capitalized form of a word when referring to a Salesforce object (for example, Lead) or a specific location (for example, the **Leads** tab) and lowercase form when referring to the more general concept (for example, capturing a lead). As we will see, the usage of common sales terminology by Salesforce can make things somewhat confusing if care is not taken.

We will explore terms such as Leads more later in *Chapter 4, Design and Build – The Lead Generation Process*. However, this is a good example to illustrate the point. A common case can be sales and marketing talking about leads. The term Lead can have a different meaning, depending on which team you are in – for example, Sales Ready Lead and a Marketing Ready Lead. Marketing teams commonly deliver leads to sales. Sales are responsible for converting leads into customers. Their ability to do that depends on the level of information and qualification. In Salesforce, a Lead is simply a record with a value entered for the Last Name. Marketing might consider a lead to be the name and contact details of a person who visited the organization's booth at a tradeshow. Sales might consider a lead to be the name, contact details, and confirmation that they have a serviceable need and budget.

The good news is that this problem can be resolved by having a glossary/nomenclature of business terms with definitions that are used during the solution implementation and beyond. An asset/artifact like this is also a useful resource for people new to the project, system, or organization.

Design thinking

Design thinking is a problem-solving approach. It requires you to think about the person's experience, not just the function that is being performed. This puts the focus on human needs. It is increasingly used to find solution options for complex problems. You may already use design thinking in your organization to solve organizational or industry-size problems.

Some of the key components of design thinking are as follows:

Having a deep understanding of your users

Framing the problem

Keeping the focus on the users' desired outcomes

Including diverse teams in your ideation

Generating as many ideas as possible

Prototyping ideas early

Constantly revisit and reinvent

For your Sales Cloud implementation, this means understanding the outcomes your users need, not just what buttons and reports they ask for. As an expert in Salesforce, you might be able to recommend better solutions that they would not be aware of.

If you are not familiar with design thinking, find out if this is already used as a problem-solving approach in your organization. If not, not there are courses and content online to get you started. Alternatively, you can approach a services company to help you adopt the principles in your organization. Applying the principles of design thinking to the way you frame problems and originate ideas can be a great way to come up with solutions your stakeholders value.

Documenting findings

Capturing and documenting all the information you have gathered about the sales process is important so that you can playback and validate your findings. It also helps you communicate what's required to people working with you on the implementation. They will also form the basis of your test cases.

Personas and actors

From the information you have gathered, it is a good idea to define your main personas. These are the actors who will be using your system – the people you are designing for. By defining them, giving them a role and a human name, and defining what they need to achieve and their pain points, it is a constant reminder that you are designing for people.

The roles of your personas will be the subjects of your user stories. We will review this in the Capturing user stories section.

Examples of commonly used Personas are sales leadership, sales manager, and account executive/salesperson.

Diagramming

A diagram is a powerful way of conveying a concept and is universally preferred. As a general rule, salespeople like to pick up the phone and talk, not read lengthy technical documents. They connect with people with a focus on needs and outcomes and craft stories about how their solutions meet the needs and deliver the outcomes. For the best outcomes, meet them where they are. Listen to their needs, understand the outcomes they want, and show them through visuals and words how your technology solution will provide that.

You may want to adopt how the organization approaches its sales process as a guide to the way that you document and present information. Where possible, use templates that already exist in your organization.

A good way to document the as-in and to-be is via process diagrams with swim lanes. *Figure 3.2* shows how the change in process for a web enquiry takes shape:

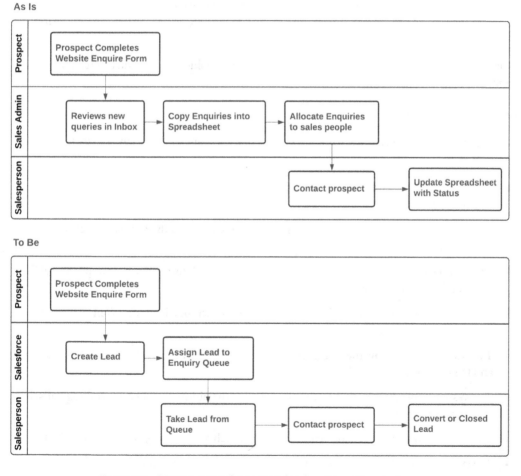

Figure 3.2 – Diagramming the as-is and to-be state with swim lanes

Agreement and acceptance from stakeholders of where the organization is now and where they would like to get to – the goal – is important as it sets the tone for the rest of the project. Diagrams can convey this quickly and efficiently. Painting a picture for your stakeholders of where the project will take them helps build excitement and positivity, which, in turn, means they will help you get to your shared goal.

Capturing user stories

A common way of capturing requirements is by writing user stories. This method puts the stakeholder at the center and captures what they want to do and why they need to do it. The format forces you to understand the why which is important as it informs the suitability of a solution.

In addition to the standard format of As a `<persona>`, I want to `<requirement>` so that `<justification>`, user stories also have **acceptance criteria**. These are statements that provide additional context and are conditions that a solution must satisfy. Acceptance criteria should be testable, meaning once a solution has been built, the statements can be tested and the outcome will be pass or fail. Acceptance criteria also help the business stakeholders and implementation team confirm they have a shared understanding.

It is best to form and capture user stories as you speak to stakeholders so that you can read them back to confirm you have a shared understanding.

Example user stories

As a salesperson, I want to view the relevant contacts in a company so that I can prepare for my calls with them:

- The salesperson should be able to view a list of contacts associated with a specific company in the CRM
- The system should display the relationship of each contact with the company, such as job title, department, and role
- The salesperson should be able to view the contact's contact information, such as phone number, email address, and physical address
- The system should allow the salesperson to add new contacts or edit existing contact information for a specific company
- The system should allow the salesperson to view the history of interactions with the contact and the company
- The system should provide the salesperson with the ability to schedule and log calls and meetings with the contacts
- The system should be accessible from any device, such as a desktop, laptop, or mobile device
- The system should be secure and only accessible to authorized users

A couple of these acceptance criteria refer to non-functional needs and are not specifically about what the user can do, but they're still important to capture. A non-functional requirement typically relates to security, performance, accessibility, or the platform – that is, desktop/laptop.

Harmonizing the sales process

If an organization is moving its sales operations to a central system such as Sales Cloud for the first time, there will likely be a lot of subtle variation in the way individual salespeople work. These variations may not be known until someone starts asking about the details. For system design, the details matter. Where possible, standardization and simplification of a process make systems easier for people to follow, easier to implement, and easier to maintain and manage. This means some people might need to change the way they work, which can be uncomfortable, so all efforts should be made to help people who are affected.

Sales leadership must be fully engaged and support the harmonization of the sales process so that any differences or conflicts can be worked through and resolved. Technology can't fix a bad process or resolve people's conflicts. Any process simplification and optimization should be carried out and signed off before time is spent on a solution design. Failure to do so means any process issues roll on, get associated with the system, and extend the implementation time. The system needs to be viewed as part of the solution not the cause of a problem.

Executive sponsors can make the biggest difference here and can be done by listening to stakeholders' concerns, making timely decisions, sharing the reasoning for decisions, and communicating the value of having a shared way of working.

Overcoming objections

Objection handling is a common part of the sales process. You may encounter some objections as you gather information. Often, the greatest benefits of implementing a central system are for sales leadership – for example, increased activity and forecast visibility.

Sometimes, for salespeople, it can mean more questions about what they are doing and more data to fill in. This can result in some initial resistance and reluctance to share information and ultimately adopt the new system. This is not always the case as automation and improvements in sales enablement can benefit sales users, but it is worth reviewing how the benefits map to different stakeholder groups.

To overcome this, it is important to know the answer to "What's in it for me?" for each stakeholder group. When working with someone from that group, either one-on-one or as part of a group, it is important to reinforce that message.

Here are some examples:

- Talking about the benefits of each interaction
- Looking for pain points in the current process and how they can be removed with the system
- Talking to sales leadership about incentives and rewards (not specifically monetary)
- Where there is disagreement, elevate the conversation back up to a level where there is agreement and refer to the decision-making process

If you are experiencing resistance, it might be appropriate to consult with sales leaders to see if they can help alleviate your concerns.

> **Tip**
>
> A lot can be learned from observing and analyzing how the organization sells and applying those techniques to how you approach selling the system to the stakeholders. You can also get recommendations from the project's sponsors.

Now that you have the tools to understand the sales process, we'll look at the Sales Cloud data and security model in more detail.

Sales Cloud data model and security

In this section, we will explore the functionality of the **Sales Cloud data model** and **security**. Sales Cloud is built on the *Salesforce Customer 360 platform*, which means it benefits from the secure and scalable infrastructure, as well as other capabilities.

It is assumed that you understand the core concepts of the Salesforce Customer 360 platform data model, where data is stored in Objects with individual records. Generally speaking, access to Objects is controlled by **profiles** and **permissions**, and the visibility of records is determined by the **sharing model**.

We will take a look at the Objects that are available in Sales Cloud and explore what they are best used for and how they relate to each other. We will then take a look at the tools available to secure them and the data they hold.

Before we get into those in detail, we will review the breadth of Sales Cloud's capabilities.

Sales Cloud's capabilities

Sales Cloud has a wide range of capabilities. This includes all the infrastructure and security capabilities. What's available depends on the edition you have. There are five editions – Essentials, Starter, Professional, Enterprise, and Unlimited. You can confirm which edition you have on the **Company Information** page in **Setup**. Go to **Setup** > **Company Settings** > **Company Information**. You will find the additions in the Detail section in the second column.

To confirm the capability in the edition of Sales Cloud you have, you can ask your account executive, review the Sales Cloud Comparison Pricing Sheet at `https://www.salesforce.com/content/dam/web/en_gb/www/datasheets/sfc-22019-r-sales-cloud-comparison-pricing-sheet.pdf`, or search for the feature in the Salesforce Help and review the **Required Editions** section. The following refers to capabilities available in Enterprise Edition and above.

Figure 3.3 provides a capability map that shows the common core sales business capabilities required by sales functions:

Figure 3.3 – Example business capability map

This capability map provides examples of a few of the capabilities you would expect an organization to require. The terminology will differ in each organization and you would expect to see more capability than what's been illustrated here.

Sales Cloud data model

OOTB Sales Cloud has over 60 Objects for capturing data relating to sales activities and processes. Objects are analogous to tables in a standard relational database and are where your data is stored. Relationships are created between the Objects that define how the different types of data relate to each other and how they can be reported on.

With so many Objects available to use, it is important to understand the OOTB data model so that you can map your organization's data to it. The existing data model will likely deliver 80% to 100% of what you need, but you have the option to create additional **custom objects** and fields to support your process if you require. We'll explore this in *Chapter 12 – Modeling Additional Processes with Sales Cloud.*

The following entity relationship diagram shows how all the main Sales Cloud Objects relate to each other:

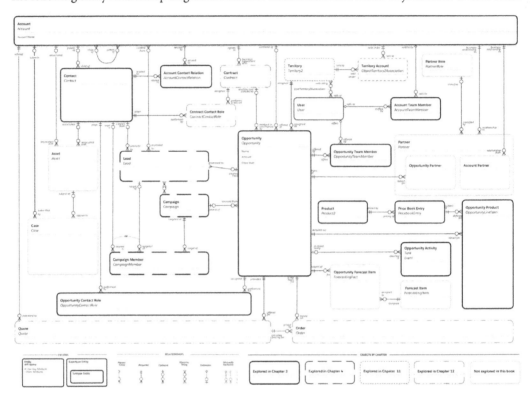

Figure 3.4 – An overview of the entity relationship diagram of all main Sales Cloud Objects

As you can see, several Objects make up Sales Cloud. To view *Figure 3.3* in greater detail, you can visit this link: https://packt.link/gbp/9781804619643. The Objects that we'll explore in this chapter are listed in the following table, along with their API name and their intended use. The other Objects in the entity relationship diagram will be discussed in more detail in *Chapter 4, Design and Build: The Lead Generation Process,* and *Chapter 12, Modeling Additional Processes:*

Object Name	Object API Name	Usage
Account	Account	Used to store data about organizations. This is a top-level object.
Contact	Contact	Used to store data about people. Contact should be related to an Account. It is a child of Account.
Opportunity	Opportunity	Used to store data about financial deals. Is a child of Account.
Product	Product2	Used to store data about products and services offered by the organization.
Price Book	Pricebook2	Used to store data about a Price Book – that is, pricing for each of the organization's products.
Opportunity Product	OpportunityLineItem	Used to store data specifying which products are being sold on the opportunity. Products can only be added to an Opportunity if the Opportunity has a Pricebook2 ID.
Price Book Entry	PriceBookEntry	A junction Object. Used to create many-to-many relationships between Product2 and Pricebook2 – that is, a specific price for a product in the related Price Book.
Account Contact Relation	AccountContactRelation	A junction Object. Used to create many-to-many relationships between Accounts and Contracts.
Opportunity Contact Role	OpportunityContactRole	A junction Object. Used to create many-to-many relationships between Opportunities and Contacts.
Opportunity Activity	Task Event	Used to store data about business activities, such as calls and meetings, carried out by Users. Activity is a collective name for Task and Event records.
Account Team Member	AccountTeamMember	A junction Object. Used to create a relationship between Account and User. Only one record can exist between each Account and User combination.
Opportunity Team Member	OpportunityTeamMember	A junction Object. Used to create a relationship between Opportunity and User. Only one record can exist between each Opportunity and User combination.

Table 3.2 – The Sales Cloud Objects provided in this chapter

The Objects that are described in this table allow data to be captured that relates to the company and employees or individual consumers, the deal, the products and services offered, the activities carried out, and the people involved in crafting the deal. These are the objects that are most relevant to modeling the core sales process and the ones that we'll learn about in this chapter.

The following is an entity relationship diagram of the Objects and relationships we'll learn about in this section:

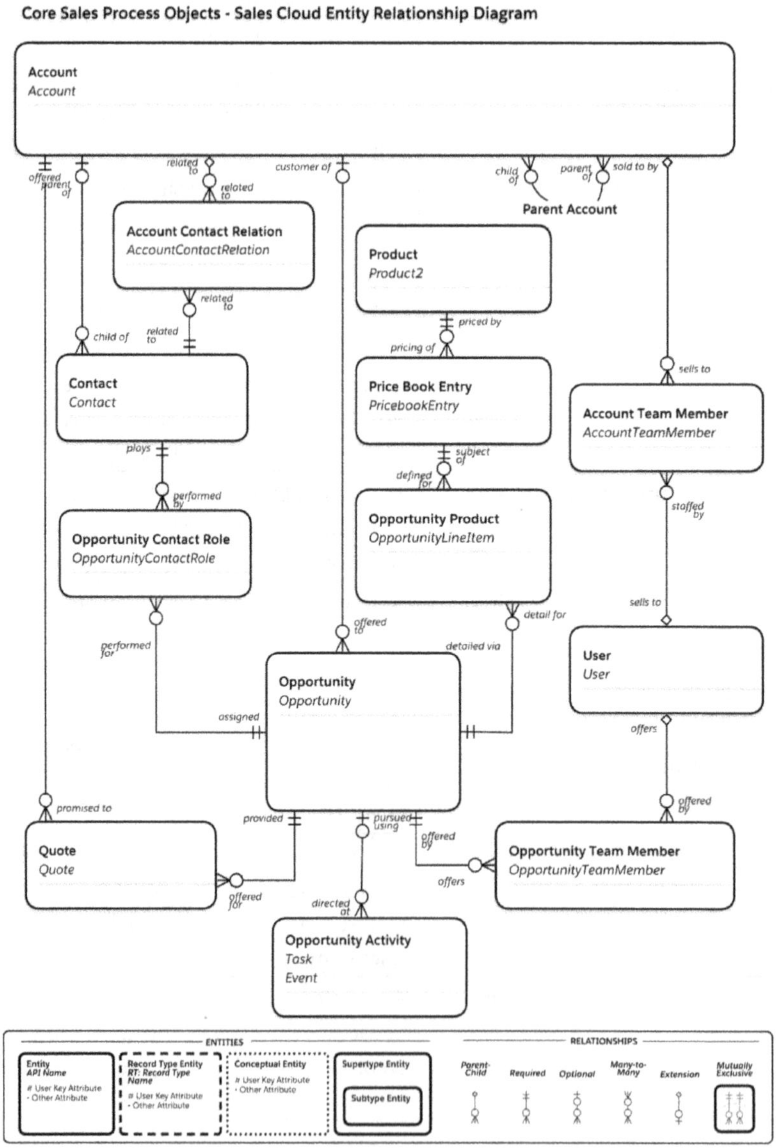

Figure 3.5 – An overview of the entity relationship diagram
of the Sales Cloud Objects that will be covered in this chapter

To view Figure 3.5 is greater detail, you can visit this link: `https://packt.link/gbp/9781804619643`. We will look at the functions of all the Objects in *Figure 3.5* in the remainder of this chapter. We'll start with Accounts and Contacts, then Opportunities, Product and Price books, and Activities, and then Account Teams, Opportunity Teams, and Opportunity Splits.

But first, in the next section, we'll explore the security tools the Customer 360 platform has to control access to data and capability.

Sales Cloud security

In this section, we'll take a high-level look at the tools that are available to execute data in Sales Cloud. These are common across the Customer 360 platform. It is assumed that you have a working understanding of these tools. We are not going to cover these in depth as this is a topic in itself and it would extend this book considerably. There are links in the Further reading sections if you would like to read about these topics in more detail.

Common core security tools

The security controls that are common across the core platform can be grouped into two main categories:

1. What Users **can do**, including create, read, edit, and delete permissions on objects
2. What records Users **can see**

Tools that control what Users can do, including create, read, edit, and delete (CRED) permissions on Objects, are as follows:

- Profiles
- Permission sets
- Permission sets groups

The following are tools that control what records users can see:

- **Organization Wide Defaults (OWDs)**
- Sharing Rules
- Role Hierarchy
- Manual Sharing
- Restriction Rules
- Scoping Rules

The core Customer 360 platform has a suite of tools to manage access control to data and capabilities. In more recent years, several new tools have been released to provide more granular options and reduce the amount of management required. In the following sections, we'll provide a brief overview of the tools available as a reminder. Sharing and visibility are big topics, and it is recommended that you reference additional materials for more detail.

Profiles, Permission Sets, and Permission Set Groups

Profiles used to be the only way to control the permissions a User had. This meant that a separate Profile needed to be created if only one additional permission was required. This led to an unmanageable situation where an org might have almost as many Profiles as Users. Salesforce released Permission Sets in 2012, and then later Permission Set Groups so that groups of permission could be assigned to individual users. Salesforce has announced the intention to retire Profiles, something that's currently scheduled for Spring 2026.

As you set up a solution, the best practice is to use Permission Sets and Permission Set Groups as they offer the flexibility to grant Users exactly the permissions they need. It is also possible to mute permissions in Permission Sets, allowing permissions to be removed from a single User.

OWDs and Sharing Rules

OWDs and Sharing Rules are the primary organization-wide tools to define who can see which records. OWDs must be set to the tightest level of restriction required by the organization. Sharing Rules can then be created to allow access to groups of Users that need it.

It is important to note that Professional Edition has less granularity on sharing rules than Enterprise Edition.

The best practice recommendation from the Salesforce Architect Evangelist team is to set OWDs to Public Read Only if business requirements allow it.

Role Hierarchy

The Role Hierarchy can allow visibility to records owned by users lower than a person in the hierarchy. As its name suggests, it should be set up to reflect an organization's role structure, but its purpose is to allow record access, not capture an org chart. This means that it can be valid to put a person's subordinate above them in the Role Hierarchy if the business need is for them to view and edit their seniors' records.

Manual Sharing

Manual Sharing allows Users to manually give another User access to a record. This is used to manage special or edge cases.

Restriction Rules

This is a relatively new tool that allows more detailed restriction rules to be added so that a User can only see a subset of the records they are granted access to by the OWDs and Sharing Rules.

These are evaluated at runtime, which makes records quick to load. Salesforce will disable these if they are affecting the performance of the multi-tenanted environment.

Scoping Rules

Scoping Rules refine a User's view but do not create a hard restriction. They can be used to improve the User's experience. Although a User might have read-only permission on all records, on a day-to-day basis, they might only be interested in their teams' records. This is a good option to remove the noise of the other records without a hard restriction.

This option can be selected in List Views, making them accessible to Users. Unlike Restriction Rules, criteria can be based on SOQL, although this is not currently available from the UI, only the API. Using dot notation in SOQL means queries can use criteria from different Objects, which gets over the limitation that List Views can only access fields on the immediate Object. This makes this quite a powerful feature.

There are restrictions on how many can be created.

Sales Cloud-specific considerations

Sales Cloud has some specific considerations, and there are some you should be aware of. First, setting the visibility of Tasks and Events is not as straightforward as it is for other objects. This is because of a common business requirement that means Sales Ops can view and edit the activities of their Sales Team, and the polymorphic relationships these Objects have with other Objects. Restriction Rules offer a new option to ensure Users only see the Activities they need. **Allow Forecasting** is a permission for the User, similar to the **Marketing U**ser checkbox, to be able to edit Campaigns.

All the visibility required for the solution should be reviewed together to determine the approach while considering all the available tools.

Reports and forecasting/reporting metrics

Forecasts are an important part of business planning. They are used to inform when parts and resources are needed so that products can be manufactured and delivered on time. They also predict when revenue will be available to hire employees, run marketing programs, and invest in product and system improvements.

It is important to identify the metrics that an organization wants to measure and track early in requirement gathering so that the system can be designed in a way that allows these to be reported on. The data required to generate these metrics needs to be included in the data model and additional calculation fields might be required to allow the metric to be reported on in the desired way.

Every organization has a combination of metrics that they track and also have a way of preparing their forecast that is unique to them.

Sales Cloud capabilities

We will now explore the capabilities in Sales Cloud, first with Dashboards and Reports, then Collaborative Forecasts. With these, Users can visualize the data in the Sales Cloud and manage their organization's Sales Forecast.

Reports and Dashboards

Sales Cloud includes the standard Reporting and Dashboard capability that is available in the Customer 360 platform. The reporting is driven by the parent/child relationships that have been created between Objects. When you create a report, you select a **Report Type** value, which determines what Objects the report includes and the granularity of the report. For example, a **Report Type** value of **Accounts** will have one row per Account, whereas a **Report Type** value of **Opportunities with Products** will have a row for every Product on every Opportunity.

In general, you will only be able to access the field on the Objects that are named in the **Report Type** field; however, there are some exceptions with some other fundamental Salesforce Objects. Accounts and Opportunities are examples. If you select a **Record Type** value where the primary Object (one listed first) is **Opportunity**, then you will also be able to access all of the parent Account fields. This is due to the special relationship that Opportunities have with Accounts. The same is true with Cases and Accounts.

Some report types also have filters based on My Team. This uses the Role Hierarchy (or territory hierarchy) and shows the records of all their subordinate. This can be a great feature of reporting on sales team performance as one report can be used by many sales managers, and they only see their sales teams' records.

Collaborative Forecasts

Collaborative Forecasts are only available in Sales Cloud. When Collaborative Forecasts are set up, the **Forecast** tab can be made available. Users can see their Opportunity data rolled up and presented in different ways to understand how they are performing. Forecast managers can see the aggregate data of their team. They can explore the data by product family and timeframe, depending on how Collaborative Forecasts are set up. They can view the aggregate amounts by four forecast categories. How amounts appear in these categories are defined during setup. Some of the features of Collaborative Forecasts are as follows:

- Drill down into individual Opportunities
- View by team members
- Adjust the amount and add a note

- Change currency
- View on mobile
- Share forecast
- See against quota
- Hide rows with zeros

There is the option to view aggregated forecast amounts with or without cumulative amounts. With cumulative amounts, the **Pipeline** category also includes the values from **Best Cases** and **Commit**. **Best cases** also include the value from the Commit. Cumulative is the most commonly used but it is down to each organization.

Pipeline Inspection

As of Summer 2023, Pipeline Inspection is included in the Sales Cloud license. Before that release, it was an additional feature license. Pipeline Inspection provides a summary view of performance metrics, deal data, and actions that have happened on a set of Opportunities. It is available from the **Opportunity** tab. Now, you can change views on this tab between **List View** and **Pipeline Inspection**.

This consolidated view means that sales reps don't need to click on opportunities to see the value of business won, total pipeline, the increase, the decrease, and deals that have moved in and out. For key metrics, the system will track and display changes, such as the amount and closed date. There is also an option to see this information visualized on charts.

In addition to the information-rich list provided, there's also a side panel called **Activity and Insights**. To see all the possible insights, you need access to the Sales Einstein feature, which was an additional license at the time of writing. The **Activity** tab shows past and future activities, as well as the **Next Step** field and a summary of the Activities. It is also possible to send emails from here. This page provides sales reps will all the information they need to take action on their deals.

Next, we'll cover the key considerations and what happens in practice.

Key considerations

The following are some common considerations:

- Do your sales managers need to override their team's forecast?
- Are the forecast categories of Pipeline, Best Case, and Commit used in your organization?
- Do you want to view the target against the Quota?
- Does the organization want to view absolute or cumulative pipeline figures?

In practice

In practice, some organizations use the standard Reports and Dashboards functionality and find this to be enough.

Forecasting is not automatically enabled, so it must be **Enabled** in **Setup**. Access to forecasting is granted by a checkbox on **User Record**. A forecast hierarchy is required for forecasting and the Role Hierarchy must be set up first.

An admin sets up the forecast types that are available to Users. Four forecast types can be enabled at one time. The available types are **Opportunity**, **Opportunity Product**, **Opportunity Split**, and **Line Item Schedule**.

Advanced Territory Management allows multiple hierarchies to be set up and separates the hierarchy used from the Role Hierarchy. We will explore Advanced Territory Management in *Chapter 11, Territory Management*.

Accounts and Contacts

In this section, we will look at the capabilities of Sales Cloud for capturing and managing organizations and people, then explore some of the key considerations and what happens in practice.

Sales Cloud capabilities

In the Customer 360 platform, organizations are represented in the Account Object and people are modeled in the Contact Object. The relational model provides the flexibility to capture organizational structures. It is also possible to turn on the capability to relate a person to multiple Accounts as a person can be an employee of one company and a board member of another. In both cases, they may influence the purchasing process.

In the beginning, Salesforce focused on supplying software to B2B companies, where the focus was on the organization. They expanded into B2C, where the person is the main entity, not an organization. In this context, the Account record had no purpose. To reflect this operating model, Salesforce created the Person Account, a hybrid of the Account and Contact records.

In this section, we'll look at Business Accounts and Person Accounts in more detail. Then, we'll explore the options for modeling complex organization and stakeholder relationships.

Business Accounts

Business Accounts refer to Accounts that use the Account and Contacts model. This terminology is usually only visible in an Org if Person Accounts are turned on and is a way of identifying between them. This is the default model that is available immediately in Salesforce. If your Customers are businesses, you can use Business Accounts OOTB without needing to enable anything else.

The following table summarizes key information about the Business Account Object and its Fields:

Key Information	
The API's name	Account
Required fields	Account Name (Text)
Standard relationships*	Parent Account (Hierarchy)
	D&B Company (Lookup to D&B Company) Retired
Other key fields	Type (Picklist)
	Industry (Picklist)
	Account Source (Picklist)
	Billing Address (Address)
	Shipping Address (Address)
	Description (Long Text Area)

Table 3.3 – Key information about the Business Account Object

*Lookup relationships to the User Object for Owner, Created By, and Modified By have not been included as they exist on all Objects.

This table shows the API name, which will be referenced in any code, and the number of standard fields. I have listed any required fields, where a value must be entered to save a record, and listed the relationship fields and key fields that I have seen used most often.

Person accounts

Person Accounts are a composite of the Account and Contact records. When you view them in the user interface, they are presented as a single record but they have both an Account ID and a Contact ID. They appear in the **List View** area on both the **Account** and **Contact** tabs. You can identify and filter Person Accounts using the **Is Person Checkbox** field.

These are not turned on OOTB. The feature needs to be enabled, and once it is, it cannot be disabled. Before enabling it, you must understand the implications and the impact on your Org and only turn it on if it is appropriate. The recommendation is to enable it in a sandbox first and assess the impact on your Org. The setup wizard for the feature helps you understand and acknowledge the impact before you enable it. The best practice is to enable it in a sandbox first and assess the impact there. Up until recently, you had to contact support to enable this as it has a significant impact.

There are two key points to be aware of. The first is that an Account record and a Contact record are created for each Person Account, increasing your storage. The second is that these records and Contact fields appear in the Account list views, which some Users find very confusing.

It is possible to use Business Accounts and Person Accounts in the same Org, but you will want to create separate List Views and Reports so that it is clear to your Users which ones they are viewing.

Although both of these are Accounts, you will see that the Person Account API name is different. An additional Object is now listed in **Object Manager**, but it only has a subset of options; the majority of the options are still under the standard Account Object. You will see the number of fields on the Account Object has increased.

The following table summarizes key information about the Person Account Object and its fields:

Key Information	
The API's name	PersonAccount
Required fields	Last Name (Text)
Standard relationships*	Parent Account (Lookup to Account)
Other key fields	Is Person (Checkbox)
	Email (Email)
	Phone (Phone)
	Lead Source (Picklist)
	Mailing Address (Address)
	Email Opt Out (Checkbox)

Table 3.4 – Key information about the Person Account Object

```
*Lookup relationships to the User Object for Owner, Created By and
Modified By have not been included as they exist on all Objects.
```

In *Table 3.4*, you can see the API name, which will be referenced in any code, and the number of standard fields. I have listed any required fields where a value must be entered to save a record and listed the relationship fields and key fields that I have seen used most often. It is worth noting that there are more standard fields than the Business Account as Contact fields have been added.

Contact

The Contact Object captures information about people either as employees of organizations or as individual consumers. Unless you're using Person Accounts, every Contact needs to be related to an Account. If the Account field is blank – that is, an orphaned Contact – the Contact will not appear in the UI and reports.

Contacts can be related to Opportunities using Opportunity Contact Roles. This allows the salesperson to model the buying group. We'll explore this more later.

The following table summarizes key information about the Contact Object and its fields:

Key Information	
The API's Name	Contact
Required Fields	Last Name (Text)
Standard Relationships*	Account Name (Lookup to Account)
	Reports To (Lookup to Contact)
	Individual (Lookup to Individual)
Other Key Fields	Email (Email)
	Phone (Phone)
	Lead Source (Picklist)
	Mailing Address (Address)
	Email Opt Out (Checkbox)

Table 3.5 – Key information about the Contact Object

```
*Lookup relationships to the User Object for Owner, Created By, and
Modified By have not been included as they exist on all Objects.
```

Contacts to Multiple Accounts

Contacts on Multiple Accounts is a feature that allows Contacts to be related to multiple Account records. This can be valuable when a person influences an organization other than the one they work for.

To get the full value from the feature, it must be used consistently across an organization. Users have to know when they should use the primary Account relationship and when to use the multi-relationship. Inconsistency will leave Users confused and ultimately, they will stop using it.

Key considerations

The only required field on **Accounts** is the **Name** field. This is the record reference field and appears throughout the platform for Users to identify and access records. For this reason, it must be human-readable rather than, for example, a code or reference number. For that sort of identifier or the legal name of the company, it is best to create an additional field. It is important to have that information in the system so it can be searched and merged into communications, but you don't want to force Users to learn this.

Classifications are important on Accounts. They get used as filter criteria in reporting. If the value can be derived, you may want to consider a formula field as this is one less piece of data a person has to enter.

Alternatively, picklist fields are a good option as these mean the values are consistent. This does require the field values to be mutually exclusive, which is not always possible. Multi-select picklist fields are always a last resort as they allow double reporting.

Another key consideration is what level of detail to model for your customer Accounts. Is one record enough? Does this allow your salespeople to capture the level of detail they need to understand how that organization makes purchasing decisions? Do individual departments have budgets and autonomy to make buying decisions on the products and services you offer?

Salesforce has the flexibility to model hierarchy in a self-referring relationship. You can also view the hierarchy. During requirement gathering, be sure to explore how your organization wants to represent customer records and agree on a consistent approach.

If you only require Person Accounts, there is no system setting to disable Business Accounts. You can remove the Record Type from Users' profiles, which means they can't create them.

In practice

In practice, there are some capabilities that sales business users request. We'll explore some of these in this section. This includes modeling complex Account and Contact structures, key Account planning, and managing duplicate records.

Modeling complex Account and Contact structures

A common requirement is to model complex Account structures. Within large organizations, it is unlikely that a single department is involved. It is also possible that an organization can sell to multiple parts or locations of an organization – in some cases, without the other customer party being aware. In this case, there are important decisions about what level to model customer organizations. This is a business decision, not a system decision.

When it comes to applying this in Sales Cloud, the most important factor is to be consistent in how Accounts are set up. Inconsistency will confuse Users and impact adoption. An easily understood naming convention is also important. From this, Users should be able to tell the organization and level/ department the record represents. You will also want guidelines on what level of Account the Opportunities should be related to. Depending on how you report, you may want to create a lookup relationship on Opportunities and automation to automatically relate Opportunities to the Account at the top of the hierarchy.

The **Parent Account** field is not on the page layout by default, so you will want to add it. There is an Account setting that turns the **View Hierarchy** link on and off on the **Account** page, so you will want to confirm that is enabled.

Key account planning

Key account management (KAM) is a systematic approach to developing relationships and growing business in a set of selected accounts. It involves developing a detailed understanding of the people in an organization, their relationship to each other, and their sentiment toward your organization and its offerings. It also involves the organization's goals and challenges and creating a plan to address them.

Sales Cloud provides the functionality to capture all the people in or related to an organization using the standard Account Contact parent-child relationship and the Contacts to Multiple Accounts junction Object. Key person attributes can be captured on the Contact record. A common requirement can be to be able to visualize people's relationships in a diagram.

In Sales Cloud, it is possible to view the hierarchy of how people relate to each other using the Reports To relationship field and the View Contact Hierarchy Action. If not already available, the View Contact Hierarchy Actions can be added to the Contact Page Layout.

There are tools on AppExchange that offer more information-rich visuals that can capture more complex relationships and sentiments. As an alternative for very bespoke requirements, you could build a junction object and Lighting Web Component to visualize these relationships exactly as your organization requires.

In addition to modeling relationships, another key requirement is documenting an Account plan. Depending on your Account Plan requirements, a solution might be to create a Custom Object related to the Account to capture the associated data. Alternatively, it can be documented in a collaborative documentation tool such as Salesforce Quip or Google Docs and linked to the Account record. There are also tools on AppExchange that present the information in the Salesforce UI.

Data quality

Data quality is very important, particularly when it comes to recording people's data. A centralized system such as Sales Cloud is only as good as the quality of the data it holds. For Users to use and trust a system, they need to be confident the data in it is accurate so that they are happy to base decisions on it. Duplicate data means reporting is inaccurate and data is not correctly associated with recorded.

Salesforce has duplicate management functionality, known as **Duplicate Rules**, that either prevents or warns Users when they are creating or editing duplicates. This can be configured by a system administrator. OOTB, Salesforce has standard matching rules for Accounts, Person Accounts, Contacts, and Leads. These also match Contacts with Leads.

This functionality is worth exploring and understanding to determine if it will add value to your solution, even if it is not an explicit requirement.

Opportunities, products, and price books

In this section, we will look at the capabilities of Sales Cloud for capturing deals, explore some key considerations, and look into what happens in practice.

Sales Cloud capabilities

These Objects are used to capture sales deals in Salesforce. I will use the term sales deal or deal rather than Opportunity to avoid confusion with Salesforce terminology. The Opportunity record is the primary record for capturing sales deal information. The other Objects and functionality described here all provide additional capabilities that may be relevant to your use case.

Opportunity

The Opportunity Object captures the overall details of the deal, such as the name, value, and when it is expected to be confirmed, as well as the stage the deal is in during the sales process. It is a child of the Account where all the organization information is captured. OOTB doesn't include any options in terms of capturing product information – there are specific Objects to model this as a deal can include many products and services and different prices might be offered to different customers.

A sales deal can include many people. There are no standard fields in the Opportunity to create a relationship with Contacts as this is not the best way to model a many-to-many relationship. For example, a deal can involve many people and a person can be involved with many deals. These relationships are captured in the Opportunity Contact Roles Object, which will be covered later in this section.

The following table summarizes key information about the Opportunity Object and its fields:

Key Information	
The API's name	Opportunity
Required fields	Opportunity Name (Text)
	Stages (Picklist)
	Close Date (Date)
Standard relationships*	Master Detail to Account
	Lookup to Contract
	Lookup to Price Book
	Lookup to Campaign
Other key fields	Probability (%) (Percent)
	Expected Revenue (Currency)
	Next Step (Text)
	Type (Picklist)
	Lead Source (Picklist)

Table 3.6 – Key information about the Opportunity Object

```
*Lookup relationships to the User Object for Owner, Created By, and
Modified By have not been included as they exist on all Objects.
```

Sales processes

In Sales Cloud, a sales process defines a set of Opportunity Stages. OOTB, the sales process contains all the active Stage values. You can create new sales processes and select which Stages appear in each one. This allows you to create as many as is appropriate for your business requirements.

For more than one sales process to be available, you will need to create different Opportunity Record Types– one for each sales process. This also allows you to apply a different Page Layout to each Record Type, which can improve the user experience as the page is optimized for the process. A common example is that a renewal process may have fewer stages than the original sale – it might even auto-renew. In this case, two processes would be set up: New Business and Renewal. New Business would have all the Opportunity stage values and Renewal would only have a subset.

Opportunity Product (Opportunity Line Item)

The Opportunity Line Item Object captures the products and services that are included in the deal. The data that populates this Object comes from the Product and Price Book Entity records. The data from some of the key standard fields is automatically transferred but automation will need to be added to transfer any data captured in custom fields.

When Users select Products, they can specify the number and enter an alternative price to the one in the Price Book. The system automatically calculates the value of the deal and puts it in the Amount field. When Opportunity Line Items exist on the Opportunity, the Amount field becomes Read Only on the Opportunity.

At the point Opportunity Line Items are created, they inherit data from Products. These values are not linked to those on the Product, so if the Product data is updated, the Opportunity Line Items do not change.

Users select products via a Product selection screen. It is possible to modify the fields that are displayed on the selection screen. It is edited on the Page Layout.

The following table summarizes the key information about the Opportunity Line Item Object and its fields:

Key Information	
The API's name	OpportunityLineItem
Required fields	Opportunity Product Name (Text)
Standard relationships*	Lookup to Opportunity
	Lookup to Product
	Look up to Price Book
	Look up to Price Book Entry
Other key fields	Quantity (Number)
	Product Code (Text)
	List Price (Currency)
	Sale Price (Currency)
	Line Description (Text)

Table 3.7 – Key information about the Opportunity Line Item Object

```
*Lookup relationships to the User Object for Owner, Created By, and
Modified By have not been included as they exist on all Objects.
```

Product

The Product Object captures information about the products and services your organization offers. Product classification is important, and the Product Object has a few classification fields, including Product Family. Product Family is a field that is available in Collaborative Forecasts.

Active field Products will not be available for selection from the Price Book if the **Active** checkbox is not ticked. For a Product to be available to add to an Opportunity, it must be added to the Standard Price Book with at least one currency. A Product must be added to the Standard Price Book before it can be added to a Custom Price Book.

There is a Product Code field that can be used to capture product codes.

The following table summarizes key information about the Product Object and its fields:

Key Information	
The API's name	Product2
Required fields	Product Name
Standard relationships*	None
Other key fields	Active (Checkbox)
	Product Code (Text)
	Product Family (Picklist)
	Type (Picklist)
	Product Class (Picklist)

Table 3.8 – Key information about the Product object

```
*Lookup relationships to the User Object for Owner, Created By, and
Modified By have not been included as they exist on all Objects.
```

Price Book

The Price Book Object captures lists of the Product records you offer. Price Books can have Products with multiple Currencies. You can think of a Price Book as a catalog that your users can browse through, and Opportunity Line Items as products that have been taken off the shelf and are sitting in their basket. Only one Price Book can be selected per Opportunity. Product records are related to Price Books by Price Book Entries, which we will look at next.

Only Products with a Price Book Entry in the same currency as the Opportunity Currency will be available to select from an Opportunity.

The following table summarizes key information about the Price Book Object and its fields:

Key Information	
The API's name	Pricebook2
Required fields	Price Book Name (Text)
Standard relationships*	None
Other key fields	Active (Checkbox)
	Is Standard Price Book (Checkbox)
	Description (Text)

Table 3.9 – Key information about the Price Book object

```
*Lookup relationships to the User Object for Owner, Created By, and
Modified By have not been included as they exist on all Objects.
```

Price Book Entry

The Price Book Entry is a junction Object that allows a Product to appear in multiple Price Books with different prices and currencies. The record is created by Sales Cloud when a Product is added to a Price Book.

To be available to select, each Product must be added to the Standard Price Book, which means that each Product must have a Price Book Entry relating it to the Standard Price Book. For custom Price Books, you can use the Use Standard Price checkbox to apply the List Price from the Standard Price Book to remove the need to re-enter data.

The following table summarizes key information about the Price Book Entry Object and its fields:

Key Information	
The API's name	PricebookEntry
Required fields	Product ID
	Price Book ID
	List Price
Standard relationships*	Lookup to Product
	Look up to Price Book
Other key fields	Active (Checkbox)
	Use Standard Price (Checkbox)
	List Price (Currency)
	Product Code (Text)

Table 3.10 – Key information about the Price Book Entry Object

```
*Lookup relationships to the User Object for Owner, Created By, and
Modified By have not been included as they exist on all Objects.
```

Multi-Currency

The Customer 360 platform can support multiple currencies. When Multi-currency is turned on, it adds fields to the records with currency fields – one to allow the user to select the currency for the record, and then companion fields for each of the currency fields on the record to display the currency value in the User's currency. This companion field can be disabled by the system administrator.

System administrators can choose to set up a single conversion value for each currency or enable **Advanced Currency Management**, which allows a conversion rate to be applied for a given period. Commonly, this would be monthly. The timeframe will be dictated by the organization's accounting team.

Opportunity Contact Role

Opportunity Contact Role is a junction Object that allows Contacts to be related to multiple Opportunities and Opportunities to have multiple Contacts. For each relationship, a role can be specified. A single Contact can be marked as the Primary using a checkbox. If another Contact is marked as the Primary, it replaces the existing Primary but the relationship is preserved.

The following table summarizes key information about the Opportunity Contact Role Object and its fields:

Key Information	
The API's name	OpportunityContactRole
Required fields	Contact ID
	Opportunity ID
Standard relationships*	Lookup to Contact
	Lookup to Opportunity
Other key fields	Primary (Checkbox)
	Role (Picklist)

Table 3.11 – Key information about the Opportunity Contact Role object

```
*Lookup relationships to the User Object for Owner, Created By, and
Modified By have not been included as they exist on all Objects.
```

Key considerations

There are several different Objects available to model the sales deal. They are not all required. In the simplest form, you can use Opportunities with a single sales process and use Opportunity Contact Roles to model the buying group.

Use the Product functionality if you have deals that have a mix of products and services, and you need to report and forecast the revenue buy product types and product lines.

Here are some key decisions you will need to make:

- Is there more than one sales process?
- Should all salespeople see all records?

- Should you use products?

- What naming convention should you use for Opportunity names?

- Should a product family be used, and do you know how to use one?

- What deal and product categories should you use?

You will also want to determine what roles you need to represent your buying group so that you can customize the Roles for Opportunity Contact Roles.

When planning how you want to use Price Books, it is important to remember that you can only associate one Price Book with an Opportunity. For example, this means that if a customer can buy products and services together, they must be available in one Price Book.

In practice

Your salespeople will spend the majority of their time managing, reviewing, and updating Opportunity records. All the information relating to a deal should be captured on or related to these records, yet the task of updating them should be kept as effortless as possible.

When it comes to fields, understand their purpose, when the data becomes available, who needs it, and who is responsible for sourcing it and entering it. Consider leaving out data that doesn't have a defined use or place it in optional, less prominent places on the page. In *Chapter 5, Designing and Building – Sales User Productivity*, we will explore the Path capability, which allows essential fields to be highlighted at each stage.

Record types can be used to allow different sales processes, and the page layout and picklists can be customized for the specific process.

Activities

In this section, we will look at the capabilities of Sales Cloud for capturing and managing sales activities such as calls and meetings. Then, we'll explore some key considerations and what happens in practice.

Sales Cloud capabilities

In Salesforce, "activities" is a collective term that's used for Task and Event objects. Unlike other standard Objects, these two Objects have two polymorphic relationship fields – **WhoId** and **WhatId**. This allows these records to be related to different types of Objects via the one relationship field – for example, either the Opportunity or Account. This very flexible type of relationship field is not available to create in **Setup** as a custom field.

To create custom fields for the Task and Event Objects, you need to create them on the Activities Object. By default, Task and Events that are related to Contacts also appear on the Activity Timeline of the Contact's Account. This automatic behavior can be changed so that these Activities don't appear. This setting can be found in **Setup** by going to **Setup** > **Sales** > **Activity Settings**.

Another unique point about Activities is the **Subtype** field. This is a picklist whose values can't be modified. It is used by the system to capture the Activity type. The values are **Task**, **Call**, **Email**, **LinkedIn**, **List Email**, and **Cadence**. **Cadence** is a value that can only be set by the Salesforce Sales Engagement tool. The value here determines the icons that are used in the Activity Timeline. It is also worth noting that the **Subtype** field is not available in reports. If you have a use case for custom types of activities, you can customize the picklist values on the standard **Type** field on Task Objects.

The following table summarizes key information about the Task and Event Objects and their fields.

Key Information		
The API's name	Task	Event
Number of standard fields	23	22
Required fields	Assigned To (Lookup to User)	StartDate (Date/Time)
	Status (Picklist)	End Date (Date/Time)
Standard relationships*	Relates To (WhatId)	Relates To (WhatId)
	Name (WhoId)	Name (WhoId)
Other key fields	Status (Picklist)	Subject (Text)
	Subject (Text)	Type (Picklist)
	Type (Picklist)	Location (Text)
	Subtype (Picklist)	Subtype (Picklist)

Table 3.12 – Key information about the Task and Event Objects

```
*Lookup relationships to the User Object for Owner, Created By, and
Modified By have not been included as they exist on all Objects.
```

Key considerations

Tasks and Event records behave differently from other Objects. As we have already covered, there is a **Subtype** field that is used by the system to determine how records are displayed in the timeline. The **Relates To** (**WhatId**) and **Name** (**WhoId**) fields are both polymorphic relationship fields, which means that they can look up to more than one Object. For example, **Name** (**WhoId**) looks up to both Lead and Contact. This means they behave differently to the standard one-to-many lookup and master-detail relationships. Because of this type of relationship, you will see there is a "Task and Events" report and an "Activities with Object" report – for example, Activities with Leads. The former returns Activities across multiple Objects and can perform slowly. "Activities with Object" reports are more performant but custom fields will not appear in these, so if you need that data available, you will need to create a Custom Report Type.

The **Assigned to** field captures who the Activity is assigned to. It is available in reports and Dashboard filters. However, if you want to add reports to your Dashboard that are based on other Objects, the **Assigned to** field will disappear from the filter. Even though the **Assigned to** and **Owner** fields typically have the same function that is responsible for the record, filters don't see them as the same.

In practice

You will want to make sure you understand the visibility requirements for User Tasks and Activities so that you can select the appropriate security tools.

There is limited space on the related list and Activity Timeline, so train your Users to put descriptive information in the **Subject** field, not just *call* or *meeting*; otherwise, they will spend a lot of time clicking in and out of Activity records.

You will want to consider how you want to report on Activities and confirm that it's possible early in your design. The **Subtype** field is not available in reports, so if you need this information, you may need to create a custom field to display it. The date fields that are available on Task and Event objects are not consistent, so you may need to create a custom field to consolidate these if you want to summarize that information in a report.

A common requirement is for colleagues to be able to edit each other's Tasks and Events. The ability to edit and view Activities is controlled but the Role Hierarchy and sharing model settings. If a person is above a user in the Role Hierarchy, they can view and edit their Activities. If **Org Sharing Setting for Activities** is **Controlled by Parent**, then a user can edit Activities if they have permission to edit the parent record. You can't create Sharing Rules for Activities, which means it is not possible to define a group of users that can modify each other's Activities.

Account Team, Opportunity Team, and Opportunity Splits

In this section, we will look at the capabilities of Sales Cloud for recording and giving access to those who are working on deals. Then we'll explore some key considerations and what happens in practice.

Sales Cloud capabilities

Account Team allows Users to collaborate on Accounts. It captures the role they have with the specific Account and the access they should have. It also shows a list of all the users on the Account so that people know who is involved. It is possible to set up a default Account Team, which removes manual work when setting up the Accounts.

Opportunity Team allows Users to collaborate on Opportunities. It captures the role they have with the specific Opportunity and the access they should have. It also shows a list of all the Users on the Opportunity so that people know who is involved.

Finally, Opportunity Splits allow revenue to be shared on Closed Opportunities. These values can be rolled into quota and pipeline reports.

Account Team, Opportunity Team, and Opportunity Splits can be enabled from the **Account and Opportunity Settings** area in **Setup**.

The following table summarizes key information about the Account Team and Opportunity Team Objects and their fields:

Key Information		
The API's name	AccountTeamMember	OpportunityTeamMember
Number of standard fields	9	6
Required fields	User (Lookup to User)	User (Lookup to User)
	Team Role (Picklist)	Team Role (Picklist)
	Account Access (Picklist)	Account Access (Picklist)
	Opportunity Access (Picklist)	Opportunity Access (Picklist)
	Case Access (Picklist)	
Standard relationships*	Account (Lookup to Account)	Opportunity (Lookup to Opportunity)
Other key fields		

Table 3.13 – Key information about the Account Team and Opportunity Team objects

```
*Lookup relationships to the User Object for Owner, Created By, and
Modified By have not been included as they exist on all objects.
```

Translating sales process requirements into a design

Now that you have reviewed the main Objects in Sales Cloud and the key considerations, and seen examples of how it can work in practice, you are in a good position to translate your requirements into a design.

You want to leverage all the standard functionality first. Try not to get caught up with the names of the Salesforce terminology. Just because you sell products doesn't mean you need to use the Product and Price Book capabilities. If you sell services, not products, you still might need to use the Product capability.

Start with the data model. Determine what Objects you need. If you aren't sure, list the fields that you have identified and then determine what Object they belong in.

One of the first decisions to be made is what Account model to use – organization or person-centric? If your organization only sells to businesses, the decision is simple.

Do you have any type of data that doesn't fit into the objects described in this section? You might need another standard object that will be covered in the next section, or you might need a custom object.

Group user stories into capabilities. Identify the data that will need to be captured for each of the groups to determine which Objects the stories involve. You typically expect a group of stories to touch a small number of Objects.

You will want to record all the fields that you need in a Data Dictionary. This captures the name of the field, the Object, and what the field type should be. If it is a picklist, the values should be listed. It can take a surprisingly long time to agree on the values in picklists, so if there is any question about this during the requirement-gathering process, make sure there is a defined process and timeline for getting these agreed on.

With something complex such as Account modeling, it is good to agree on a sample set of organization data and if there are a couple of options try them out in a Sandbox or Developer Org and get user feedback. This setup is important, so it is good to get feedback early.

Summary

In this chapter, we started by exploring common sales frameworks and what they can tell us about the type of Sales Cloud setup we might need. We went on to look at techniques for gathering more information about the specifics of the sales process used in our organization. Next, we reviewed the Sales Cloud's capability and then looked at data Objects in detail. We ended by discussing how to approach translating the requirements that have been gathered into a solution design.

In the next chapter, we will explore the Objects and key functionalities available to model the lead or demand generation process.

Further reading

User stories

- *Trailhead: User Story Creation:*

  `https://trailhead.salesforce.com/content/learn/modules/user-story-creation`

Sales Cloud capabilities

- *Salesforce Data Security Model – Explained Visually:*

  `https://developer.salesforce.com/blogs/developer-relations/2017/04/salesforce-data-security-model-explained-visually`

- *Trailhead: Data Security:*

  `https://trailhead.salesforce.com/content/learn/modules/data_security`

Dashboards and Reports

- *Trailhead: Reports & Dashboards for Lightning Experience:*

  `https://trailhead.salesforce.com/content/learn/modules/lex_implementation_reports_dashboards`

Salesforce role-based websites

- `Architect.salesforce.com`
- `Admin.salesforce.com`
- `Developer.salesforce.com`

4

Design and Build: The Lead Generation Process

The **lead generation process** is often simple to describe in steps but complex in terms of delivery and departmental responsibilities. This function can be fast paced and high volume with stretch targets. As a business scales, a lot can be demanded from the tools that support this process.

This chapter gives you the tools you need and the confidence to explore, understand, and document how your organization generates business, and capture the associated requirements. We will explore the similarities and differences between lead generation and **demand generation**, and then consider how they apply in both a **business-to-business** (**B2B**) and **business-to-consumer** (**B2C**) context. This will help you understand the differences between the two and inform your conversations with business stakeholders. We will then review the capabilities in the Sales Cloud that support lead generation.

Our focus in this chapter will be on two main objects, Leads and Campaigns, and their supporting functionality. These Standard Objects have some specialized capabilities, which you will be aware of if you have studied for the Administration Exam. We will look at the data and explain how they interact with the Objects discussed in *Chapter 3 – Design and Build: The Core Sales Process*. Although we assume that you are already well aware of the Customer 360 Platform security features, we do highlight any specific security considerations that you may come across. We go on to explore the characteristics of the Objects, their feature settings, and their supporting functionality, including **Lead Conversion** and **Web-to-Lead**.

Once we have explored all the standard capabilities that support the Lead Process, we will look at how to approach translating the requirements into a solution design.

As noted, before in *Chapter 3* there is no singular perfect design for a set of requirements. Some solutions are just more appropriate for a business need than others. This is why it is so important to spend time understanding the needs of the business and the requirements of the systems' users prior to any customization.

In this chapter, we're going to cover the following main topics:

- Understanding how your organization generates business

- Lead generation data and security model

- Leads

- Campaigns

- Other relevant Objects

- Translating lead generation process requirements into design

Supporting tools and information

For this chapter, you will require a tool to capture system requirements. A spreadsheet application such as Microsoft Excel or Google Sheets is a good way to quickly capture, share, collaborate, and refine requirements.

For your Sales Cloud implementation, you should consider using the tools your organization uses as a standard, as they will be widely understood and accepted. Requirements can be managed in spreadsheets for simple and very small team projects, however, specific requirement management or project management tools offer tailored functionality and will help improve collaboration and organization on larger projects with more people involved. These tools often offer traceability through the life cycle so you can map the requirement to the configuration changes. Some examples are **JIRA** by Atlassian or the **Agile Accelerator**, an application built on Salesforce that can be installed from AppExchange.

For this chapter, you will require a tool to document the lead process. At the very start, this might be with a paper and pen, or the digital equivalent. For sharing with stakeholders or adding to a document, a diagram can be created in a presentation tool such as Microsoft PowerPoint or Google Slides. These are often used as they are commonly available but for large or detailed diagrams, they can be challenging. Diagramming applications have the shapes and the functionality, making them easier to use. **Lucidchart** has a library of Salesforce shapes but not everyone has access to it in their company.

Understanding how your organization generates business

In this section, we will explore how organizations generate business and the industry terminology that's used. We start by looking at common ways organizations approach generating interest for their products and services. We compare and contrast the differences between **demand generation** and **lead generation** so you can understand the characteristics of these industry concepts. We also review commonly used strategies and channels. This will help you get an understanding of the foundational concepts and the terminology, which you can use as a basis for your specific organization knowledge. It will help you talk to business stakeholders about what they need.

In this area of capability, more so than any other, terms can be used interchangeably, but have different meanings to different people with different roles or goals. I highlight this as differences in understanding can take up time and cause frustration. For example, marketing might consider a lead to be the name and contact details of a person who visited the organization's booth at a tradeshow. Sales might consider a lead to be the name, contact details, and confirmation that they have a serviceable need and budget. however, in Sales Cloud, a **Lead** is simply a record with a value entered for **Last Name**. For clarity, I will use Leads with a capital L when referring to the Sales Cloud **Lead Object** and leads with a lowercase l when referring to a person who has the potential to purchase a product or service.

The macro-environment that organizations operate in has changed in recent years with the introduction of legislation that defines how **personally identifiable information** (**PII**) is acquired, stored, and processed. The introduction of this type of legislation started in Europe but it is becoming increasingly relevant worldwide. We will discuss why it is important to be aware of these, particularly for lead generation activities, and list some of the most notable legislation so far. Consent for data use is at the cornerstone of all of this legislation.

By the end of this chapter, you will understand some of the common strategies used for generating leads, understand that there is important but changing regulation on personal data, and be able to gather detailed information on what happens in practice and document it in a way that is appropriate for your stakeholders.

Customer buying journey

As the name suggests, the customer buying journey is the journey a person or organization goes through in order to purchase a product or service. As presented by the Chartered Institute of Marketing, the following diagram shows the five stages in the customer buying journey.

Figure 4.1 – The customer buying journey

This journey is defined in different ways by different institutions and organizations depending on their perspective, so there are many variations. There are a lot of different ways and terminology to break down how interactions are carried out in this journey and by whom, which we will talk about in the coming sections. Some of these terms and concepts overlap in their objectives and content so your organization may use some or all of them to describe what they do. Throughout your work designing a system for both the lead generation and sales process, it is essential to remember that this is about helping internal people, help external people through a process. Learning about or applying these strategies and approaches should not mean that you lose focus on the fact that people buy from people.

Demand generation versus lead generation

The terms demand generation and lead generation are important but different elements of a marketing strategy. They focus on the different stages of the purchasing journey:

- **Demand generation**: This is about creating awareness and interest for a product or service in the wider market. It is a broadcast approach aimed at reaching people who were previously unaware and unknown to the organization. Overall, this creates interest and increases demand, which in turn increases sales. An example might be a **product launch**. It is always at the beginning of the purchasing journey.

- **Lead generation**: This is the process of finding and attracting people who have the potential to buy a company's products or services. The aim is to get contact information from those who have an interest in a product or service. Their needs can then be qualified and handed over to the sales teams for conversion into customers.

The standard Sales Cloud functionality is best suited to lead generation activities where there is a personal selling element, rather than demand generation activities where there can be a requirement for mass outbound massaging. Sales Cloud has the capability to send personalized templated emails, but the send volumes are small in comparison to marketing automation tools are designed for communication at scale. Salesforce does have a Sales Engagement functionality that can be added to Sales Cloud for an additional cost. Sales Engagement tools increase the efficiency by which sales teams can deliver high-quality interactions with their prospects and customers.

In the next section, we will explore how demand generation and lead generation are applied in a B2B and B2C context.

B2B versus B2C

For B2B organizations, demand and lead generation have an important role. Demand generation focuses on sharing information about products and services and their benefit via content such as webinars, blogs, white papers, and testimonials. Lead generation is more targeted, identifying companies or individuals. Contact information is acquired via signup forms for informational content, free trials, webinars, live events, and so on, and then a business development or salesperson works with the contact to identify if they have a short-term need and budget and identify anyone else that might need to be involved.

For B2C organizations, the focus is more on-demand generation as the market is larger, and commonly sales volumes are higher than B2B. Marketing activities are on a mass scale such as advertising and social media. Once a person has engaged with the brand and shared their email, personalization can provide a targeted message via channels such as email. The purchase process is more often than not self-service. Lead generation for sales via a salesperson is less common and usually for bespoke or high-end products. An example might be travel or bespoke home services such as kitchens or bathrooms.

In the next section, we will explore other concepts and strategies that you will want to be aware of when talking to and gathering information from business stakeholders.

Channels and strategies

Two other concepts that you will want to be aware of when you are talking to stakeholders are channels and lead-generation strategies. Your organization will use a mix of these and the people who are responsible for delivering lead-generation activities in your organization will be experts in these areas.

Communication channels

Communication channels are the medium that your organization uses to communicate with external stakeholders. The following are the most used, but this is not an exhaustive list:

- In person
- Email marketing
- Chat
- Web

In recent years, we have seen an increase in the number of available channels to include more digital channels such as chatbots and instant messengers as technology and people's digital adoption have evolved.

Lead generation strategies

There are many different lead-generation strategies that an organization might adopt. A combination might be used, and, in a large organization, these strategies are delivered by different teams:

- Content marketing: This involves creating informative content about the organization's products and services, and distributing it
- Event Marketing: This involves hosting and attending events and promoting products and services
- Account-based marketing: This focuses on identifying target accounts and building relationships with key people rather than individual leads
- Personalization: This involves understanding the preferences and characteristics of prospects and delivering personalized content and campaigns

Having a basic understanding of what strategies and channels your organization uses before you engage with stakeholders will help you understand the language and likely objectives so you can quickly focus on the details.

Personal data regulation

In recent years, there has been a significant increase in regulation around personal data. There has been regulation on the storage and use of financial and health data for many years. However, the type of data that is subject to regulation and countries that have implemented it has increased, and in some countries, data that is considered PII is subject to regulations. As the purpose of lead generation is to capture the information of individuals for selling and marketing purposes, these activities are impacted by this new type of regulation.

In 2018, the **General Data Protection Regulation (GDPR)** came into force in the **European Union (EU)**. Since then, individual countries and states have implemented similar types of regulation, and this is set to continue. According to the **United Nations Conference on Trade and Development (UNCTAD)**, since 2021, 71% of countries have adopted some form of legislation. Further information can be found on their website, which is linked in the *Further reading* section. Here are some examples, however, this is not an exhaustive list:

- GDPR – EU
- **Data Protection Act (DPA)** 2018 – UK
- **California Consumer Privacy Act (CCPA)**

The HIPAA privacy rule that many people have heard of is a set of US federal laws that requires appropriate safeguards to protect the privacy of protected health information and sets limits and conditions on the uses and disclosures that may be made of such information without an individual's authorization. While this must be considered for lead generation activities in health care, its scope is not as broad as the general data protection legislation that was just outlined.

Organizations have to assess whether their operating practices are subject to this regulation. If they collect or process personal data in a region that has this regulation, it is likely that they will. Each organization has to decide how they implement their processes and systems to comply with the regulation.

As a system designer, it is important to engage with the people who have the responsibility to ensure compliance with relevant regulations and incorporate their requirements. A system alone can't ensure compliance.

Next, we will explore what is meant by a Lead, which will explain why personal data is collected.

What is a Lead?

The term "Lead" can mean different things to different people. It has more than one meaning in this book. It is important that as you work with stakeholders, you seek to define this, and any other terms, for your organization to eliminate confusion. The following are examples of how the definition of Leads varies based on stakeholders' requirements:

- **Marketing Ready Lead (MRL)**: A person who has engaged with marketing content and activities but is not ready to engage with sales

- **Sales Ready Lead (SRL)**: A person who has indicated that they are ready to make a purchase, for example, by making a pricing inquiry

Gathering information on the lead generation process

In *Chapter 3 – Design and Build: The Core Sales Process*, we talked about many of the practicalities of gathering information and documenting it. In this section, we will explore why it is important to gather detailed information about the process, how it is managed today (the As-Is), and what it should be in the future (the To-Be). We will explore the who and the how of gathering information on the sales process.

Identifying Your marketing and sales stakeholders

There are several groups of people who you will want to engage with to understand how Leads are gathered and managed within your organization. They each perform different activities. These include the following:

- **Marketing leadership** sets the marketing strategy and targets, which will define the demand generation and lead generation activities that will take place. They are accountable for the success of the strategy and associated activities. For this group, you want to focus on making it easy to capture and track their activities. They will want to be able to measure the performance and **return on investment (ROI)** of activities.

- **Marketing executives** are responsible for capturing leads and nurturing them to the point they are ready to hand over to the sales team. Nurturing activities may include emails and online events. For this group, you will want to focus on making it easy to capture the data, prepare it, and track it for any further activities.

- **Sales leadership** sets the sales strategy and targets. They are the consumer of the demand and lead generation activities – the internal customer. For this group, you will want to focus on understanding when a lead becomes sales-ready so the system supports this handover.

- The **data controller** is responsible for how the organization stores, processes, and secures personal data. They will be able to confirm what the organization has confirmed consent for and the processes that people and systems need to follow to ensure compliance. For this group, you will want to focus on the processes and security requirements reporting that they need to ensure compliance.

The titles might have slightly different names and some organizations might have one person performing multiple functions, but all the activities performed need to be known to understand the process. By talking to representatives of all functions, you will get the best understanding of the process.

> **Tip**
>
> Ask the executive sponsors to introduce and position what you are doing so stakeholders understand that it is important to the organization and its goals.
>
> Ask that individuals be given time out of their schedules to work with you. You will get limited time and attention as stakeholders are also trying to deliver their normal workload.
>
> Ask to talk to a range of individuals, high performers whose behavior the organization wants to model, those who are likely to champion the system, and those who are new to the process. They will all have different but valuable perspectives.

In the next section, we will explore the importance of asking good questions.

Asking good questions

To reiterate from the previous chapter, the aim is to understand the business requirement including what it will allow the user to do. Getting past the initial request by asking why can reveal new and significant information. It can reveal that a completely different solution is required.

Don't be afraid to ask for further information. You can use questions such as the following:

- Why would you want to do that?
- What will that help you achieve?
- Why can't you do that now?

The following note box gives examples of questions to ask about the lead generation process.

> **Note**
>
> What documentation do you have on the lead generation process?
>
> What language do you use internally to describe sales inquiries? Is it leads?
>
> How do you generate leads?
>
> What function is responsible for generating leads?
>
> How do you qualify leads?
>
> Who qualifies the leads?
>
> What stages are there in the Lead qualification process?
>
> How are leads assigned?
>
> How do you report on Lead generation activities?
>
> Are there targets in Lead generation?
>
> What are the biggest challenges?
>
> Tell me about your lead generation process.

Now that we have some context, a foundational understanding of the processes our system needs to support, and we have explored how we gather detailed requirements from our stakeholders, we will review the Sales Cloud functionality that is available.

Lead generation data and security model

In this section, we will explore the functionality in the Sales Cloud Data Model that is most commonly used for lead generation. Sales Cloud is built on the Salesforce Customer 360 Platform, which means it benefits from the secure and scalable infrastructure. We explored the tools available for security in the previous chapter, *Chapter 3, Design and Build – The Core Sales Process*, which you might want to review.

We will take a look at the Objects available in Sales Cloud, explore what they are best used for, and how they relate to other key Objects in Sales Cloud. However, before we get into those in detail, we will first review the business capabilities required for lead generation and how those map to functionality in Sales Cloud and other products in the Salesforce portfolio.

Sales Cloud capabilities

For your individual organization, it is important to confirm the specific business capabilities. The following capability map provides an example of the capabilities required to deliver lead generation.

Figure 4.2 – Lead generation capability map

From the capability map, you can see there are a number of capabilities required, and some of these will also be required by other business functions, for example, activity management. The diagram also indicates where Sales Cloud has full, partial, or no functionality to support the capability. The exact functionality available depends on the edition you have. To confirm the capability in the edition of Sales Cloud you have, you should talk to your account executive or review the Sales Cloud Pricing sheet. In the next section, we will look at the objects in the data model that support lead-generation processes.

Sales Cloud data model

For lead generation, the primary Object in the Sales Cloud is the Lead Object. This single Object is a holding place to capture a wide range of data while detailed information is being gathered. At the point it is confirmed that the organization wants to develop a longer-term relationship with the person, the Lead is converted, which separates out the data into the Account, Contact or Person Account, and Opportunity records. We will review the Lead conversion process in more detail in the *Lead conversion* section.

The benefit of this approach is that only a single record is initially created, rather than three, so if there is no mutual benefit in developing a relationship, then only one record needs to be updated. This makes it easy for users to work quickly through high volumes of inquiry records. It also keeps data storage volumes down.

Lead records are used to capture a transitory expression of interest. The information they capture is relevant for a relatively short period of time. They are not long-term reference records about a person, organization, or a product or service purchased. Once a Lead has been converted, it is no longer visible in the user interface, but some reporting is available on converted Leads.

Campaigns are also used for lead-generation activities. They are used to capture information about individuals and programs of mass audience activities. Examples include online or physical events. Leads and Contact records are associated with Campaigns to create audiences. Campaigns can be related to each other in a hierarchy so an overall program Campaign can group and summarize the activities of multiple child activities.

The diagram that follows shows how Leads and Campaigns relate to other Objects, primarily Account Contact and Opportunities.

Lead Generation Process Objects - Sales Cloud Entity Relationship Diagram

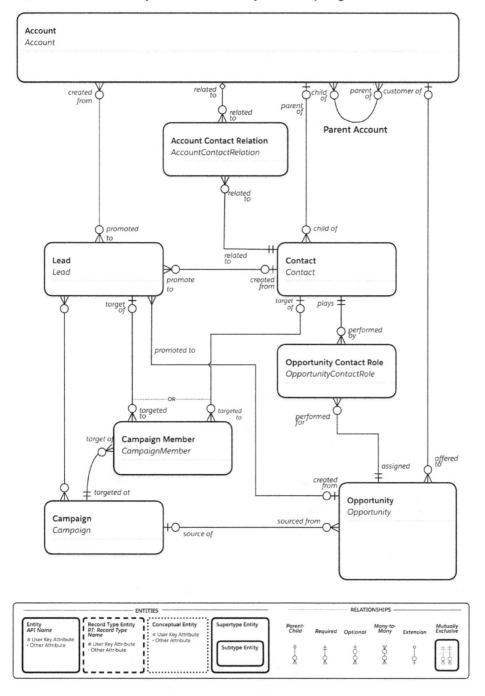

Figure 4.3 – Entity relationship diagram (ERD) Leads and relate Sales Cloud Objects

From the entity relationship diagram, you can see that the Lead and Campaign Objects are related to a number of other Objects, including each other via the Campaign Member junction Object. The next diagram shows the ERD for Leads, Campaigns, and Campaign Members.

The following is a table introducing the Lead and Campaign Objects we will review in this chapter. We covered the composition and features available for Accounts and Contacts in *Chapter 3, Design and Build – The Core Sales Process*.

Object Name	Object API Name	Usage
Lead	Lead	Used to store data about people who have expressed an interest in an organization's product and services.
Campaign	Campaign	Used to store data about programs or activities, for a mass audience, typically for marketing purposes. Examples might include an event or promotional email.
Campaign Member	Campaign Member	Used to relate people, Leads, and Contacts to a Campaign. Examples might include the invite list to an event or the mailing list for a promotional email.

Table 4.1 – Table describing the primary lead generation Objects

In the next section, we will look at the data model that is available across the Salesforce Customer 360 Platform for managing consent.

Salesforce Consent Data Model

The Salesforce Consent Data Model is a standard set of Objects that Salesforce has developed to manage consent at multiple levels. It moves towards modeling a person as an individual not just single points of contact (i.e., multiple Lead inquiries). It allows consent to be modeled at multiple levels of granularity (i.e., at a channel level, such as an email, or communication-specific, such as a newsletter). It has the flexibility to enable each organization to decide at what level they want to manage consent. Levels can be added as regulation and business needs change.

It is important to be aware of this capability, which has already been developed and is available in Sales Cloud. For organizations that have business requirements relating to consent and personal data regulation, looking at this capability is the starting point. Depending on the business needs, all or part of this data model might be relevant so should be assessed before building a custom solution. This provides a place to capture the information but doesn't automatically share it with systems or engagement or allows people to update their preferences so solutions of this will also have to be considered and designed.

The benefit of this capability is that the data model has already been designed and built and these records don't count towards the data storage total, which would be a consideration for any bespoke solution.

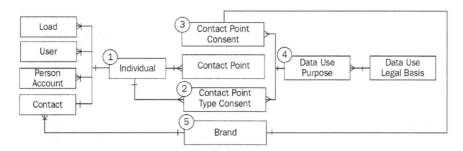

Figure 4.4 – ERD of the Salesforce Data Consent Model

There are links to more information on this in the *Further reading* section at the end of the chapter. Next, we will explore the Sales Cloud security features that relate specifically to Leads and Campaigns.

Sales Cloud security

In the previous chapter, *Design and Build – The Core Sales Process*, we reviewed the common core security tools. These are all relevant for Leads and Campaigns. If you have not already reviewed that section in the earlier chapter, I recommend you do so. In this chapter, we will review be looking at the security considerations that are specific to Leads and Campaign functionality.

Lead ownership

All Customer 360 platform records must have an Owner. The default Owner is the User that created the record. When a record is created by an automated process, such as Web-to-Lead, the User is set to the Default Lead Owner, which is defined in Lead **Settings**. To set this, go to **Feature Settings | Marketing | Lead Settings**. The location for setting the Default Lead Owner can be seen in *Figure 4.5*.

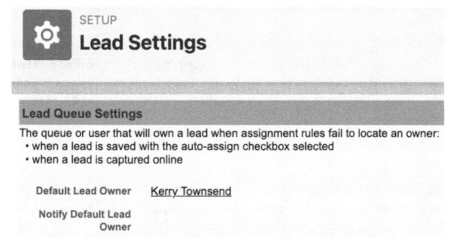

Figure 4.5 – The location for setting the Default Lead Owner

Leads, and some other standard Objects, can also be owned by Queues, which are sets of users. Queues are good when a group of people are working on a collection of records and allow records to be created before it has been decided who should own them. This is particularly relevant when Leads are created by an automated process and need to be picked up by the next available Users. For Users to be able to take ownership of a Lead from a Queue, they must be a member of the Queue. Roles, Public Groups, or Users can be added as members of a Queue. The best way to manage this is to create a Public Group and add it as a member of the Queue. Users can then be added and removed from the Public Group as they join or leave a team. The ability to add and remove people from Public Groups can be given to Managers or Team Leads via the delegated administration functionality without having to give the User full System administration privileges. Next, we will look at how Users can transfer records they don't own.

Transfer Leads Permission

In addition to create, read, update, and delete permissions, like other Objects, Leads also have a Transfer permission. All Users can transfer Leads that they own to another User, however, only Users with the Transfer Leads permission can transfer Leads owned by other users. The Transfer Leads permission is usually reserved for team leaders and Managers so that Users can't take Leads from other team members. The best way to provision this permission is by creating a Permission Set or Permission Set Group for lead generation Managers.

View Converted Leads

Although standard Converted Leads are no longer viewable in the **Lightning Experience Sales Cloud** UI, they are searchable. A User can be given permission to view and edit with the View and Edit Converted Leads permission. This is usually reserved for Admins who might need to correct data inaccuracies. Assess the impact of any changes before making them as they could change historical reporting which will have to be explained.

Campaigns

In addition to create and update permissions on the Campaign Object, Users also need the **Marketing User** checkbox checked on their User record to be able to add Leads and Contacts as Campaign Members and modify Campaign records. This is a setting that is often missed as it can't be added to a Permission Set.

Leads

In this section, we will look at the capabilities of Sales Cloud for capturing and managing expressions of interest in a product or service, then explore some of the key considerations and what happens in practice.

Sales Cloud capabilities

So far, we have seen how the Lead Object relates to other important Customer 360 Platform Objects and some of the common key security considerations. In the following sections, we will go into more detail about the Lead Object itself and the supporting functionality.

Lead Object

The Lead Object captures information about people who express an interest in an organization's products and services. The Lead Object only has a lookup relationship and that is to the Individual Object which is the person Object of the Salesforce Consent Model that we reviewed in a previous section. The Lead Object is used to capture several types of data, which is separated into other Objects if there is the potential for a sale and the Lead is converted.

In your Org, you might still see that there is a lookup relationship to the Dun & Bradstreet company. You will see that it is not visible in free Dev Orgs. This Object was part of the Data.com functionality that allowed you to subscribe and import company data from Dun & Bradstreet. Data.com was retired in February 2021 and is no longer available. For this reason, Objects and fields related to this will not be referenced in this book even though they might appear in your Org.

The following table summarizes key information about the Lead Object and its Fields.

Key Information	
The API Name	Lead
Required Fields	Last Name (Text)
	Company (Text)**
	Lead Status (Picklist)
Standard Relationships*	Individual (Lookup to Individual)
Other Key Fields	Lead Source (Picklist)
	Industry (Picklist)
	Rating (Picklist)

Table 4.2 – Key Information about the Lead Object

```
*Lookup relationships to the User Object for Owner, Created By, and
Modified By have not been included as they exist on all Objects.
```

```
**The Company field is required when Person Accounts are not enabled
in the Org. This can't be reversed. We reviewed Person Accounts in
Chapter 3 – Design and Build: The Core Sales Process.
```

It is worth noting that the Lead Source field is a special standard field. It also appears on the Contact Object and uses a shared set of values, which is also used in the Account Source field on Accounts. If you modify the values on either Lead, Contact, or Account, the changes will be reflected in all three fields. Next, we will consider the Sales Cloud Lead process.

Lead processes

A **Lead process** is the specific steps an organization takes to qualify a Lead. An organization might have different variations of its Lead process for different types of inquiries, products, and services. In Sales Cloud, the Lead process is captured in the Lead Status field. Multiple Lead processes can be active at the same time.

The **out-of-the-box (OOTB)** Lead process in Sales Cloud has four options. That is three main steps, assuming Closed – Converted and Closed – Not Converted are subtypes of the status Closed. They are as follows:

- Open – Not Contacted
- Working – Contacted
- Closed – Converted
- Closed – Not Converted

Here is a table of the Sales Cloud statuses, other commonly used statuses, and suggested activities for that stage.

Lead Status Values		Activities
OOTB Values	**Commonly Used Values**	
Open – Not Contacted	New	Created but no one is working on it and it might not be assigned.
Working – Contacted	Working	Has a User Owner that is actively working on qualifying the inquiry.
Closed – Converted	Converted	The Owner has confirmed the Lead meets the organization's criteria to Convert has been converted into an Account & Contact or a Person Account. An Opportunity might also have been created depending on the process.
Closed – Not Converted	Closed	The Lead does not meet conversion criteria and no further work is carried out.

Table 4.3 – Lead process statuses and likely status activities

Another Status that is often used is **Unqualified**. Users can find this a little confusing as it can be interpreted as still needing to be qualified or that it has been disqualified. Efforts should be made to avoid ambiguity as this can result in misclassification.

> **Note**
>
> It is very important to clearly define when a Lead should be converted. The point of conversion must come before any potential sale should appear in pipeline reporting. A typical point to convert a lead is when it is confirmed that a person's contact details are correct and reachable, they are looking to make a purchase and the organization has a product or service that could meet their need. This does, however, vary from organization to organization and should not be assumed. Once converted the process cannot be rolled back. We explore the Lead Conversion functionality in more detail later in the Lead Conversion section.

To update a Lead Process, you first add the new statuses to the **Lead Status** picklist in **Object Manager > Leads > Fields & Relationships**. Then, update or add a process in **Platform Tools > Feature Settings > Marketing > Lead Processes**.

To have more than one active Lead Process, you will also need to create different Lead Record Types, one for each Lead Process. You can associate a Lead Process with each Record Type. This is done in **Object Manager > Leads > Record Types**.

You can specify what Record Types Users can create and which one is their default using Permission Sets or Profiles. If a User has access to multiple Record Types, they will see a screen when they create a Lead allowing them to select the one they want. If they only have access to one, the record will automatically default to that. Users will see records or Record Types they are not able to create if the Sharing Model allows.

Record Types can also have different Page Layouts. This can improve the user experience as the page can be optimized for the process. There is also another way of contextualizing the Page Layout by enabling Dynamic Forms. This means only one Page Layout is required which reduces overall maintenance. We will cover customizing the UI in more detail in *Chapter 5, Design & Build – Sales User Productivity.*

Lead Conversion

Once the qualification steps have been completed a Lead either needs to be Converted or closed with no further action. When converted, a Contact and Account (B2B) or Person Account (B2C) is created and, optionally, an Opportunity can be created. The process is triggered by clicking the **Convert** button from the Lead record. There is no purely declarative way to convert Leads en masse. Lead Conversion can be automated with APEX code and this code can be initiated (invoked) by a Flow. We will explore APEX and Flow more in *Chapter 5*. There are also solutions on AppExchange that provide functionality to Convert Leads in bulk. We explore how to expand your solution with apps from AppExchange in *Chapter 14*.

Here is the screen the User is presented with when they click the **Convert** button with the default settings.

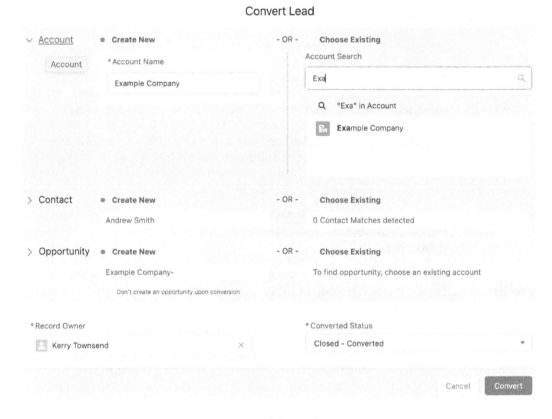

Figure 4.6 – Lead Conversion screen

On the **Convert Lead** screen, the User has the option to create new records or select existing records. It is important to note that if a User selects an existing record, the data from the Lead record doesn't overwrite fields that already have values in the existing record.

If Duplicate Matching Rules are active, then possible matches are suggested in the **Choose Existing** section. If Duplicate Matching rules prevent duplicates from being created this might have to be resolved before the conversation process can be completed.

By default, the Converted Lead Status is the Converted Lead Status Picklist Value that was specified in the Lead Status field. The User has the option to change this along with the Record Owner on the **Convert Lead** screen.

During the conversion process, field values of standard fields are automatically transferred to standard fields on the Account, Contact, and Opportunity. The mappings of the most commonly used are shown in the following table.

Lead Mapping	
First Name	Contact: First Name
	Person Account: First Name
Last Name	Contact: Last Name
	Person Account: Last Name
Company	Account: Account Name
	Contact: Account
	Opportunity: Opportunity Name and Account Name
Phone	Account: Phone
	Person Account: Phone
	Contact: Phone
Mobile	Contact: Mobile
	Person Account: Mobile
Lead Owner	Account: Owner
	Contact: Owner
	Opportunity: Owner
Lead Source	Account: Account Source
	Contact: Lead Source
	Opportunity: Lead Source
	Person Account: Lead Source
Description	Contact: Description

Table 4.4 – Lead mapping on Conversion

You can see from the table the fields from the Lead Object can populate multiple fields on the created Objects. A list of the mappings of all the standard fields can be found on Salesforce Help. A link to this is provided in the *Further reading* section at the end of the chapter.

Custom Lead fields can be mapped to custom fields on the Account, Contact, and Opportunity. The mappings are set on the **Lead Mapping** page from the **Action** buttons on Leads Fields & Relationships.

A common request is to want to map Standard Lead fields, to either a different Object or to a Custom field. This is not possible. A Custom field will need to be created on both the Lead and target Object, mapped to each other, and added to the Page Layout. The Standard fields will need to be removed from the Page Layout and any data migrated. A common example is wanting to direct the Description field to the Opportunity Object rather than the Standard mapping, which is to the Contact Description.

The option to create an Opportunity from the conversion screen can be removed if it doesn't make sense for your organization's process. This is done with a feature setting, which we will explore in the next section.

Once Converted, a Lead record is no longer searchable. If a Lead is a Campaign Member, the conversion process replaces the Lead with the new or existing Contact record, so the person is still related to the Campaign. Next, we will look at the settings available for Leads, of which there are a number related to the conversion process.

Feature Settings

The **Lead Feature Settings** set Org wide settings for the Default Lead assignment, Conversion Settings, Merge Settings and Lead Email Notifications when the Owner is assigned by code. They can be found in **Feature Settings | Marketing | Lead Settings**, as shown in *Figure 4.7*.

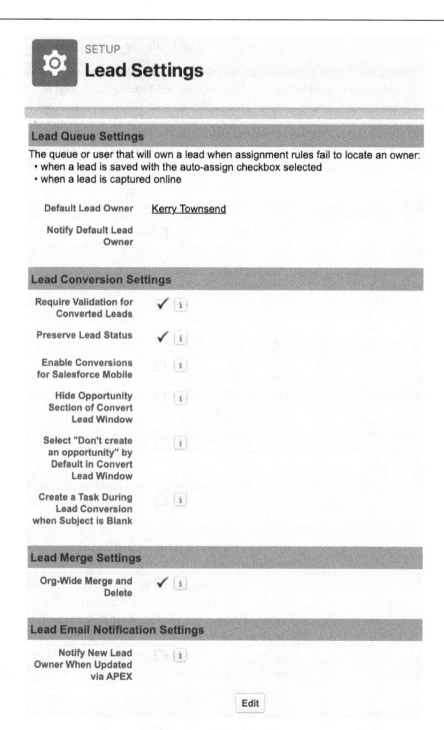

Figure 4.7 – Lead Settings

The figure shows the organization-wide settings available for Leads that can be turned on and off.

Default Lead Owner is the Owner Assigned when they don't meet the criteria for any Lead Assignment Rule. If no Lead Assignment Rules are active, all web-generated Leads are assigned to the Default Lead Owner.

You can see that there are a number of options to customize the Lead Conversion behavior, along with the merge and email notification. The following table lists the remaining feature options and what they do.

Feature Setting	Functionality
Require Validation for Converted Leads	When enabled, this means that required fields, Validation Rules, workflow actions, and APEX triggers are triggered when a lead is converted.
Preserve Lead Status	When enabled, it prevents the Lead Status from being set to a new Lead Owner's default status. The Lead Owner changes to the person who converted it.
Enable Conversions for Salesforce Mobile	When enabled, Users can convert Leads on the Salesforce Mobile app.
Hide Opportunity Section of Convert Lead Window	When enabled, the Opportunity section is removed from the Lead Conversion dialog, which means an Opportunity can't be created.
Select "Don't create an opportunity" by Default in Convert Lead Window	When enabled, the Don't created an Opportunity upon conversion checkbox is checked by default.
Create a Task During Lead Conversion when Subject is Blank	Only applicable in Classic; when enabled, this creates a Task even if the `Task Subject` field on the Lead Conversion dialog is blank. The new Task button is not clicked on the conversion successful screen.
Org-Wide Merge and Delete	Once activated, and assuming the Org operates with the broadest available Lead sharing parameters ("Public Read/Write/Transfer"), this configuration empowers all Users to merge and delete Leads..
Notify New Lead Owner When Updated via APEX	Only applicable in Lightning; when enabled, this sends a notification to the new Lead Owner when the ownership is changed via APEX.

Table 4.5 – A summary of Lead Settings and their functionality

From the table, you can see that there are a number of ways that the Lead conversion experience can be customized depending on an organization's requirements. The **Require Validation for Converted Leads** and **Preserve Lead Status** are usually enabled by default. Another setting that is frequency enabled is **Select "Don't create an opportunity" by Default in Convert Lead Window** so that a lot of unnecessary Opportunities are not created.

In the next section, we will review the Queue functionality and how it allows a wider group of people to have ownership permissions on records.

Lead Queues

The Customer 360 Platform Queue functionality is used when a group of Users is working on a collection of records. Initially, records are assigned to a Queue and individual Users can take ownership of a record from the Queue when they are available and ready to work on it. There are often lead generation use cases where Queues are the best option. There are a number of Objects that can use Queues including Service Cloud Cases, but it is worth noting that Queues are not available for Accounts, Contact, and Opportunities.

The following screen shows the options a User sees when they create a Queue.

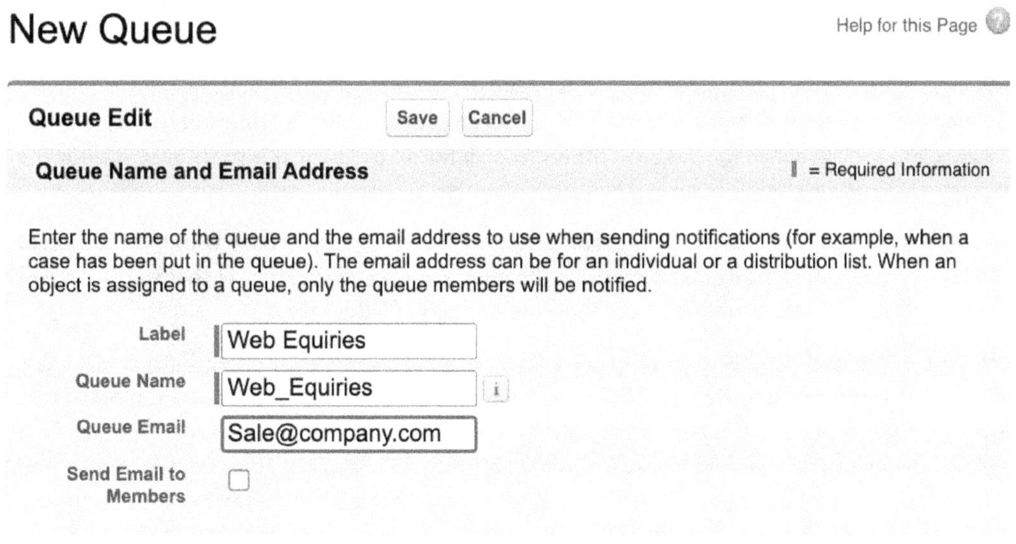

Figure 4.8 –The New Queue screen

Each Queue requires a Label, Queue Name (API Name), and a Queue Email. The Queue Email will receive a notification once these are set up. This is an option to notify all members of the Queue. Queue Members are the Users who can take Ownership of Leads from the Queue.

If the Sharing Model for Leads is Public Read/Write/Transfer, Queue Members are not required as everyone has the Transfer permission. For Public Read / Write and Private, Queue Members can be specified. Queue Members can be specified as User, Roles, Roles, and Subordinates or Public Groups. The latter two are simpler to maintain as they don't require access and permission to modify the Queue definition. The simplest is via Role as User will automatically inherit the permission if they are assigned a Role that has access. If more granularity is required, then a Public Group is the next best option.

Also, for maintainability and clarity for Users, the number of Queues should be kept to the minimum number that satisfies the business requirements.

To enable traceability and accountability, Leads should not be worked on before Lead Ownership is transferred to the User updating it. Validation Rules can be added to prevent the record from being updated when it is owned by a Queue or preventing a specific status while it is owned by a Queue. How exactly this type of rule is implemented should be informed by the specific business requirements. It is important to remember that it should only apply to update and not create.

Web-to-Lead

The Web-to-Lead functionality provides a predefined pattern of bringing inquiry data into Sales Cloud from a public website. Without a prebuilt pattern like this, an integration would need to be built by each Sales Cloud customer.

The Web-to-Lead functionality allows you to generate the HTML code of the Lead fields. Users can select the fields they want to include in the form, including any that they might want to keep hidden, and Sales Cloud will generate the basic HTML. Although not a Lead field, it is possible to include the Campaign ID so a Lead can be associated with a Campaign.

This basic HTML code will need to be incorporated into your company website with the addition of the styling and any client-side data validation. There are services on the market that validate email addresses before the form is submitted but these are not part of Sales Cloud.

Web forms can attract spambots, which repeatedly submit the form creating spam Leads making it hard to identify genuine inquiries. With Web-to-Lead forms, you can enable Google reCAPTCHA. This is a Google service and not part of the Salesforce service. To use this, you need to register for a Google reCAPTCHA account, which, at the time of writing, is free to do. To use it, you must agree to the service terms and conditions. You will want to confirm that it is available in your geographical area. When you sign up, you will register your domain and receive a public and private key pair.

On the **Web-to-Lead** setup page, you enable reCAPTCHA with **Require reCAPTCHA Verification**. You enter the reCAPTCHA key pair when you generate the HTML on the same page that you select the fields to be included.

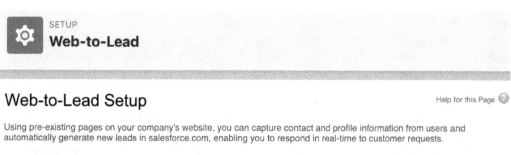

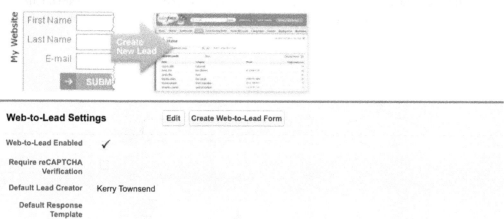

Figure 4.9 – The Web-To-Lead setup

There is an Org limit of 500 web Leads per day. If the daily limit of 500 is exceeded, the information captured of all additional Leads is emailed to the Default Lead Creator. It is important that this is a monitored inbox. It is possible to request an increased daily limit from Salesforce by raising a Support Case. When the limit is exceeded, the additional requests are queued in and submitted when the 24-hour limit is refreshed. The queue holds a maximum of 50,000 and also captures Web-to-Case excess requests.

If you routinely generate more than 500 or your Salesforce increased limit, you will want to explore developing a bespoke solution.

Be aware of any Validation or Duplication Rules on Leads that would prevent Lead records from being created by an automated process as the error messages that would have been seen in the UI will not be displayed to a person submitting a web form. Add except criteria so the rule doesn't fire.

Lead Assignment Rules

Lead Assignment Rules allow Leads to be assigned to an Owner based on a set of criteria. The alternative is manually assigning Leads, which is time consuming and repetitive. Allowing Users to take ownership of Leads has the risk that they might only take what they think are the best Leads.

Depending on where they are assigned from, they may need the Read/Write/Transfer permission, which means they can take Leads from other Owners. This is a permission that can be abused. The Transfer permissions are not required if the Leads are being transferred from a Queue and the User is a member of the Queue.

To assign Leads, a set of Assignment Rules is set up. It is possible to have more than one set of Lead Assignment Rules although only one can be active at a time. These rules have an If... Else format. The first criteria is evaluated and if it is met then the Lead is assigned, and no further criteria are evaluated. If the criteria are not met, the next criteria is evaluated, and so on until there are no further rules; in which case, the Lead is assigned to the Default Lead Owner. The following figure illustrates how the logic works.

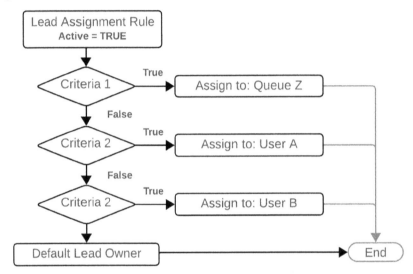

Figure 4.10 – Lead assignment evaluation logic

To ensure all Leads are assigned to someone in the Sales team, it is good to have a rule at the end with no criteria that assigns Leads to a Queue or someone who will be able to assign them. It is important to test these thoroughly to make sure that all possible combinations are accounted for, otherwise inquiries may be allocated to the Owners and not followed up appropriately.

Lead Auto Response Rules

Lead Auto Response rules provide an automated way of sending an email response to the person who submits a Lead to acknowledge the inquiry. An acknowledgment means that inquirers are not left wondering whether their inquiry has been submitted.

Lead Auto Response Rules are set in the same way as Lead Auto Response Rules. As with Assignment Rules, it is possible to have multiple sets of Auto Response Rules, although only one can be active at a time. These rules have an `If...  Else` format. The first rule is evaluated and if the criteria are met, then the Lead is assigned and no further rules are evaluated. If the criteria are not met, each rule is evaluated in the order of execution until a set of criteria is met or there are no more rules; in which case, the Lead is not sent an email. To ensure all Leads are sent a response, it is good to have a rule at the end with no criteria that sends a generic response.

Lead Scoring

With large volumes of leads, a scoring approach can be implemented to indicate those that are most likely to buy. In its simplest form, the scoring can be based on data attributes such as job title and email domain, but it can also be based on behavioral data (i.e., email clicks or form submissions if that is available).

Duplicate management

The Customer 360 Platform has the functionality to identify and merge duplicate records. This is important as duplicate records can result in duplication of effort and a poor customer experience.

A common approach is to create rules that prevent Users from creating duplicate records in the user interface. However, having this type of prevention rule is not appropriate if there are automatic methods of creating Lead records, such as Web-to-Lead. In this case, duplicates need to be allowed with a process for identifying them and merging records where appropriate.

Unlike other records, there may be use cases where it is appropriate to allow duplicates to remain. For example, if one Org is used for multiple brands and a person inquires about different product lines, it would be appropriate that a Lead for the same person might exist.

Duplicate Rules can be set up to prevent duplicates, to alert, or just to report. OOTB Salesforce has standard rules for matching Leads, Contact, Person Accounts, and Accounts. There are also rules that match Leads with Contacts. There is a component that can be added to the Page layout that highlights potential duplicates and links to a page where Users can inspect and merge duplicates.

Key considerations

The only required field on Leads is the `Last  Name` field. This is the record reference field and appears throughout the platform for the User to identify and access records. For this reason, it is important that it is human readable rather than, for example, a code or reference number. For that sort of identifier or for the legal name of the company, it is best to create an additional field. It is important to have that information in the system so it can be searched and merged into communications, but you don't want to force Users to learn these pieces of data.

Classifications are important for Leads. They are important to ensure that Leads are directed to the right people for follow up and qualification. Picklist fields are a good option for these as this means the values are consistent and there are a finite number of options. Multi-select picklist fields are always a last resort as they allow records to appear in multiple categories which can result in double reporting in number counts.

Converting to Person Accounts

When you use the Person Account model, the Company field on Leads has no purpose. For Orgs where Person Accounts are enabled, leave the Company field blank to convert the Lead to a Person Account rather than a Business Account. Enter a value for Company for the Lead to convert to Contact and Account. You will need to modify the Lead Page Layout so Company is not required at that level.

When to create a Lead versus Contact

A question that Users often ask is when to create a Lead versus a Contact for an inquiry when the person is from an organization that is already a customer. This varies from organization to organization depending on the business process and strategy. If an Account-based strategy is followed, then the managing team will want to be aware of any activity as early as possible and the Opportunities are likely to be known so in this case it might be appropriate to move them to a Contact as soon as possible.

Part of the qualification process is to establish whether the contact information is valid. People often enter incorrect contact information on web forms to get access to content without sharing their personal details. For this reason, a level of qualification is always recommended before Lead data is moved to Contacts.

> **Other lead considerations**
>
> Is more than one Lead Process required?
>
> Should all Lead Users see all records?
>
> Should an Opportunity be created every time a Lead is converted?
>
> What naming convention should be used for Opportunity names?
>
> What Lead categories are required?

Now that we have worked through some of the key considerations when using the Leads functionality, we will take a look at how functionality is practically applied.

In practice

In practice, Lead Processes are kept quite simple as Lead records are not expected to have a long life. If the contact details are good and a person has a need that can be met by a product or service, then they are converted for dedicated attention from a salesperson.

The number of fields on Leads is typically quite small to keep it simple to complete the information. It is usually limited to clarification to allow lead routing and reporting and a small number of free-form text fields to capture their needs and context so that a rating or score can be applied.

OOTB, there is no relationship between Leads and Accounts or Products. A common request is to mark or relate Leads to these. The requirement to capture product information can usually be satisfied with a simple picklist of Leads as their exact product requirements will be confirmed later in the buying process.

Salesforce has a product called Sales Engagement (formally **High Velocity Sales**), which has functionality for outbound sales calls. It allows the creation of call lists and uses AI to analyze calls for buying intent and agent coaching points.

In the next section, we will explore the Campaigns Object and its uses as this can be used to track activities that capture Leads.

Campaigns

In this section, we will look at the capabilities of Sales Cloud for recording and managing activities or programs of activities that target multiple people, then explore some of the key considerations and what happens in practice.

Sales Cloud capabilities

These Objects are used to capture data about the activities in Salesforce. The `Campaign` record is the header record that captures the summary information. The Campaign Member Object relates people, Leads, and Contacts, to the `Campaign` record.

In this session, we will explore the Campaign and Campaign Member Objects.

Campaign

The Campaign captures the overall details of a mass audience activity, for example, an online or physical event. It includes data such as the activity name, type and status, associated costs, and responses. It also includes an **Active** checkbox, which is an important Sales Cloud field as it determines whether the Campaign is available for the User to add Members to. The following table summarizes key information about the Campaign Object and its Fields.

Key Information	
The API Name	Campaign
Required Fields	Campaign Name (Text)
Standard Relationships*	Parent Campaign (Lookup to Campaign)
Other Key Fields	Active (Checkbox)
	Type (Picklist)
	Status (Picklist)

Table 4.6 – Key Information about the Campaign Object

`*Lookup relationships to the User Object for Owner, Created By, and Modified By have not been included as they exist on all Objects.`

OOTB, the Campaign Object (and Campaign Member), has broad and basic options set up to illustrate how it can be applied. For this reason, organizations don't always initially understand the full potential of Campaigns. Creating a few Record Types for the different types of mass activities you want to track, reducing the picklist options, so they are relevant for the activity type, and customizing the Member Statuses (covered in the next section) quickly makes it more targeted and easier to use.

In addition to adding Leads and Contacts to a Campaign, you can also associate Opportunities. An Opportunity can be related to one Campaign via the `Primary Campaign Lookup` field on the Opportunity. The value of the Opportunities related to a Campaign is summarized in the Campaign even though the relationship is not a Master Detail relationship. This is an example of some of the special relationships that exist between standard Objects.

Also, OOTB Campaigns have eight special fields that behave as rollup summary fields, although their field types are `Number` and `Currency`. They summarize data related to Leads and Contacts from Campaign Members, as well as Opportunities associated with the `Primary Campaign` field. Opportunities. The fields are as follows:

- `Leads in Campaign` (Number COUNT)
- `Converted Leads in Campaign` (Number COUNT)
- `Contacts in Campaign` (Number COUNT)
- `Responses in Campaign` (Number COUNT)
- `Opportunities in Campaign` (Number COUNT)
- `Won Opportunities in Campaign` (Currency SUM)
- `Won Opportunities in Campaign` (Currency SUM)
- `Value Won Opportunities in Campaign` (Currency SUM)

These are all system calculated and can't be edited by the Users. As the relationship between Campaign and Opportunity is not a Master Detail, it is not possible to create custom fields of type Rollup Summary that summarize Opportunity data onto a Campaign.

Campaign Hierarchy

The Campaign Object also has a `Parent Campaign` field, which is a lookup to itself. This allows the modeling of multi-activity mass audience events, making it much more flexible. For example, an online promotional event might have multiple activities such as one or two promotional emails, the event itself, and a follow-up email. For this scenario, a parent Campaign can be created to capture the overall timescales, objectives, and performance, and child Campaigns can be created for each of the tactical activities to record targeted attendees' responses.

There are standard fields that also summarize the information from the Campaigns in the hierarchy. These fields are as follows:

- `Budgeted Cost in Hierarchy` (Currency SUM)
- `Actual Cost in Hierarchy` (Currency SUM)
- `Expected Revenue in Hierarchy` (Currency SUM)
- `Num Sent in Hierarchy` (Number SUM)
- `Leads in Hierarchy` (Number COUNT)
- `Converted Leads in Hierarchy` (Number COUNT)
- `Contacts in Hierarchy` (Number COUNT)
- `Responses in Hierarchy` (Number COUNT)
- `Opportunities in Hierarchy` (Number COUNT)
- `Won Opportunities in Hierarchy` (Currency SUM)
- `Won Opportunities in Hierarchy` (Currency SUM)
- `Value Won Opportunities in Hierarchy` (Currency SUM)

As you can see from the list, there is quite a lot of information available when the Campaign Hierarchy is available. Next, we will learn about adding Leads and Contacts as Campaign Members.

Campaign Member

The Campaign Member is a junction Object that allows Leads and Contacts to be related to multiple Campaigns and Campaigns to have multiple Leads and Contacts. The Campaign Member has a small number of fields that are unique to it but the majority of the fields on the Object are for capturing information from the Lead or Contact such as First Name, Last Name, Email, Lead Source, and Email Opt Out.

For each relationship, a Campaign Status is assigned to the person. This Status can be updated during the life of the Campaign meaning a person's interaction with a campaign can be captured and reported on. The following table summarizes key information about the Campaign Object and its Fields.

Key Information	
The API Name	CampaignMember
Required Fields	Campaign (Lookup to Campaign)
Standard Relationships*	Campaign (Lookup to Campaign)
	Lead (Lookup to Lead)
	Contact (Lookup to Contact)
Other Key Fields	Responded (Checkbox)
	First Responded Date (Date)

Table 4.7 – Key Information about the Campaign Member Object

```
*Lookup relationships to the User Object for Owner, Created By, and
Modified By have not been included as they exist on all Objects.
```

Campaign Members can be added individually from the Campaign Related List on Lead or Contact Record, they can be added from a report where the primary Object is either Lead or Contact. They can also be uploaded from a file although this has data quality and duplication implications.

When you are working with multiple child Campaigns that are part of a program of activities, you can create reports of Members with specific Statuses from one Campaign and use them to add or update Members on any Campaign.

Campaign Member Statuses

The Campaign Member Status can be powerful in tracking how a Lead or Contact has interacted with a Campaign. OOTB, the Status values are Sent and Responded. Often, Users are not sure how to use these as not all Campaigns send something, and the term "Responded" can be broadly interpreted. In addition, for a set of Statuses, one or more can be marked as Responded, this is independent of the Status value Responded.

The count of Members with a Status that is marked as Responded is displayed on the Campaign. It can be used as a measure of success for a Campaign if the Statuses marked as Responded are meaningful.

Below is a table of Campaign Types and possible Member Statuses to get you thinking about what Statuses you might work for your organizations. The Statuses marked as Responded are in *bold italics*.

Campaign Type	Event	Email	Web Form
Campaign Statuses	Selected	Selected	*Responded*
	Invited	Send	
	RSVPed	*Clicked*	
	Attended	*Opened*	
		Bounced	

Table 4.8 – Lead Mapping on Conversion

The best way to approach this as an organization is to determine the types of Campaigns you want to track. Decide on a list of Statuses for each campaign type. You want values that either indicate what the next action is with that person or are used for reporting. They describe which of those statuses for each type should be considered Responded. You can set up different Record Types for each Campaign so that only the relevant Statuses are displayed.

Customizable Campaign Influence

Campaign influence is a Salesforce functionality that allows standard and customizable revenue attribution models. If you are not familiar with attribution models, they define the value of a deal that can be attributed to a Campaign. Organizations are always trying to understand what actions and activities have the most impact on winning business. Campaign attribution is a complex topic, which we will not get into in detail here.

Sales Cloud has two types of campaign influence functionalities: Customizable Campaign Influence and Campaign Influence. The latter is only available in Classic so we will only focus on Customizable Campaign Influence. Customizable Campaign Influence can be enabled by going to **Feature Settings** > **Marketing** > **Campaign Influence** > **Campaign Influence Settings** and selecting **Enable**.

Once enabled, you can set auto-assignment rules that apply to both the standard and any custom models. These rules allow you to restrict the Campaigns that can be considered influential. For example, in the context of the length of your sales cycle, you may want to restrict the timeframe that a Campaign can be marked as influential. You may want to restrict the types of Campaigns that can be marked as influential, for example, if you use the Campaign Hierarchy you may only want parent Campaigns to be associated. Custom fields can be used in auto-association rules.

In the UI, **Customizable Campaign Influence** shows as a related list (Campaign Influence junction object) and a set of reports to show how Campaigns impact Opportunities. With the standard model attribute, 100% of the value of an Opportunity is to the Campaign selected in the `Primary Campaign Source` field. With this model, the system creates the `Campaign Influence` records automatically based on auto-association settings. Users can't create these records manually.

With the custom attribution model, Users can create Campaign Influence records manually. It is also possible to create Campaign Influence records via the API. If you want Users to be able to create records manually from the related list, you need to set the custom to Default. If you don't want Users to create records manually, then set the model to **Locked**.

Once functionality has been enabled, you get a new report called Campaigns with Influenced Opportunities. Three other report types can be created using the Campaign Influence Object: Opportunities with Campaign Influence, Contacts with Campaign Influence, and Accounts with Campaign Influence.

If you are using Marketing Cloud Account Engagement with Sales Cloud, three additional attribution models become available: **First-Touch**, **Even Distribution**, and **Last-Touch**. There is a link in the *Further reading* section where you can read more about these.

Key considerations

The biggest consideration with Campaigns is what Campaigns are practical and beneficial to track in Salesforce and for each of those which Campaign Member Statuses are appropriate. Another key consideration is where to add the parent Campaign and associated field to allow a parent/child hierarchy. This can be powerful if you run programs of Campaigns.

There are a few questions to consider:

- What Campaign types do you want to track?
- Do you have the data to run the Campaigns you want?
- What metrics need to be tracked?
- What teams need to use Campaigns?
- Can audiences be identified based on criteria?
- Who will select audience lists?
- Do salespeople need to be able to add, remove, or approve people on Campaign lists?

While Tasks can be logged against Campaigns, the functionality is not a tool designed for managing Campaign development project management (i.e., assets). It can be used to capture costs to compare with returns to calculate the ROI.

In practice

In practice, campaigns are used in a wide variety of ways. The functionality can be used for any activities that involve a group of customers/potential customers, Leads, and Contacts. In a lot of organizations, this functionality is underutilized. This can be for a few different reasons, but common ones are that organizations just don't realize the functionality is available or Salesforce is considered to be a tool for the sales team that no one from the marketing teams has access to.

It is usually the marketing function that will get the most benefit from the Campaign functionality as it can allow them to see what activities returned in sales.

Getting the most from this functionality does require sales and marketing teams to work together. Marketing teams need to communicate what Campaigns they are running and what they need from sales for them to be successful. There can be a manual element of Sales to ensure Opportunities are attributed to Campaigns.

Align Campaign classifications with marketing budget categories so it is easy to see the value of business generated. This means reports can be created in Sales Cloud that can be easily compared to the budget. The most common example is events. There might be money allocated in the budget for different types of events (i.e., internally hosted or externally hosted events), making it very easy to differentiate, which then makes reporting more efficient.

Other Objects

In this chapter, we have learned about the Lead and Campaign Objects, but there are other Objects that are used with these, most notably the Activity Objects, Task, and Event. We review these in more detail in the previous chapter, *Chapter 3, Design and Build: The Core Sales Process*.

With lead generation, activity management is very similar to the sales process, the focus is on recording past or future actions (i.e., calls, emails, meetings, etc.) with the aim of giving potential customers a consistent, timely experience that moves them through a process.

Activities allow managers to track how much work is required to qualify leads. Adding classification fields to Activity Objects allows leaders to assess what types of action make a difference. Without structure and guidelines in this area, there can be a lot of variation in the way the User describes each action by simply using the Subject. You would never want to have to start reviewing the description in reports to understand performance.

There are a number of ways that the logging of Activities, Tasks, and Events, can be logged. Tasks are used to log calls. Calls where a voice mail is left are logged and a follow-up task should be created as a reminder of when to call again. To make it very quick and easy to log this type of activity, a **Quick Action** button can be created that prefills the information. We explore Quick Actions in more detail in *Chapter 5, Sales Productivity*. Making it easy for Users to complete the actions required of them means they are more likely to complete them, so leaders get the reporting they need.

Although technically not Objects, Reports and Dashboards offer essential functionality to enable the lead generation process. These allow leaders to measure and analyze performance, and share this with the team to encourage the desired team behaviors. You will want to work with sales and marketing leaders to define a core set of these. Consider what reports will also show the success of the system such as Days to Convert, making the assumption this time will be shorted with a tool that improves sales efficiency.

Lead generation is an area where managers usually want to track performance quite closely and in real time. Lead generation today is a strong indication of sales performance in the future. Reports offer a powerful way to track performance but remember, to improve overall sales performance, it is important to combine data with insights and opinions from the team.

Translating lead generation process requirements into design

Now that you have reviewed the capability of the primary Objects in Sales Cloud, that that are used for the lead generation we can start to translate the requirements into design. As said before, you want to make sure you leverage all the standard functionality first before any custom solution. You also want to use the organization's terminology where possible; however, be cautious about renaming stand Objects and Fields as this has a maintenance cost.

Always start with the simplest option and, when possible, play this back to Users to get feedback and only add complexity if required. For example, if the organization has requested a lot of fields on the Lead record, or they have many free text fields, you might want to show a version that only shows the essential classification fields to make sure they are aware of the user experience impact of extending the admin burden on Users.

Implementing a new system gives an opportunity to simplify and streamline, you should make recommendations on options for doing this; however, the business will make the final decisions. The following is the minimum you should expect for a baseline solution:

- At least one lead process.
- A Default Lead Owner setup.
- An approach for bringing leads into Sales Cloud either Web-to-Lead or file upload.
- Set up basic Lead Assignment Rules and, if appropriate, a simple Auto Response.
- A basic set of fields including some picklist fields that will be used for reporting.
- A simple page layout with only fields that Users will fill in. Keep the required fields to those that are essential.
- A clear definition of when a Lead should be converted and what information is required in order to do so.

- If the business has clear rules and the data is available in Sales Cloud a Lead Source formula.

- A set of reports.

If you are using Campaigns, you will also want to include these in your baseline solution:

- A campaign naming strategy.

- A basic set of picklist classification fields for reporting

- Agreed criteria on when a Campaign is marked as active

- An agreed set of campaign member statuses that will be used across all Campaigns

- A process for communicating upcoming Campaigns to Sales Cloud Users

- Guidelines on when Users should associate an Opportunity to a Campaign via the `Primary Campaign` field

Now that we reviewed some tips for translating your requirements into a solution and reviewed what would be required in a basic solution, we will summarize what we have learned.

Summary

In this chapter, we started by exploring the differences between demand generation and lead generation then what the standard Sales Cloud is. We went on to look at techniques for gathering more information about the specifics of the sales process used in our organization. Next, we reviewed Sales Cloud's capability and then looked at the data Objects in detail. You learned about the Sales Cloud functionality that relates to Leads and Campaigns and the main things you should consider when designing with this functionality. We ended by discussing how to approach translating the requirements gathered into a solution design.

In the next chapter, we will explore the Objects and key functionality available to model the lead or demand generation process.

Further reading

Personal Data Legislation

- *UNCTAD: Data Protection and Privacy Legislation Worldwide*:

  ```
  https://unctad.org/page/data-protection-and-privacy-legislation-
  worldwide
  ```

Lead Conversion

- *What happens when I convert leads*:

  ```
  https://help.salesforce.com/s/articleView?id=sf.faq_leads_what_
  happens_when.htm&type=5
  ```

- *Lead Conversion Field Mapping*:

  ```
  https://help.salesforce.com/s/articleView?id=sf.lead_conversion_
  mapping.htm&type=5
  ```

Customizable Campaign Influence

- *How Customizable Campaign Influence works*:

  ```
  https://help.salesforce.com/s/articleView?id=sf.campaigns_
  influence_customizable_understanding.htm&type=5
  ```

- *Campaign Influence Implementation Guide*:

  ```
  https://resources.docs.salesforce.com/latest/latest/en-us/sfdc/
  pdf/campaign_influence_implementation_guide.pdf
  ```

Design and Build: Sales User Productivity

In the previous two chapters, we looked at Sales and Lead Generation Processes, respectively. We explored how to understand and capture the requirements of your business. We also explored the data structure and functionalities that Sales Cloud has for these processes so that you can design data models that are appropriate for our use case. In this chapter, we build that foundation and look at the functionality that provides increases in Sales productivity. You will learn about the importance of the Sales' User experience and optimizing the options you have to optimize it for your use case. You will also learn about the tools available to automate actions, options for tracking activities, and the mobile app for Users who spend more time out of the office than in. In each section, we start with the functionality that is typically easiest to implement and progress to those that take greater consideration or require additional licenses.

The benefits gained from the functionality in this section are typically why organizations implement a centralized system or an enterprise-grade system such as Salesforce. However, we need an appropriate data model to build this on, which is why we started with those.

In this chapter, we're going to cover the following main topics:

- The importance of **user experience** (**UX**) design

- Sales Cloud **user interface** (**UI**) design

- Automation

- Email and calendar integration

- Going mobile

- In-app guidance

Supporting tools information

In this chapter, we look at user interface design and automating processes, which are two areas it is important to get User feedback about as early as possible before investing time in a complete solution, particularly for Pro Code solutions.

You can use a sandbox or dev org to create a visual mock-up or prototype of your solution. If you don't have one available for this purpose or you need to mock up examples very early in the process, you can use an UI wireframe tool such as Avonni Creator or Sketch. The latter has libraries for Salesforce components. If neither of these are available, then you can take screenshots of your existing UI and manipulate these in a presentation or drawing tool that allows you to manipulate the images.

If you are working on a Sales Cloud implementation, you should document any significant decisions or automations that you design in a documentation tool such as Confluence, if your organization uses it, or in a word processor such as Google Docs or Microsoft Word.

The importance of user experience (UX) design

User experience, often shortened to **UX**, is about considering a person's holistic experience and designing a solution that meets their human needs.

In this section, we explore what is meant by UX design and why it is important to think about it when you configure Sales Cloud for your Users.

What is UX design?

UX design looks at a person's whole experience. There are many factors that impact this, including but not limited to their previous experiences, the environment they are in, their attitude to technology, and their goal. It addresses all aspects of a person's interactions with a system. The aim is to meet the exact needs of the User in a frictionless way, resulting in an efficient and pleasant experience.

This requires you to put yourself in your Users' shoes to not only understand their needs but also understand the pressures and challenges they face. For example, some of your Sales Users might be office-based and some field-based. This means they will be accessing the system from multiple devices with different form factors and sizes. You need to understand what these are and adapt and test your designs accordingly.

Designing everything assuming all users have the screen size or number of screens you use might disappoint some Users. Many Salespeople have to complete tasks while they are out of the office travelling in between meetings. This is a very different experience than working from an allocated space in an office.

Why is it important?

A customer's opinion of an organization is shaped by the people they interact with and the ability of those people to respond to their needs. The ability of customer-facing employees to meet and exceed a customer's needs depends on their own employee experience. Employees with access to the information they need and are empowered to do so offer the best solutions for the customer.

The ease with which an employee can complete a task with the systems they have access to impacts their overall engagement and satisfaction in their role, which then impacts performance and loyalty. Retaining high-performing employees is usually a key objective of an organization. Employees are more likely to stay at organizations where the systems make it easy to perform the tasks required of them. It can also be a differentiator in hiring, particularly if a candidate has been referred by an employee, as they are likely to be positive about the employee experience.

Measuring Sales Cloud adoption will give you an indicator of how good your Users' overall experiences are. We explored adoption in detail in *Chapter 1, Preparing for Success*. Low adoption or low adoption amongst specific groups of users might indicate that some improvements are required to be made to the overall experience.

In the next section, we consider how having a set of design principles can help you deliver a better overall user experience.

Design principles

To provide a consistent user experience, you need to make consistent design choices during Sales Cloud solution designing and building. For example, consider where you place information on the page or place buttons. If every page is different, users will find the system confusing or frustrating. It will increase the number of errors they make and if they use it at all. You want to avoid all of these. Consistency is relatively easy when you only have one person customizing Sales Cloud, but if you have a team, it is easy for different styles to appear. This becomes more pronounced with Pro Code solutions.

A documented set of **design principles** can provide a solution to this. A design principle is the way a certain element of **user interface** (**UI**) or system design should be approached. For example, you might specify that all Record Pages have a Highlight Panel unless there is a specific reason for them not to. We review both of these elements in the next section on Sales Cloud UI design.

Documenting these principles means you can share them with all team members so they can apply them from the start and minimize any work. Each organization needs to define its own principles, specific to its use case and audience. The following are elements to consider:

- Consistent use and placement of UI design elements such as components, fonts, colors, and whitespace
- Consistent language for action buttons
- Consistent approach to dialog boxes

- Consistent completion and use of language in Help Text

- Consistent error messages and message handling

- Minimized number of systems each stakeholder group interacts with

- Consistent tab order for navigation fields and Objects with the keyboard

- Present/request information only when relevant

Some of these elements have more impact when custom code development is carried out. This is not an exhaustive list but gives an indication of the types of elements that should be considered.

Salesforce Certified User Experience (UX) Designer

The significance of UX design discipline in the development and adoption of Salesforce solutions is such that Salesforce has developed a curriculum and certificate on the topic. This certification is not just about Salesforce UI features, it requires an understanding of how to select research methodologies and tools and incorporate human-centered design into your solution. You can find more details about the certification at `trailhead.salesforce.com`. There are links to more information in the *Further reading* section at the end of the chapter.

With the introduction of Salesforce Lightning, the options for customizing UI have significantly increased. Understanding the options and how to apply these is a skill set in itself. There are now many declarative ways that you can use to modify and improve a user's experience and productivity that we explore in the next section.

Sales Cloud User Interface (UI) design

Salesforce offers a range of tools to customize the User Interface, which in turn impacts the overall User experience. These can be classified into two categories: **Low Code** and **Pro Code**. Low Code refers to declarative tools where development is via point and click. Pro Code tools are the tools where some coding expertise is required. In this section, the majority of the tools we explore are Low Code. We look at the following:

- Lightning Apps

- Page Layouts

- Compact vs. Comfy

- Dynamic Forms

- Highlights Panel

- Path

- Home Page

- List Views

- Search

- Scoping Rules

We also take a very high-level look at the Pro Code options for when the declarative options don't provide the right solutions. We look at the following:

- **Lightning Web Components (LWC)**

- **APEX**

- **VisualForce (VF)**

As we reviewed in *Chapter 2, Defining the Approach*, you should aim to deliver your requirements with Low Code tools and advance to either buy or utilize Pro Code tools for complex requirements or situations where a code-based solution offers performance benefits. Both of these have additional maintenance overhead, which it is important to assess.

Org-wide branding

Branding your Org is a relatively quick and simple way to indicate to users that this Org is designed specifically for them. You can find Org-wide branding from **Settings** > **User Interface** > **Themes and Branding**. Here you can create a **New Theme** where you can add a logo, specify brand colors, and upload background and banner images. It is typical to add the company logo and a more prominent brand color.

This brand applies to the whole Org. In the next section, we learn how you can create Apps to provide focused workspaces for Users that perform different tasks.

Lightning Applications (Apps)

Salesforce can be used by multiple stakeholder groups to perform different functions, for example, Sales, Customer Support, and Finance. Although they all benefit from working in a single system with a consolidated data set, when they log in, they are most productive when they can get straight to what they need. Lightning Apps allow you to give Users a view of the system that is customized to their role. These apps can be assigned to groups of users. For Sales Users, it is typical to have Sales Apps that has many, if not all, the Tabs for the Objects we have explored in the previous two chapters.

Users are given access to apps by assigning them via a permission set or to their User profile. For Professional Edition, Profiles must be enabled for Apps to be assigned. The apps a user has access to can be selected from the App Launcher in the top-left of the user interface.

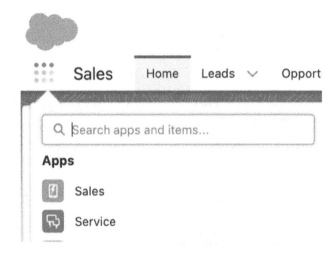

Figure 5.1 – The Lightning App Launcher

From *Figure 5.1*, you can see that clicking on the App Launcher brings up a dialog where you can search for or select apps. Clicking on **View All** brings up a list of all the Tabs a user can see. When a user logs back in, they return to the last App selected. It is possible to make access to external systems available as Apps in the App Launcher so a user can navigate to them from Sales Cloud. This makes Sales Cloud a Salesperson's primary system that they can access other systems from, making their experience as simple as possible.

Apps are created from the App Manager in Setup. The App Manager is also where you create Connected Apps. It is important to note that these are different. These are how you allow external systems access to Salesforce data. We will not be talking about Connected Apps in this chapter. To find the App Manager, go to **Settings** > **Apps** > **App Manager**. You can set the order and suppress the visibility of existing apps in the App Menu. Go to **Setup** > **User Interface** > **App Menu**.

In the App, define the following:

- Name and branding
- Form factors – desktop, mobile, or both
- Navigation – standard or console
- Utility bar
- Included Tabs

Typically, for Sales Cloud implementations, the Sales App is used as a starting point and Tabs are added and removed depending on the organization's requirements. Users can add Tabs to their view of the app. You can edit an app by clicking on **Edit** from the pull-down menu for the app in the **App Manager**, which you can see in *Figure 5.2*.

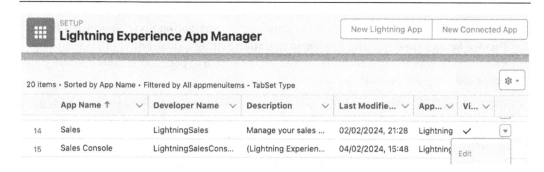

Figure 5.2 – Editing apps in the App Manager

Clicking on **Edit**, seen in *Figure 5.2*, brings up an editing screen, which you can see in *Figure 5.3*.

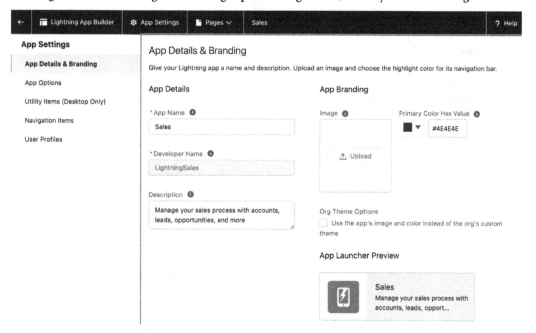

Figure 5.3 – The app editing screen

From *Figure 5.3*, you can see that there are a number of setting options, which are as follows:

- **App Details & Branding**: The first page of the app edit screen allows you to change the name and apply branding for the app. Applying branding to an app provides users with a visual indication that they are in the right screen.

- **App Options:** This lets you select options such as the **Navigation Style, Supported Form Factors, Setup Experience** and **App Personalization Settings**. These settings change how the user interacts with the app, including removing the option to personalize. This is where you define if the app will be used on a desktop, mobile, or both.

- **Utility Items:** This is only relevant for apps used on the desktop. This is where you can enable the **Utility Bar** and select which productivity tools users can access. The **Utility Bar** is located at the bottom of the page and persist on all screens. Examples include **Notes** and **My Appointments**.

- **Navigation Items:** This is where you select the Tabs you want and the order they appear in.

- **User Profiles:** Here, you can select the User Profiles that can access the app. Salesforce are transitioning from Profiles to Permission Sets, so you will also want to add access to the app via a Permission Set that is applied to the stakeholder group.

In the next section, we look at the declarative options for modifying the page layouts in Sales Cloud.

Page Layouts

With the introduction of Salesforce Lightning Experience in 2015, there are two places in Sales Cloud where you define the page layouts: **Page Layouts** (Record Pages) and **Lightning Page Layouts**. We will explore these in turn.

Page Layouts (Record Pages)

Page Layouts control the elements you see on Record Pages. This is historically how the User Interface in Sales Cloud was modified with limited options to modify the page structure. In **Setup**, you can find these under the individual Objects in **Page Layouts**. *Figure 5.4* shows where you can find the record **Page Layouts** and the **Lightning Page Layouts**:

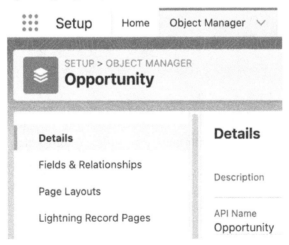

Figure 5.4 – Object Page Layouts

You can access both the Page Layouts and Lightning Record Pages from here. We look at the latter in the next section.

Lightning Page Layouts

The introduction of the Lightning Experience increased the different types and structures of pages available. Administrators have the flexibility to place standard and custom Lightning Components in locations on the page that best suit their Users. Lightning Pages are created and modified in the Lightning App Builder.

There are four main types of Lightning Page:

- **Home Page**: A Home Page is the default page a User visits when they log into Salesforce. You can have different Home Pages for different Apps and different User Profiles (not Permission Sets at the time of writing). These are only available on desktop. We will explore the Home Page in more detail in the Home Page section.

- **Forecasts Page**: It is possible to customize the Forecast Page on desktop in Lightning Experience when Customizable Forecasts are enabled.

- **Record Page**: It is possible to customize the Record Page for each Sales Cloud Object. This means that you can create a Lead and Opportunity Layout that is specific to your Users' needs. These are available on both desktop and the Salesforce Mobile App. We will explore the Home Page and Mobile app in more detail in a later section, *Going mobile*.

- **App Page**: You can create a Home Page for a third-party App, giving them access to the most important items or a page that includes Lightning Components that you added to your Sales App. These are available on both desktop and the Salesforce Mobile App.

There are a couple of other page types, for example, for Service Cloud Voice, but we will not be reviewing these as part of this book.

- You can access the Lightning App Builder from **Setup** > **User Interface** > **Lightning App Builder**. It can also be accessed via the Object Manager for the individual Objects to create and modify Record Pages: **Setup** > **Object Manager** > **Object** > **Lightning Record Pages**, as shown in *Figure 5.4*.

By default, Lightning Record Pages show the fields and Related Lists that are defined on the Page Layout. This means the structure of the page is defined in the Lightning App Builder and the Fields and Related Lists are defined in the companion Page Layout. When Dynamic Forms are enabled, which fields are visible on the page are defined in the Lightning App Builder and no longer in the Page Layout. We explore the functionality that enables this, Dynamic Forms, in more detail in the later section, Dynamic Forms.

Next, we look at how you can modify the white space on a page with Compact or Comfy.

Compact vs. Comfy

Compact and Comfy are page Density Settings. They determine how much text vs. white space there is on the page. When the Lightning Experience was first released, it introduced a lot more whitespace on the page; this is now the Comfy setting. This made the Page Layouts longer and required more scrolling. There were immediate requests for an alternative option, with spacing more comparable to the classic page layout spacing. In response to this, the Compact option was added.

Admins can choose the default for their Org in **Settings** > **User Interface** > **Density Settings**. Users can choose to override this setting for the Profile menu by clicking on the profile picture in the top-right corner. *Figure 5.6* shows how you select between **Comfy** and **Compact**:

Choose the default display setting for your org. Users can select a different setting from their profile menu under Display Density.

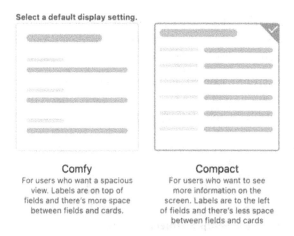

Select a default display setting.

Comfy
For users who want a spacious view. Labels are on top of fields and there's more space between fields and cards.

Compact
For users who want to see more information on the screen. Labels are to the left of fields and there's less space between fields and cards

Figure 5.5 – Screen to set Comfy or Compact

In the next section, we look at the newest way to set up record page layouts that includes dynamic options to make them contextual.

Dynamic Forms

Dynamic Forms were released in Winter 2021. They enhance the Lightning Page Layout, providing more flexibility on where fields can be placed on the page compared to the more restrictive traditional Page Layout. In addition to selecting the fields and the order they are displayed in, it is also possible to apply conditional visibility logic to fields so they only appear when criteria are met. An example would be to make fields visible depending on the Opportunity Stage. This would mean that fields for procurement and contracting might only become visible later in an Opportunities life. *Figure 5.6* shows how you apply visibility filters to fields with Dynamic Forms:

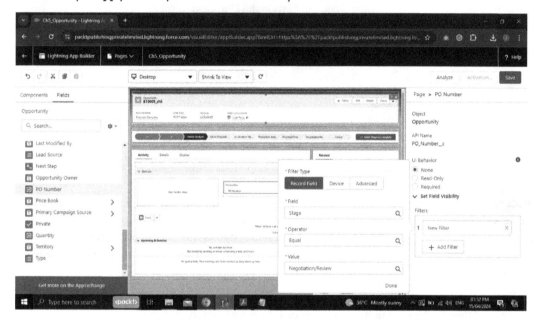

Figure 5.6 – Create visibility filter dialog for Dynamic Forms

At the time of writing, Dynamic Forms are available for the following standard Objects: Accounts (including Person Accounts), Cases, Contacts, Leads, and Opportunities. The intention is to roll this functionality out to all Objects. However, we should keep in mind that this is subject to Safe Harbor statements.

With this capability, page maintenance can be simplified as a single Lightning Page can be maintained when previously it would have required multiple Page Layouts. Field visibility can be based on other fields, roles, profiles, and form factors.

Dynamic Forms are not enabled by default on existing Lightning Page Layouts. There will be a prompt to migrate the page when you are in edit mode, and the recommendation is to migrate fields and sections into an Accordion component to improve page performance. *Figure 5.7* shows the route to upgrading existing Lightning Page Layouts.

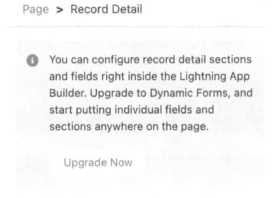

Figure 5.7 – Dialog about how to upgrade to Dynamic Forms

Fields and Field Sections can be added directly to Lightning Pages that are created from scratch. Unlike with Page Layouts, a field can be added more than once. However, it is not recommended to have both a Record Detail and field section on the same page as it results in unexpected results. If the page is to be used on Mobile, then a component will be added to the bottom of the page called **Record Detail – Mobile**.

You can enable and modify Dynamic Forms from the Lightning Page Layout from **Setup** > **Object Manager** > **Object** > **Lightning Record Pages** or **Edit Page** from the **Setup** Menu:

Figure 5.8 – Edit Page from the Settings Menu

In the next section, we look at the dynamic options for Related Lists.

Dynamic-Related List

Dynamic-Related Lists provide an additional level of customization for an Object's list of child records. Using the `Dynamic Related List-Single` component, you can specify a name, chose the number of records that are shown, select the actions shown, order the fields, and apply a filter to limit the records.

Next, we look at another component that can be added to the record page.

Highlights Panel

The Highlights Panel is a component that can be added to Record Detail Pages. It is banner shaped and fits well at the top of the page in the Header section. It keeps a subset of data visible at the top of the page while Users have the option to view more detailed data or perform actions in other sections of the page. In *Figure 5.9*, you can see an example of the Highlights Panel:

Figure 5.9 – The Deal Highlight Panel

The fields that you can see visible are defined in the Compact Layout. By default, the fields displayed are all Standard fields. From a Compact Layout, up to the seven fields appear in the Highlights Panel; the first field is highlighted in a larger font. You can assign a different Compact Layout for different Record Types.

For Sales Cloud Objects, such as Accounts and Opportunities, it is useful to add status/ stage, region, and unique identifier fields so that the User can quickly get assurance that they are looking at the right record and understand its status in a process. If you are using Path, which we cover in the next section, it can be used to display the status.

It is worth noting that the Compact Layout also defines the fields and their order for other UI elements, including the following:

- Hovers over lookup fields
- Object Record Highlights in the Salesforce Mobile App
- Fields shown on the expanded Activity Timeline

As the Compact Layout defines the fields displayed in multiple areas in the UI, it is important to select a set of fields that work for all.

The buttons defined on the Highlight Panel are defined in the Page Layout unless the panel has also been upgraded to be dynamic. If this is the case, visibility filters can also be applied to buttons.

In the following section, we look at a page component to help users follow a process.

Path

The Path functionality is designed to guide Users through a business process, such as the Sales Process. Key features include a visual indicator at the top of a page that shows progress through the process and the ability to highlight key fields (up to five) and provide guidance for each step of the process. Path is available for Lightning record pages and the mobile app. The Path component is a collapsible element on the page. It is most typically displayed under the **Highlights Panel**:

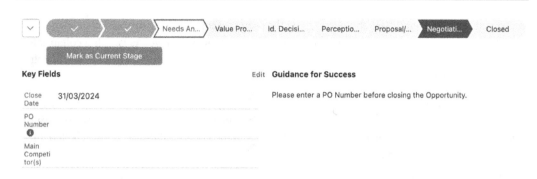

Figure 5.10 – A Path on the Opportunity record

This can be a very powerful way of keeping Users focused on what is important at a given time and getting consistent use of the system. It is particularly useful for Users that are new to Salesforce or the business process.

Path is available for the following Sales Cloud standard Objects and custom Objects:

- Accounts (business accounts and person accounts)
- Assets
- Campaigns
- Cases
- Contacts
- Contracts
- Leads
- Opportunities
- Orders
- Quotes

It is also available for some non-Sales Cloud Standard Objects, but they are not listed here as they are out of the scope of this book.

Opportunities and Leads have the Path status bar component on the Page layout even if Path is not enabled. A different Path can be set up for each Record Type.

When you are talking to your stakeholders during the requirement-gathering process, you will get an understanding of how prescriptive the actions and activities are at each stage. As Path is a collapsible element, it is worth considering even if there is flexibility when information is collected. It will help new Users as it provides guidance that they can refer to.

Path needs to be enabled in **Setup**. Go to **Setup** > **Path Settings**. In the settings, you have the option to have the Path remember if the User had the Path open when they last viewed the page. Selecting **Remember user's Path preferences** means the page loads as the User left it. If this is not selected, the Path is always collapsed when the page is loaded.

Some standard Objects have a specified Closed Stage that can be set; otherwise, you will need to consider how you manage the last stages of the Path.

> **Opportunity Stage Duration**
> It is worth noting that Opportunity Stage Duration is rounded up to the nearest day in Paths. Event one minute will display as one day.

In the next section, we learn how you customize the Home Page.

Home Page

The Home Page is typically the first page that Users see every time they log in. This makes it the ideal place to present Users with information that signpost them to what they should focus on first on any given day and how they are doing in comparison to their wider objectives.

From Spring 2024, a page called **Advanced Sellers Home** can be enabled on the Home Page on the Sales, Sales Console, and Sales Engagement App. Sellers Home is designed to give sales Users a focused start to the day. There, they can see a summary of Account, Opportunity, Contact, and Lead data along with goals they have sent and their upcoming activities. This may already be enabled in your Org if it is new, but if not, you can enable it from **Setup** > **Feature Settings** > **Home**. At the time of writing, the only element of this page that can't be customized is the component that shows goals.

If the Seller Home Page is not appropriate for your Users, you can create a custom Home Page that is focused on their needs. There are a number of components that are available for the Home Page. The following are some of the most relevant for Sales Users:

- Performance
- Assistant
- Today's Tasks
- Today's Events
- Recent Records

- Chart

- Dashboard

- Tabs

- Items to Approve

- Key Deals

- Accordion

- Rich Text

On the standard Home Page, by default, the component in the top left-hand corner of the Sales App is the Performance component, which shows a quarterly performance chart of Opportunities with some additional metrics. This is a unique component that doesn't have any Admin customization options. It shows the sum of your Closed Opportunities for the quarter and the sum of all your open Opportunities with a probability of over 70%. The goal value displayed is an amount the User enters on the chart and is independent of any Quota targets in the system.

It is important that you use this valuable space on the page to display information about how the User or organization is performing to help them feel connected with the company's goals. If the performance chart is not displaying information that achieves that, you can replace it with a Chart or a Dashboard. We explore reports and Dashboards in a later section, *Analyzing and visualizing data*. Showing the top three charts from a Dashboard that is designed to summarize personal or team performance can be a good option for this section of the Home Page. Adding a topline preview of a Dashboard that you want a set of Users to view daily is also a great way to remind them to do that and make it easy for them to find. Assistant, Today's Tasks, Today's Event, and Recent Records are also components you would expect to have on all Sales-focused Home Pages.

The Items to Approve component is important if you are using a Salesforce Approval Process for approving Opportunity discount levels. The Key Deals component allows the User to select from the available Opportunity List Views and shows the top three records. Neither of these have Admin configuration options. The Rich Text component gives you a section on the screen where you can write text. This could be a simple header for a section or it could be a section that is updated regularly with company performance information or Sales Cloud maintenance of improvement notices.

List and Inspection Views

List Views are a powerful tool for helping Users get to a record or set of records they need to get to quickly. When Users click on an Object Tab, they are taken to the Objects List Views. Users have options to customize List Views for their specific requirements.

Starting with Pipeline Inspection from March 2023, there are now a number of Inspection Views available in Enterprise edition. These are available from the Object Tab and are interchangeable with the traditional List Views. These Inspection Views summarize the action that has been taken with the listed records. At the time of writing, there are Pipeline, Lead, and Contact Inspection, all of which provide insight for Sales Users.

Pipeline Inspection provides a range of summary metrics for the group of Opportunities listed. This includes the value of the whole Pipeline as well as the value of new and lost Opportunities within a specific timeframe. Additionally, it provides a summary of changes including increases and decrease in value. This information can also be visualized on some charts. A side panel provides a summary of the activity that has happened on an Opportunity. You can also include a Push Count, which counts the number of times an Opportunity has been pushed into a new calendar month.

With the List Views, there are a lot of options that let Users quickly find, view, and update records. From the pulldown menu on an Object Tab, you can select a Recent View or Recent record or create a new record.

The following are some of the features and options available with List Views that allow Users to work with and manage the data they have available to them:

- Recent Items is the default List View
- Pin the List View they want to see by default (pin to the right of the name)
- Create New records where permissions allow
- Users can create lists that only they can view
- Edit individual record fields from a List View (some fields are not editable)
- Mass update records in Views where all the records are the same Record Type
- View Records in a View in different formats: Table, Split, Kanban
- Mass change the Owner of Leads
- See all the Records owned by a Queue (view is automatically created for each Queue)
- Visualize Data in the View on a Chart
- View the filters used to define the View
- Sort the Columns of a view to see the highest values or missing data
- Drag and Drop columns into a different order
- Clone existing List Views

These are some of the most commonly used Sales Cloud options for List Views. If Users are used to being able to manipulate data in a spreadsheet, they will ask how they can do common tasks in Sales Cloud. List Views offer quick access to common views of data and the option to update multiple records. Reports offer the options to summarize data into tables and aggregate data, which we will cover in a later section, *Analyzing and visualizing data*. From Spring 2023, it is possible to perform some field edits from a Report Run page by clicking **Enable Field Editing**.

Tips

It is good practice to have a set of organization-wide List Views for each Object that are created and maintained by the Admin(s), but you can then encourage Users to create their own List Views specific to their tasks. The Org-wide Views would be visible to all Users, and User-created Views should only be visible to themselves or groups of Users, most likely in the same role.

It is worth noting that since the introduction of Lightning, there have been two versions of the Recently Viewed list. One of these is new with Lightning and has additional functionality, such as the ability to display a chart. The other is the original View and determines the columns that are shown on the Recently Viewed Home Page component.

List Views are limited to showing 2,000 records. If you have criteria that show more records than that, you can bring the data into a report and export it to view more than 2,000 records. If Path is enabled, the fields shown on the Kanban card will be the key fields from the Path.

Scoping rules

Scoping rules restrict a User's default data set, although they can choose to expand this to all the data they have access to. This is a good tool when the Sharing Model is Public Read and Users are feeding back that search results and list views are showing them records from regions that they are not interested in.

A Sales Cloud use case could be that when a User is searching for companies in Salesforce, they are seeing results that show all the locations globally. For their day-to-day work, they only want to see locations in their region. Scoping Rules can be used to reduce the default data to their region while still allowing them to find the global data when they want to see it. For example, this is seen in the case of account planning.

Lightning Web Components (LWCs)

Lightning Web Components are the modern way to extend the Customer 360 platform. It allows client-side processing, whereas previously any processing was carried our server-side with APEX.

LWCs allow a range of customization options, including presenting data from an external system in real time.

If you are considering extending Sales Cloud capabilities, it is important to develop them in line with your design principles and create components that have a familiar look and behavior to other UI elements. Where possible, the Compact and Comfy density settings we reviewed should be observed.

VisualForce

Historically, VisualForce was the only way beyond the declarative tools to modify the User Interface. For this reason, there are many thousands of VisualForce pages powering customer solutions and AppExchange solutions. This has now been superseded by Lightning Web Components and these should be considered before using VisualForce.

Analyzing and visualizing data – Reports and Dashboards

In this section, we will explore the tools available in Sales Cloud to report and visualize data: Dashboards and Reports. Reporting on and visualizing data can be a powerful way of driving User behaviors, improving data quality, and confirming that processes are followed.

Sales Cloud has a baseline of Report Types out of the box based on the standard Objects' relationships. The following are some of the examples:

- Accounts with Contacts
- Opportunities (this includes Account data)
- Opportunities with Contact Roles
- Opportunities with Product
- Leads with converted lead information

Some other reports that can be particularly powerful for reviewing performance are as follows:

- Opportunity History
- Opportunity Field History

When a new relationship field is created, a companion '*with*' Report Type is created; for example, if you created a lookup relationship from a Custom Object to Opportunities, a Report Type of Opportunities with Custom Object would be created.

Dashboards are a collection of Charts that are all based on data from Reports. Charts and a well-designed Dashboard can convey a lot of information with very little screen space. They can also be easy to understand by all types of Users. The following are examples of common types of Dashboards set up in Sales Cloud:

- Company Sales Performance
- Sales Team Performance
- Sales Leader Board
- Individual KPI Tracking
- Lead Generation KPI Tracking

Salesforce Labs have created a package of Reports and Dashboards, which is available for all Sales Cloud customers to install for the AppExchange. We explore what is available from the AppExchange in more detail in *Chapter 14, Extending with the AppExchange*. It is free, so lots of companies install it as a starting point to get an idea of what is possible and modify it as they need for their requirements.

It is assumed that you have a basic understanding of how to create and run Reports and Dashboards on the Customer 360 platform. If not, there are several videos created by Salesforce that explain the basics. These can be found in the Salesforce Help page; links have been provided in the *Further reading* section.

In the remainder of this section, we will recap some of the main formats and explore some of the features and options that are useful for Sales Cloud reporting. We will look at the following:

- Report Formats
- Without Reports
- Cross Object Filters
- Show Me Filter
- Editing Fields Inline
- View Dashboard As
- Dashboard Filters
- Managing Dashboards and Reports
- Performance

Report Formats

There are four different Report Formats available:

- **Tabular**: A list of data
- **Summary**: Grouped by rows
- **Matrix**: Grouped by rows and columns
- **Joined**: Up to five different reports joined by common fields

The Summary format is the most commonly used as it allows data to be grouped and summed or averaged. For example, it can be grouped by Salesperson (owner) with Won Opportunity Amount summed.

Matrix Reports allow data to be grouped by Salesperson and Closed Month so performance can be compared month by month.

The Joined format allows up to five reports to be combined. This means that a single report can show a cross-organization summary of a customer by combining a report of Opportunities and Cases.

Without Reports

As standard, Sales Cloud creates "*with*" Report Types, so these reports only show parent records where the lookup child relationship has been created. It is also possible to create '*with*' and '*without*' reports using custom Report Types. Opportunities with and without reports would list all Opportunities and display the data for the child Object where it existed. When you create a new custom Report Type, you can specify if the relationship with the child Object is with or with and without.

When you create Custom Report Types you can specify which fields appear by default when the report is first created. If you don't select fields, it will just show the Name fields. You can hide Report Types that your organization doesn't use.

Cross Object Filters

Cross Object filters allow you to add criteria based on Objects that are not included in the report. This also allows without reporting, which can be powerful. An example would be a report of Accounts without Closed Won Opportunities, or, for a services company, if the service contract information is in Sales Cloud, it could be possible to create a Report of Account with Contracts with a termination date in the past without a current active contract.

Show Me Filter

Within Reports, you can filter fields, but there are also a set of filters based on the owner. Within Opportunities, there are an increased number of filters available depending on what team and role structure you are using. Many of these are also available for Forecasts and Activities.

In the Show Me filter, the options available are as follows:

- My Opportunities
- All Opportunities
- My Team's Opportunities
- My Selling Team's Opportunities (if you are using Opportunity Teams)
- Filter By Role

The Role Hierarchy filter allows you to select a Role in your Role Hierarchy. You can further narrow this down to a person, selecting the person by name. This will show all the records they own and those of their subordinates. This means a set of Reports can be created that report a team's performance based on the Role Hierarchy.

Editing Fields Inline

Edit fields inline on the Report Run page. To edit fields in a report, you must click the **Enable Field Editing** button, and you have to have edit access on the Object and field and field edit access on the page layout for your Profile. There are some fields that can't be edited, including Opportunity Amount and Polymorphic fields such as the Activity related to field and Owner field.

View Dashboard As

For Dashboards, you have the option to show the data in the way a specific User would see it or to make it dynamic so one Dashboard presents different records depending on who is looking at it. This means that you can create one Dashboard called My Sales Performance and it will display the appropriate information to the person that is logged in. To achieve this, the reports added to the Dashboard will all need to be filtered by My Opportunities or My Activities, and View Dashboard As will need to be set to The dashboard viewer. This type of Dashboard is called a Dynamic Dashboard. It is possible to have up to five of these in an Org.

Managing Dashboards and Reports

Dashboards and Reports are easy to create. They are a great way for Users to work with and understand data in Sales Cloud. However, the number of Reports and Dashboards can quickly get out of control. People create and clone reports but forget to go back and delete the ones they no longer need. Once there are a lot of reports, people get confused about which ones they should use and just create more.

It is good practice to have some guidelines on who can create reports and where and how often they should be reviewed. Organization and access to reports and Dashboards are managed in Folder.

It is recommended that a core set of business-wide reports is managed by the Admin(s) in folders that only they can add to. Users should be able to create the reports they need and save them in folders for their team or their private report folder depending on who needs access.

Performance

If you find your Report is running slowly, then check if you can filter it further. Can you shorten the timeframe of the data you are looking at or remove any columns? Can you make the filters more restrictive or change any Contains filters to Equals? A My filter value and a date range are applied when you create a new Report so the Report Builder runs quickly.

Automation

Automating repetitive tasks can really enhance a User's experience. It can also have other benefits such as increasing productivity and data quality. The Salesforce Customer 360 platform has a number of tools that can be used to automate actions. These can be grouped into two categories: Low Code and Pro Code.

Low Code

Low Code tools, in some cases no code, are tools that are point and click. Salesforce offers a lot of Low Code options across their clouds to open up development to a wide range of users. Using these tools before moving to code has a number of benefits, including a lower maintenance overhead and indicating to Salesforce which features are most heavily used. The following are examples of Low Code tools:

- Quick Actions
- Workflow Rules
- Process Builder
- Flow

Over the last few years, these automation tools have evolved and new standards have been developed. For the latest guidance on the automation tools to use for given use cases, refer to `architect.salesforce.com`.

At the time of writing, Workflow Rules and Process Builder are being phased out and Flow is the preferred tool to use for automations that would have otherwise been created with these tools. This makes the two primary automation tools Quick Actions and Flow. We explore all of these in more detail in the next section, *Automation tools*.

Pro Code

Pro Code tools provide an essential option that is powerful when there isn't a Low Code option or the scale of the solution required means that there are performance concerns with the Low Code option. These technologies both involve writing code, which is not usually part of the skill set of a typical Salesforce Admin.

The two Pro Code options on the platform are as follows:

- **APEX**: Server-side processing – a proprietary Salesforce language based on Java
- **LWC**: Client-side processing – JavaScript, HTML, and CSS

It is best practice to use Low Code options first and only move to Pro Code options if there is an appropriate option. This is because code has an additional maintenance overhead and a dependency on a specialist skill set.

Next, we will explore each of the available tools.

Automation tools

Let's take a look at the various tools that are available in the platform to remove manual tasks from users.

Quick Actions

Quick Actions are available on the desktop and in the mobile app. Custom Quick Actions allow Users to create records and invoke Flows, Lightning Web Components, and VisualForce Pages from specific areas in the UI. Quick Actions can be added to the Home Page, Records Pages, and Chatter Tab and Groups.

In Lightning, they appear in button locations. In the mobile app they appear in the Action Bar and as List-Item Actions.

There are two types of Quick Actions: **Global Actions** and **Object Specific Actions**.

Global Actions can be put anywhere in the UI where Actions can be added, and the User remains on the same page. Object Specific Actions can only be added to the Object they are built for and automatically have a relationship with the record they are created from. Examples of both are creating or updating records or sending emails. Admins can define the fields that can be displayed for Users to enter data into and any predefined values.

Workflow

Workflow Rules were the original way to automate actions on the Salesforce platform. The options for automation were field updates, sending emails, time-based workflows, and outbound messages (SOAP messages). Although limited in comparison to today's options, they removed the many use cases where code would otherwise be required.

Workflow Rules have now been surpassed and the recommendation is to migrate any existing Workflow Rules to Flow and create any new automation in Flow. From Winter 2023, Workflow Rules can no longer be created; however, existing rules can be modified and activated.

A migration tool has been created to transition existing Workflow Rules to Flow, which we look at in a later section.

Process Builder

Process Builder was the next evolution of automation on the Salesforce platform. It offered the option to create related records, which was otherwise only possible with code.

In recent times, with Flow also available, this meant there were three possible automation tools, and a decision on which one to use was required. It also meant there was an increased requirement to understand the Order of Execution of processes to make automation as efficient as possible, or at least avoid unexpected behavior.

Process Builder has now been surpassed and the recommendation is to migrate any existing Processes to Flow and create any new automation in Flow.

A migration tool has been created to transition exiting Processes to Flow, which we look at in a following section.

Flow

A version of **Flow** has been available on the Salesforce platform for many years, but it has seen significant evolution in recent years. A significant change was the ability to define actions before record updates, which became available in Summer 2020. This means that fields on a record can be manipulated before the data is committed to the database. Before this was possible, Flow updates to the record could only happen after data on the record was committed to the database, so the record was effectively saved twice. This meant that all the follow-up actions, such as evaluating Triggers, would happen twice, and if poorly designed, this could result in unexpected behaviors and an increase in processing power.

It is best practice to use Before Save flows for updating fields on the record that triggered the Flow. To send emails or create child records, an After Save Record Flow is needed, as the record needs to exist before a send or record can be associated with it.

> **Decision guides**
>
> The Salesforce platform has become increasingly complex, and it can be difficult to know what tool to use. Salesforce is aware that this is a challenge. To help organizations and system integrators, the Salesforce Architect Evangelist team have created some decision guides that are available on their website, `architect.salesforce.com`. There are decision guides for Record-Triggered Automation, Building Forms, Data Integration, and Event-Driven Architect. Use these guides to design solutions in line with how Salesforce have designed the functionality to work. Find further links in the *Further reading* section.

Code (APEX/ LWCs)

As described earlier, APEX and Lightning Web Components technology allow you to build complex solutions on the platform. APEX is a server-side technology that carries out automation in the background. LWCs have both visual and process capability. These are built with a universally used coding language, which means that a wider range of people can offer these skills.

Email and calendar integrations

A common requirement for Sales Teams is to be able to record emails related to Opportunities against the Opportunity, Contact, and Account Records. Sales Cloud has a few different options to support this. At the time of writing, they are also phasing out a previous option for synching Outlook and Gmail: Lightning Sync. This is not available for new Sales Cloud users but is still operational for those that turned the feature on before Winter 2021.

In this section, we will look at the options available for syncing emails, events, and contact data into Sales Cloud, starting with Lightning Sync.

Lightning Sync

Lightning Sync is no longer available to new Sales Cloud customers. However, this might provide an option if it is already enabled in your Org while you consider the other alternatives. Updates will be provided to maintain the functionality, but there will be no product enhancements after Winter 2021. Users do need to select or confirm what emails are added, which requires time but also offers quite granular control.

Admins control who has access. This involves Users installing an extension in Chrome and then logging into a side panel from their Gmail account. From the side panel, Users can log emails and create records. Although the setup is usually straightforward, there can be challenges when Users don't understand what is required, are not familiar with extensions, or have local problems with Chrome. There are no administration tools that resolve these, so they usually need to be addressed with good change management and training.

As an Admin, you can customize the side panel to control what Users can do. A common customization is to allow Users to create Contacts and Leads from emails. When an email is selected from a sender that is not in Sales Cloud, a button becomes available in the side panel called **Add to Salesforce**. When clicked, the User may be presented with the option to create a Lead or a Contact or both. The User can also associate the email with other related records such as Opportunities.

For many organizations, this has provided a workable solution and may continue to do so for orgs where it is already enabled. At the time of writing, it was not known when this feature will be retired, but this should be checked before planning to add new Users.

Einstein Activity Capture standard

Einstein Activity Capture is the recommended way of making email, event, and contact data available between Sales Cloud and Gmail or Office 365. Depending on the settings and data type, some of this data is not actually stored in Salesforce (hence the name capture), but it is visible in the Activity Timeline on the desktop. This does mean that not all the data visible on the desktop is available in Reports or visible in the mobile app; see later section. Customers with Sales Cloud licenses can give up to 100 Users access to Einstein Activity Capture Standard; otherwise, add-on licenses are required.

> **Einstein Activity Capture Licenses**
>
> If you have Performance, Unlimited, Sales Cloud Einstein, Inbox, Sales Engagement or Revenue Intelligence, you have access to enhanced features. The setup for both is the same, but the retention, metrics, and recommendations are different. In this section, we will mainly focus on the capabilities of the Einstein Activity Capture Standard.

One of the primary differences between Einstein Activity Capture and previously available methods is that data is automatically synced to Sales Cloud. Previously, Users would have to select and add emails or confirm they should be logged just after they were sent. Emails and Events can be excluded from being added, even if overall synching is enabled, by adding email addresses or domains to the Exclusion List. There is an Admin Exclusion List that will apply exclusions for all Users and an individual User Exclusion List so Users have a level of personal control.

Access to Einstein Activity Capture Standard is given via a Permission Set. A connection is set up between either Microsoft Exchange or Google and then a configuration is created to define the syncing behavior.

Einstein Activity Capture is the recommended way of making individual email and event data visible in Salesforce. This is the approach that Salesforce are investing time in product development. This functionality is often required by sales teams and organizations as it gives a more holistic view of a person's interaction with an organization. A limitation that some organizations will find is that email history is only retained and therefore visible for six months with Einstein Activity Capture Standard. This may be problematic for organizations that have an annual renewal. As data is stored outside the Salesforce domain (on Amazon Web Services), there are also additional considerations for organizations that have specific data residency requirements.

Sending emails from Lightning Experience via Gmail or Office 365

This option allows Sales Cloud Users to write emails in the Lightning Experience, including accessing templates, but the email is sent via Gmail or Office 365. This only applies to emails sent by individuals with connected Gmail or Office 365 accounts, not emails sent from organization-wide email addresses or sent via List Emails or automations, including Triggers. The record of the email sent is in the Gmail or Office 365 logs, not in the Salesforce email logs. Users will need to look through their sent emails in the **Sent** folder in either Gmail or Office 365.

Users need the following permissions:

- **Send Email**
- **Send Email through External Email Service**
- Users select how their emails are sent from their **My Email** settings.

Email to Salesforce

Although a very basic approach, there is also a functionality called Email to Salesforce, which provides each user with a unique email address that they can forward emails to that they want to add to Salesforce. This might be an option for Users that only have a small number of emails that should be added and don't want to set up a large number of exclusions. This feature needs to be enabled in an org, and the individual email address can be found in **User Settings** > **Email** > **My Email page**. They can include the email address as a BCC for emails they want to add. This will only apply to emails they send and will not offer a solution for Events or Contacts.

Other options

If none of the solutions described are appropriate for your use case, you have a couple of alternatives. Salesforce Inbox is another Salesforce tool that is available for an additional fee if you have Enterprise edition, or it is included with Unlimited and Performance editions. It provides email management and tracking, meeting scheduling, and analytics to review recipient engagement.

There are also a number of tools available in the AppExchange. We learn how to use the AppExchange in *Chapter 14*, *Extending with the AppExchange*. There are a number of different tools in this space; some of them are very mature now. You can find these by searching for email tools on the AppExchange and focusing on the productivity options.

Going mobile

There is a mobile app available with Sales Cloud: the Salesforce Mobile App. It offers teams that are out in the field, such as your Sales teams, the option to quickly review and update data on the move without having to open a laptop. It is available for iOS and Google devices. It is worth noting that Forecasts is only available in the iOS app.

It is designed to enable the most common on-the-move activities, such as checking the situation with a customer before going into a meeting or logging a call made while out and about. It does not have all the functionalities available on the desktop version of Sales Cloud. Check Salesforce Help for the most up-to-date list of considerations and limitations to confirm it is an appropriate solution for your Users. Not all Objects are available in the Mobile app, but all the key Sales Cloud Objects are available in a way that allows for operational tasks. For example, the Product Tab is not available, but it is possible to add Products to Opportunities.

The Salesforce Mobile App has a number of customization options, and we are not going to be able to cover them all in full detail in this chapter. Instead, we will look at the elements you should consider when deciding if you should use the mobile app. In this section, we explore some of the common use cases and offline capabilities.

Common Sales Cloud use cases

You may have a few different stakeholder groups that have a need to check and update the data in Sales Cloud when they are away from their normal working environment. This includes Salespeople and Sales Leaders, either because they need the information in response to their situation, such as a meeting, or because they are looking to maximize their available time, for example, at an airport.

Now we will consider some of the common use cases for different stakeholder groups.

Common use cases for Salespeople are as follows:

- Reviewing status, key stakeholders, and activities on an Account before a meeting
- Logging a call that was taken both inbound and outbound
- Checking what information is already know about a person at a tradeshow
- Finding a person's contact details, such as phone number or email and used device to action
- Asking for another Sales Cloud User to investigate something related to a record, if Chatter is used
- Converting a Lead and creating an Opportunity based on a conversation at an event or meeting
- Adding meeting notes directly after a meeting has taken place

Common use cases for Sales Leadership are:

- Reviewing company or team performance via Dashboards
- Calling the owner of an Opportunity to find out more about it
- Preparing for meetings while on the move

As you can see, there are a lot of use cases for the Salesforce Mobile App for Sales Cloud Users. Combined with the capability that many mobile devices have to dictate text, it can be a quick and efficient way to capture notes about activities that have happened when Sales Cloud Users are out of the office.

If you have a fully field-based sales teams that requires an optimized appointment schedule, you might want to consider the Field Service Lightning product.

Working offline

A question that always comes up when looking at the mobile app is what happens when the device is offline. In some regions and countries, mobile signals can be accessed almost everywhere, whereas in other regions, this is not the case. The good news is that it is possible to see a subset of the data and perform many of the tasks. Salesforce Mobile does have offline capability. It uses each User's previous activities to determine what Objects and records to cache so that they are available for the User to view.

The ability to view and edit data offline can be enabled and disabled. This is done by navigating to **Setup** > **Apps** > **Salesforce** > **Salesforce Offline**. The two permissions are:

- Enable caching in Salesforce for Android and iOS
- Enable offline create, edit, and delete in Salesforce for Android and iOS

When a User installs the mobile add for the first time, the Enable caching in Salesforce for Android and iOS option is automatically enabled.

We will now explore what these two permissions allow in more detail.

Offline access

Offline access caches some records and Objects locally on the device so they are available to view. It saves the thirty most recently accessed records from the five most recently accessed Objects based on desktop and mobile usage. It also caches the five most recently accesses Dashboards and Tasks from **My Tasks**.

When Users log in, the cache is empty, either because it has never been populated or because it was cleared when the User last logged out. Users can set the Objects they prefer to see online from inside the app by going to their profile menu in the top-left corner, going to **Settings** > **Offline Preferences**, and selecting the preferred Objects. Users can refresh their online cache from the App by going to their profile menu in the top-left corner and selecting **Settings** > **Offline Cache** > **Start Caching**. When the User logs out of the Mobile app the cache is removed.

The recommendation is that Users refresh their caches every time they use the app or anticipate needing it offline. This ensures their most recently access records are available.

Offline edit

Records can also be edited or created offline. When a record is created or updated it has a **Pending** status until the device is back online and the data has been uploaded. Users see messages in the app letting them know they have records that are pending sync in a few places, including the Object home page.

Users can see if there were any problems with synchronizing their change from the **Pending Changes** page in the app by going to their profile menu in the top-left corner and selecting **Pending Changes**. There are visual indicators in green, yellow, and red to show if the outcome of the sync was a success, conflict, or error. To resolve conflicts, User must go to the Pending Change page to find out more about and resolve the error. A conflict might occur because of a duplication rule or a validation rule. If an error occurs, they are taken directly to the record page to resolve it.

Settings and considerations

Capture a list of common tasks that your mobile Users will need and confirm the steps in the mobile app. You may find that you want to create some actions to help your Users works as efficiently as possible.

Settings

The mobile app has some organization-wide setting options that the Admin can configure:

Organization-wide notifications settings are as follows:

- Enable in-app notifications
- Enable push notifications

Organization-wide downloadable app settings are as follows:

- Let users see onboarding tips in the mobile app

- Let users send feedback to Salesforce from the mobile app

You can decide if these are appropriate for your Users, but rollouts where a large number of Users are involved can be distracting.

Organization-wide device access settings are as follows:

- Allow Salesforce to import Contacts from mobile device Contact lists

This last setting allows Contacts to be created in Salesforce based on the device contact list, which comes at the risk of creating Contacts that are unrelated to sales activities. This might be appropriate if all Users only have work-issued devices, but any external source that can automatically create records risks creating duplicates.

Considerations

At the time of writing, it is also worth noting that there are some other data views and functionalities that are not supported in the mobile app:

- **List Views**: You can Create, view Kanban and Split List View, mass updating records via a List View

- **Lead Conversion**: You can't select existing Opportunities; if you are creating a new Account, the fields don't prepopulate

- **Campaign members**: You can't manage Campaign members, but you can add Contacts to a Campaign

- **Add Account Team Members**: You can't add Team Members to an Account

- **Merging Duplicates**: You can't merge duplicates

- **Hierarchies**: You can't view the Account, Campaign, or Contact Hierarchies

- **Forecast Adjustment**: You can adjust your Forecast but not your subordinates

- **Einstein Activity Capture**: Emails and events captured from Einstein Activity Capture don't appear on the Activity Timeline

These are certainly considerations and limitations to make your Users aware of, but they do not significantly impact the overall productivity gains.

There are also some actions that are available but not from all the same UI locations in the desktop version. For examples, files can be updated via an Action and not the Files Related List.

In-App Guidance

In-App Guidance is not an automation tool, but it can be set up to provide in-app information and prompts on how to use Sales Cloud at the time Users are accessing the screens where actions should take place. It is uniquely positioned to present Users with helpful information right at the point when they need it.

In this section, we explore why you should use In-App Guidance and some of its common Sales Cloud use cases.

Why use In-App Guidance?

In-App Guidance offers just-in-time information for Users as they use the system. Once the prompts are created, they can be activated periodically to remind Users of system usage best practices.

With the standard Sales Cloud license, it is possible to have three In-App Guidance prompts running at any given time.

Common Sales Cloud use cases

Some common use cases for In-App Guidance are providing guidance on new Sales Cloud functionalities and guiding new Users on core Sales Process and using Opportunities, on best practice for creating reports, and on how to use Campaigns. This is a very flexible tool that can provide support to users at all stages of their journeys with the system.

Now that we have learned about In-App Guidance, we will wrap up what we have explored and learned throughout the chapter.

Summary

In this chapter, we have learned a lot about a variety of the functions available in Sales Cloud to increase productivity. We started by learning why it is important to really consider the User's experience when making choices about your Sales Cloud solution and how this can impact overall adoption. We explored how you ensure consistency in your implementation with design principles and how you can learn more about UX design by studying for the Salesforce certification.

Next, we explored a range of options for customizing the Sales Cloud user interface, including how information can be presented on the page and how key information can be elevated on the page with the Highlights Panel and Path components. We also learned about options to help Users focus their actions and make them more efficient by curating Home Page components, creating List Views, and reducing the default dataset that Users see with Scoping Rules.

We took a look at how you can create reports and visually present data to help Users understand how they and the organization are performing so they can make decisions about how they use their time. We then reviewed the tools that are available on the platform to automate processes. There has been a lot of development on these tools in recent years. We confirmed that the key Low Code tools are now Actions and Flows. The Pro Code solutions are APEX and Lightning Web Components.

Finally, we learned about the options for connecting email tools and how users can view and update Sales Cloud while they are in the field or travelling.

In the next chapter, we learn about how to bring legacy data into Sales Cloud and how to plan migrating data as part of an implementation project.

Further reading

Salesforce user experience designer

- *Trailhead: Salesforce User Experience Designer Certification:*

  `https://trailhead.salesforce.com/users/strailhead/trailmixes/prepare-for-your-ux-designer-credential`

Reports and Dashboards

- *Build a Report:* `https://salesforce.vidyard.com/watch/qGpi4cPjtUWQ7XV1jT6xnM`

Learning Flow

- Trailhead: Module: *Build Flows with Flow Builder:*

  `https://trailhead.salesforce.com/content/learn/trails/build-flows-with-flow-builder`

- *The Ultimate Guide to Flow Best Practices and Standards:*

  `https://admin.salesforce.com/blog/2021/the-ultimate-guide-to-flow-best-practices-and-standards`

Automation Champion

- *Learning Flow:*

  `https://automationchampion.com/learning-flow/`

Decision Guides

- *Record-Triggered Automation:* `https://architect.salesforce.com/decision-guides/trigger-automation`

- *Building Forms:* `https://architect.salesforce.com/decision-guides/build-forms`

Part 2: Preparing to Release

In this section, we will cover the following chapters.

Bringing Data into Sales Cloud

You've designed a system that meets the requirements and completed the build. However, to bring the system to life, it needs data. It is commonly accepted that any CRM or database-powered system is only as good as the data in it. What data, how much of it, and how to go about it are the next big decisions.

This chapter gives you the understanding and tools you need to identify, plan, and execute loading data into Sales Cloud Objects. We'll start by learning how to decide what data to load, which is informed by the requirements and limited by the sources available. We'll explore the tools that are available and consider their key attributes in order to make a selection. We'll then go on to learn about the data-loading process and what should be included in a plan to load legacy data into Sales Cloud Objects.

We're going to cover the following main topics in this chapter:

- Identifying data to load
- Selecting your data-loading tools
- Loading data
- Planning your legacy data load
- Ongoing data-loading activities

Supporting tools and information

For this chapter, you will require tools to manipulate data, tools to load data into Salesforce, and an Org with your configured solution design available. We will look at the permissions required to load data in the section on tools as it varies for the Salesforce Data Import Wizard and other tools.

For practice or a solution with limited complexity and smaller data volumes, you can use a spreadsheet application such as Microsoft Excel or a web-based spreadsheet program such as Google Sheets.

Use Google Sheets to manipulate data, the Salesforce-supplied tools to load data, and a Dev Org to practice the data load on. Microsoft Excel currently has a row limit of 1,048,576 and Google Sheets has a limit of 10 million cells or 18,278 columns. If you expect to reach these sorts of limits, you will want to confirm these limits are still current at the time of reading. Usability will become a problem here, so if you are working with large volumes, you will want to use an alternative.

If your solution is more complex, you have higher data volumes (for example, 50,000), or they are already available to you in your organization, you will want to use commercially available tools for data cleansing tasks that have **Extract, Transform, and Load** (ETL) capabilities as they have features that make the tasks easier.

To do a full rehearsal of your data load, you will need a Sales Cloud Org that has the capacity for all your data. A Partial Copy sandbox is included with Enterprise, Unlimited, and Performance Edition Salesforce licenses. A Partial Copy sandbox can hold up to a maximum of 10,000 records per selected object. A Full Copy sandbox will have the same capacity as your Production environment. These, along with additional Partial Copy sandboxes, need to be purchased via your Account Executive.

In this chapter, we will discuss some of the capabilities of the tools that are available so you can make appropriate choices.

Identifying data to load

Your solution design determines the exact data you need to bring into Sales Cloud. However, all solutions typically include Accounts, Contacts, and Opportunities. They also often include Products, Price Books, Opportunity Products, and Leads. Your business maturity will determine the volume of data available to load, and the type of business performed will determine how much historical data you need to have available.

The first and most important step is deciding what set of data to load. It is tempting and common practice to simply load all the data available without any critical analysis. During the later stages of implementation, there is usually a desire to get the system running as soon as possible, and loading all the data available may seem like the path of least resistance. However, this can turn out to be a mistake. There are consequences, including an ongoing maintenance cost, to holding data.

There are obvious costs, such as data storage, but there are also other costs, such as search speeds, report and dashboard loading speeds, and a sub-optimal user experience. There is also the cost of keeping data up to date, as there are legal obligations to do this. Some recent data legislation, such as the **General Data Protection Regulation** (GDPR), includes obligations to keep the data you use up to date and for individuals to be able to challenge the accuracy of the data that is held, which has a processing cost.

To make good decisions about data, engage with your organization's data governance team as they will be able to advise you on the organization's approach to data and the relevant legal and organizational policy requirements. Involve them as early as you can. They may have questions about the solution, or using Sales Cloud might mean that policies need to be updated, which can take time and result in implementation delays.

In the next sections, we will look at how you identify the available data, assess it, and decide what to load, and look at options for improving your existing data.

Identifying available data

The first step is to create a list of all the data that the business might want to load – a **Data Inventory**. You'll be able to get most of this information from your business stakeholders as they use these sources on a daily basis. You may need to supplement this with information from other teams, such as Data Governance, who should know all the sources of company data, and IT and Business Analytics, who may have the technical knowledge on how data can be extracted from current sources.

Key information to gather and capture, most likely in a spreadsheet, is as follows:

- **Source name**: The name that is used in the company to refer to the system or report.
- **Description**: A description of the source and data from the source that is relevant.
- **Types of data**: The type of data. You may find it helpful to classify this by its likely Sales Cloud destination (i.e., contact, deal product data, etc.).
- **Who owns it**: This is the name of the person who makes decisions about the data source; they can give you access and explain the format and meaning of the data.
- **The current source format**: This is the format the data is available in that could be imported into Sales Cloud with the correct tool (i.e., spreadsheet, on-premises database, cloud database, etc.).
- **Is this the current master source? Yes/no**: For types or individual pieces of data, this source holds the organization's definitive value. It is likely that a source is a master for some data but not all.
- **Will it be the master source post Sales Cloud? Yes/no**: This captures whether the definitive source of this type of data is migrated to Sales Cloud. For example, Sales Cloud is likely to become the master source for sales data.
- **What format is the data available in? CSV, XLS, XML, or JSON**: This captures the formats that a data source can be exported into. Multiple formats might be available, or just CSV. Ideally, you want to standardize to one format as this will make the preparation steps easier.
- **Data volume**: This is the number of records. This will have an impact on the tools that can be used.

- **How current/accurate is it?**: Some sources might hold data from the previous year or might be incomplete, which is particularly important to know if there are the same or similar types of data in multiple systems.

- **Quality**: This is an assessment of the quality of the data. This includes how complete and consistent the data is, especially for classification fields. In spreadsheets, individual users can add classifications or change the format without coordinating with others.

- **Expected destination Objects**: A list of the Objects the data will be loaded into (i.e., Opportunities, Products, Accounts, etc.).

- **Subject to retention policy? Yes/no**: Is this data subject to a data retention policy, for example, a financial retention policy?

- **Notes**: This is used to capture more detailed information about the source and its relevance moving forward. This information may be separated into further columns if you have consistent information for most sources.

The examples discussed here illustrate the information to capture about the data sources that are available. For some of this information, you won't have answers straight away and you might have to work it out, but it is important to capture this information when you get it.

Getting this information in one place allows you to identify the most relevant sources and get an understanding of the volume of data. You are typically trying to identify the source of record of a type of data, that is, the one the business relies on as being correct. You are also looking for the most up-to-date and highest-quality data.

Here is an example of what this information might look like:

Name	Description	Owner	Types of Data	Current Master Source? (y/n)	Furture Master Source? (y/n)	Available Formats	Data Volume (rows)	Accurate/ current?	Quality?	Destination Objects	Subject to Retention Policy? yes/ no	Notes
Sales Master Sheet	Spreadsheet of all closed deals	Sales Manager	Customer and Deal data	Yes	No	xls, csv	500	High	High	Account, Contact, Opportunity, Opportunity Products	No	
Events Follow up sheet	Spreadsheet with a tab of contact details gathered for each event	Marketing Team	Contact Data	Yes	No	xls, csv	5000	Medium /Low	Low – Duplicates	Leads	No	
Contract Master Sheet	Spreadsheet of all Contracts	Operations Team	Contracts	Yes	No	xls, csv	400	High	High	Contracts	Yes	
Contracts Folder	Folder on shared drive of all signed contracts	Operations Team	Contracts	Yes	Yes	Folder	400	High	High	Files	Yes	

Table 6.1 – Data inventory table

From the table, you can see that sales, prospect, and contract data have been identified and that the volume and quality vary.

In the next section, we will look at how you can assess data in the identified sources.

Assessing the data

Once you have identified the available sources of data, you will want to assess the data they hold. To do this, you will need to view the data or at least a reasonable sample of it.

There are five commonly known measures to assess data quality:

- **Accuracy**: Data that is likely to be inaccurate, such as incorrectly formatted email addresses.

- **Completeness**: Missing values, particularly for important data, such as company name in prospect data. Sales Cloud Objects have required fields, so it is important to confirm that data is available or can be constructed.

- **Consistency**: Are the values entered in a field consistent across all sources? For example, in classification fields, have salespeople created their own classifications in personal spreadsheets?

- **Timeliness/relevance**: When was the data created and last updated? For example, when was a person last contacted? This is increasingly important for **Personally Identifiable Information (PII)** as a new regulation.

- **Duplication**: Is a record recorded more than once? For example, a sale or a person who works at an organization.

You will want to review the data, assess these areas, and capture the results. Some quantitative measures that you can use to record what you find include the ratio or percentage of errors, number of duplicates, and number of empty values. You should also list the types of errors you find so you can include these in a plan to improve data quality (e.g., inconsistent Company Type classification).

If you are doing an assessment in a spreadsheet, functions that you may find useful include data validation and find duplicate functions, which can show you records that don't match allowed values or are duplicates. Filters also help you quickly identify empty cells.

Table 6.2 gives examples of common data quality issues you should look out for in lead generation and sales process data:

Data Quality Measure	Examples
Accuracy	Phone number: Do they have the correct number of digits?
Completeness	Email: Are there email addresses for key company contacts?
Consistency	Company name: The company's legal name or a shorthand version. Classification: Is there a consistent set of mutually exclusive values for classification fields such as `Type` and `Industry`? Phone: Is the phone number data constant in the formatting of area and international codes?

Data Quality Measure	Examples
Timeliness/ relevance	Lead lists: When were they acquired? Contact data for historical deals: When were people associated with historical deals last contacted?
Duplication	Contacts listed multiple times because they have more than one role in the sale, for example, Decision Maker and Finance Contact

Table 6.2 – Examples of common data quality issues

The preceding table provides a few examples of some of the common data quality issues observed in data typically loaded into Sales Cloud. The full list for each organization will be unique as it depends on each unique business context.

Something that you will want to be looking for is unique identifiers available in your source data that exist on both the record they identify and the child records that are related to them. If an identifier is not available, determine whether one can be constructed. Having a common identifier available on parent and child records means that Salesforce IDs don't have to be substituted into child records once parent records have been created. If so, you can create an external ID field in Sales Cloud to capture these and streamline your upload process.

Carrying out this sort of assessment in spreadsheets can be time-consuming. There are commercially available tools that allow you to quickly identify issues with your data and resolve them. They also offer more sophisticated matching for duplicates, including fuzzy logic name matching. If an initial assessment of your data reveals you have a data quality problem, these tools are an option. This could be either a one-off data cleansing project or as part of an ongoing strategy.

Deciding what data to load

So far, you have identified the available data and assessed it. The next step is deciding what data should be loaded. This is likely to be a collective decision by multiple stakeholders. Based on the information you have gathered about the overall requirements for the solution, the policy and regulation requirements, the quality, and the volume, you should be able to make recommendations. However, Data Governance and the Business Sponsor will make the final decision. It will be your role to inform them of any implications if they decide to deviate from your recommendations. It is reasonable to ask why the data is needed and why it is needed in real time.

In order to make your recommendations, you may want to consider the following:

- The overall objectives and success criteria of the implementation.
- What data will Users need to be available in the system to perform their roles and get the benefits promised by Sales Cloud?

- What data is required for reporting? For example, performance year on year requires last year's data.

- What data is Sales Cloud now mastering? As this may all need loading.

- Some emails are only relevant for a short period of time and increase storage quickly.

- Loading documents can mean you fill up your file storage quickly.

You are looking for the right combination of enough good-quality data to allow Users to get the benefits they were promised with Sales Cloud, without old or obsolete data that bloats the system, gets in the way and confuses Users, or just won't be used.

> **Tip**
>
> It can be a good plan to estimate your expected data storage to predict whether you will reach data limits. Data storage can be increased by increasing your license or paying for additional storage. By either reviewing your historical data or considering your sales targets, you can predict the number of Accounts, Contacts, Opportunities, and Opportunity Products you will create per year. You can assume that each record is 2 Kb so you can calculate the required storage. If you are using Person Accounts, then each of these will be 4Kb. Campaign records are also larger, at 8 kb. You will also want to estimate the volume of Email Messages. These have a higher storage volume as they are dependent on the size of the email (variable attachment and HTML). Einstein Activity Capture data is not in an org in AWS. A link to record storage sizes can be found in the *Further reading* section.

Once you have made your recommendation on what data should be loaded, and a decision has been made by the key implementation stakeholders, you can start work on preparing the data, which we will explore in the next section.

Preparing your data

During your analysis of the data, you will have identified data quality and duplication issues. There is now an opportunity to correct the identified problems and also make improvements.

At this point, you want to carry out actions to harmonize the data by defining the standard you are going to follow. Once that standard, or set of rules, is defined, you can update the data so it is consistent with that standard. The exact set of rules, or standard, that you set will depend on your business requirements.

> **Note**
>
> Sales Cloud helps you maintain data integrity with features such as a picklist. The system can be set up to restrict the data loaded to the options available, which I recommend.

The following table has some of the standards that are commonly used in Sales Cloud:

`*` Indicates that it is enforced by the system.

Field/Data Types	Standardization
Emails	Email addresses must have the `jsmith@acme.com` format with an @ sign and ending in `.com`, `.co.uk`, or other confirmed domain endings.* Incorrectly formatted data or multiple email addresses will be rejected.
Phone numbers	Standardize the format for each country (i.e., either include or exclude + or (), number of digits, etc.).
Date	The User's locale determines the format the date is presented in in the UI. The date format required for upload depends on the tool.
Date/time	The date/time format is used for created by fields. The format required for upload depends on the tool.
Addresses	Standardize state/county options.
Salutation	Limit to a predefined list with a consistent format (e.g., either Mr or Mr.).
Classifications (picklist fields)	Review options to confirm they are mutually exclusive. Where available, consider using industry-standard classifications, such as Standard Industry Classification (SIC) codes. As a minimum, standardize the classifications you use across the organization.

Table 6.3 – Table of common data standardizations

The table lists some of the common types of data and how they can be standardized. The enforcement of the email format by Sales Cloud can often cause errors as emails are often miskeyed or multiple emails are entered in one field.

Within spreadsheet tools, you can do some duplicate identification and removal. It relies on the data in the selected matching fields being exact matches, which works well for data such as emails but not for names where both full names and nicknames can be entered. If you suspect you have a duplicate problem, it will be worth exploring the tools available in AppExchange to see how they can help you meet your data objectives.

> **Note**
>
> Opening data files *in spreadsheet tools can introduce changes to the format*. For example, spreadsheet tools can remove leading zeros from phone numbers or change numbers such as unique identifiers into scientific notation. It is important to identify these and make adjustments before the data is loaded in.

If you have gaps in your data, you may want to ask people in your organization to source and update the information or see whether there are sources of this information in other departments. This can be time consuming and delay your implementation. Other options that you might want to consider are enriching your data and validating your data. Enriching involves using external sources to add missing data or additional data to your dataset, such as company addresses and classifications. Validating involves using external sources to confirm your information is valid, such as email and location addresses. You will find tools that can help you with both services on AppExchange.

> **Tip**
> I have often been asked whether the data can just be loaded as it is and data quality issues worked on once the data is in. While it is tempting to get Users into the system quickly, I always recommend correcting as much as you can before loading. Poor and incomplete data means that your reports and dashboards as not as accurate as they could be straight away. Sales Cloud is a great tool for managing business processes, but it's not a large-scale data manipulation tool. Within the UI, you can modify up to 200 records at a time, which is enough for Users managing processes but not for data cleansing.

In the next section, we will explore how you select the best tool to use to load data for your use case.

Selecting your data-loading tool

There are a range of tools available that you can use to load data into Salesforce. Salesforce provides two tools: **Salesforce Data Import Wizard** and **Salesforce Data Loader**. There are also several third-party tools ranging from free basic data-loading tools to enterprise ETL tools and integration platforms. These have different strengths, which we will explore.

It is worth noting that the tools that you choose determine the loading template you use, which defines the format and structure you need your data in. This defines the amount of transformation required on your source data. For example, the Salesforce Data Import Wizard loads Account and Contact records from one template. With all other tools this data will need to be added to two separate templates.

Some third-party tools allow you to use a database or SFTP site as the source.

Salesforce-supported tools

In the following sections, we explore the capabilities and characteristics of the two tools that Salesforce provides. The following figure shows the options in the **Setup** menu.

Figure 6.1 – Integration node in the Setup menu

Data Import Wizard

The **Data Import Wizard** is an online tool that is available from **Setup | Integrations | Data Import Wizard**. It is designed to be used by Users, such as salespeople who want to load Leads and Contacts. It has features and limitations in line with that purpose. It has some unique features that differentiate it from the other data data-loading tools available. Here is a list of some of its key characteristics:

- It is limited to 50,000 records per load.

- It is cloud-based, so it does not require installation.

- It loads data into the following Objects: Accounts, Contacts, Person Accounts, Leads, Campaign Members, Solutions, and Custom Objects

- It matches headers on Label names, not API names. This means Users can find the field names in the UI.

- It creates a relationship with other Objects with External ID or Record ID field.

- It uses the Users' locale to determine the Time Zone and Date format

- It saves operations or field mappings.

Here are some unique Data Import Wizard features:

- Accounts and contacts are loaded in one process that allows for multiple contacts to be associated with an Account in one row.

- Option to specify a Campaign and Campaign Status when Loading Leads and Contacts. This means that leads or contacts can be associated with a Campaign in a single load.

- Matching options include email and name for people name and site for accounts, which are not typical matching criteria in other tools.

- You can set some universal values for some of the processes, such Lead Owner, Lead Source, Records Type. This means you set these values for records in the template without adding the field to the template.

The key benefits of Data Import Wizard are that it is free and available without installation, and it has features that make it straightforward to load Account, Contact, and Lead data. However, there are some limitations. You can load up to 50,000 records in one load. Also, you can't load data into the following key Sales Cloud Objects: Opportunities, Opportunity Line Items, Products, Price Books Campaigns, and Activities. Error reporting is also not as user-friendly as some other tools.

Salesforce Data Loader

The Salesforce Data Loader is another free tool from Salesforce. You can download it from **Setup > Integrations > Data Loader** and install it locally.

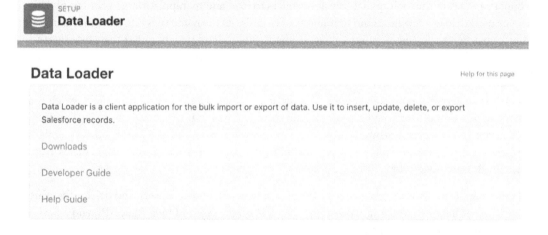

Figure 6.2 – Data Loader downloaders and guides

The figure shows the resources that are available from the **Setup** menu. There is a Windows and iOS version. Different versions are provided for each operating system release. If you are doing an initial setup and data load for Sales Cloud, it is likely that you will use this as it allows you to load Opportunity data, which the Data Import Wizard doesn't. Here are some of its key characteristics:

- Loads up to 5 million records per load

- Requires installation; can be used via the UI or automate jobs via the command line (Windows only)

- Access data in all Objects; some only become visible by selecting **Show all Salesforce objects**

- Matches headers on API names, not label names

- Create relationships with other Objects with the External ID or Record ID field

- Set Time Zone and Date format in **Settings** (European date)

- Option to save field mappings

- Can be set to use Bulk API

The key benefits of Data Loader are that you can load data into all objects and that you can load up to 5 million records. For most implementations, this provides an option to load legacy data. If you are loading data that has relationships to data in other objects, it is worth noting that some third-party tools allow you to define the relationships based on Parent Object attributes rather than record IDs and External IDs, as this can reduce the amount of data transformation required.

Salesforce Bulk API

Salesforce Bulk API is not a wizard or application like those we have talked about so far. It is, however, an important part of the tooling that Salesforce offers to load and manipulate large volumes of data. It can be used to load a few thousand to millions of records. As the name suggests, with the inclusion of the term API, this feature requires a programmatic pro-code approach, rather than a declarative no-code one. There are low -code applications such as Data Loader and Dataloader.io that have the option to use Bulk API. You should check the options available.

Bulk API is an asynchronous web service. You use it to upload data by submitting a job, which is a term used for a unit of work, and a batch of data records. The Job is processed in the background, which means you don't get real-time feedback on how many records have been processed as you might with Data Loader. You can monitor your job, including the status, errors, and when it completes, from **Setup | Bulk Data Load Jobs**.

Like other data-loading functions, you have the option to insert, update, upsert, and delete. There are two versions of Bulk API: the original version, which is simply referred to as Bulk API, and a newer version, which is called Bulk API 2.0.

Here, we will discuss some of the points where the two versions differ.

Bulk API's features are as follows:

- Data in CSV, XML, or JSON format and binary attachment processing

- Can be used using Data Loader

- Limited by quantity of batches

Bulk API 2.0's features are as follows:

- A streamlined workflow

- Data in CSV format only

- Breaks data into batches automatically

- Automatically performs **Primary Key (PK)** chunking

- Limited by total records per day

- Can be used with tools such as Dataimporter.io and Postman

It is worth noting that they are comparable in speed. As you can see, the two versions do vary; Bulk API 2.0 has been streamlined, making it more straightforward to use. However, for low-code developers, accessing the feature is not as simple as selecting the bulk option in Data Loader, the Salesforce-supplied data-loading application. As is the case in many situations, other commercially available tools do seek to fill this gap. There is a step-by-step guide on how to connect Postman to Salesforce on Trailhead in the Quick Start: Connect Postman to Salesforce trail. You will find a link to the trail in the *Further reading* section.

Bulk API is a really powerful tool for loading large volumes of data, and at some very large volumes, it may be the only option. However, to use it, you do require a more technical understanding of how it works than the other data-loading tools we have discussed. You either need to know how to make calls to the API or have access to a client-side tool that supports the version you want to use. If you are working with large data volumes, review the additional resources listed in *Further reading*, including those on `developer.salesforce.com`, to get a detailed understanding of how to use Bulk API.

Third-party tools

There are a number of third-party tools available that you can use to load data into Sales Cloud. These range from free data-loading tools to enterprise-level integration tools/platforms. The free tools are usually limited by data volume and are usually provided by companies that also offer full enterprise-offered paid tools.

When exploring what tools to use, it is important to determine whether your organization already has access to tools that you could use. If it does, you are also likely to have access to people with skills and experience you can connect with. The types of tools you should ask about are ETL tools or middleware.

In the following sections, we will look at a couple of the free tools, some of which I have purchased for more functionality-rich alternatives.

Workbench

Workbench is a free tool that was created by Salesforce but is not supported by Salesforce, which is why it is being mentioned as a third-party tool. It includes a disclaimer that it has not undergone complete quality assurance testing and that it should not be used with production data.

It has a range of capabilities that are useful for developers, including being able to insert individual records and load records from a CSV file. It has a size limit of 2 MB. I have included it here for awareness as it has import and export capabilities. As it is not a supported tool, you use it at your own risk. It can be accessed at `workbench.developer.com`. More information about the tool is available on GitHub.

Dataloader.io

Dataloader.io is a tool developed by MuleSoft, which is a Salesforce company. It is a web-based tool; you can go to it directly at `dataloader.io` or find it in the **Setup** menu from **Setup | Integrations | Dataloader.io**.

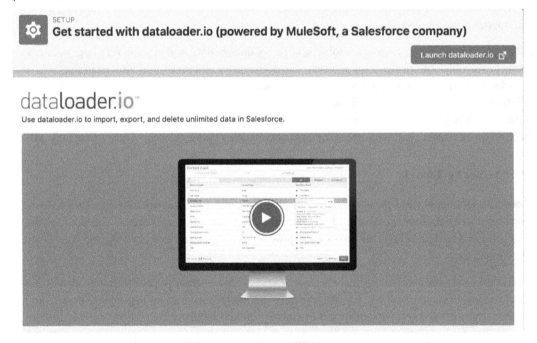

Figure 6.3 – Dataloader.io page in Setup

The figure shows the **Launch dataloader.io** button in **Setup**.

Here are some of its key characteristics:

- Loads up to 5 million records per load

- Cloud-based; does not require installation

- Access data in all objects (up to the supported API version)

- Create a relationship with other Objects with External ID or Record ID field or by matching on Parent Object attributes, for example, Record Type Name

- Set Time Zone and Date format in **Settings**

- Saves data operation configurations (jobs) so they can be run later

- Can load data from CSV, Box, Dropbox, and (S)FTP

The key benefits of Dataloader.io, and other tools like it, are that it can use fields other than Record Ids and External Ids to create relationships and it can save jobs, which you can re-run with different import files. The latter means you can set up and test your upload in advance and then simply execute it when you are ready to load the full set of data.

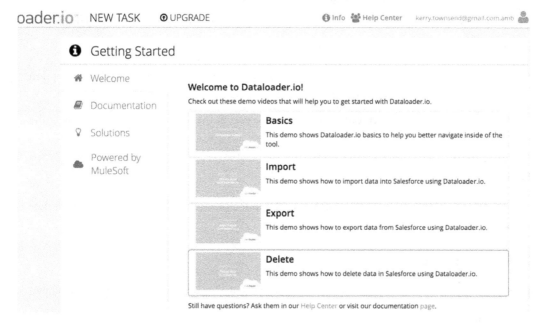

Figure 6.4 – Dataloader.io

Companies that provide Salesforce data-loading tools include Jitterbit and Informatica. Enterprise-level integration middleware tools also have built-in capability to carry out any required transformation. This means the transformation and load can be carried out together. You can find a list of data loading tools and their capabilities on the AppExchange. We learn more about the AppExchange in *Chapter 14 – Extending with the AppExchange*.

Which tool to use

As you can see, there are a number of options, and there will be more options than we have covered here. To make a selection, you should go through the following questions:

- Do I already have data-loading tools available to me in my organization?
- What Objects do I need to load data into?
- What volumes of data do I need to load?
- Is there a free tool available to me?
- Does the free tool have the data volumes and usability I require?
- Do I need to load parent and child records, and do I already have a relationship identifier?
- Do I have the budget for a data-loading tool?

The answers to these questions will help you identify whether one of the free tools is a good option or whether there are benefits to using a paid tool.

Now that you have selected which tool you are going to use, in the next section, we will look at the data-loading process.

Loading data

In this section, we will go through the steps required to load some data, starting with an overview of the process.

The loading process

The overall steps for loading data are common regardless of the tool that you use. They are as follows:

1. Define the data template.
2. Format data on the template.

3. Execute the data load:

    - Select the operation

    - Select the file/source

    - Confirm mapping and settings

    - Load data

    - Review errors

4. Validate all data has loaded correctly.

In the following sections, we will look at each of these steps in more detail.

Creating a template

Often, the easiest way to create a template for loading data is to create a record in the target system with realistic data in all the fields that you want to load. Then, using the selected tool, you can export the record. This will give you all the headings and show you an example of the format of the data. You will have one template per object.

This is a good option for tools such as Salesforce Data Loader and other third-party tools where the headings need to the API names. However, the Salesforce Data Import Wizard doesn't offer an export option. For this the headings you need are the field labels as you see them in the UI, for example Last name. In most cases the data format is also as you see in the UI. This includes the record ID's ID, which usually requires the 15-digit rather than the 18-digit ID.

In the next section, we will look at how you get data into templates.

Data mapping and formatting

In this section, we'll look at the data mapping and formatting required specifically to load data into Salesforce. Mapping simply means defining which source system fields go to which Sales Cloud fields. It is beneficial to document this mapping in a spreadsheet as the field for one source may map to different Objects in Sales Cloud. This can be used as a reference when you set up the mapping in the data-loading tool to make sure everything is mapped correctly. The following figure is an example of a mapping:

	A	B	C	D	E	F
1	**Source System**		**Sales Cloud (Target System)**			
2	**Table/ Sheet**	**Field**	**Object**	**Field**	**Type**	
3	Deal Sheet	Deal Name	Opportunity	Name	Standard	
4	Deal Sheet	Stage	Opportunity	Stage	Standard	
5	Deal Sheet	Closing Date	Opportunity	Close Date	Standard	
6	Deal Sheet	New/ Exising	Opportunity	Type	Standard	
7	Deal Sheet	Budget	Opportunity	Budget	Custom (Free Text)	
8	Deal Sheet	Authority	Opportunity	Authority	Custom (Free Text)	
9	Deal Sheet	Need	Opportunity	Need	Custom (Free Text)	
10	Deal Sheet	Timing	Opportunity	Timing	Custom (Free Text)	
11	Deal Sheet	Company	Account	Name	Standard	
12	Deal Sheet	Contact	Contact	First Name	Standard	
13	Deal Sheet	Contact	Contact	Last Name	Standard	

Figure 6.5 – Mapping spreadsheet

For the formatting, you will have one template per object, except when you are using the Salesforce Data Import Wizard for accounts and contacts when that information is consolidated into one template.

There are some data formatting considerations that are specific to Sales Cloud. This includes adding fields that may not be in the source data. The considerations have been listed as follows:

- **Required fields**: Enter a value for every record.
- **Picklist fields**: Only picklist options can be chosen.
- **Email addresses**: Should be written in the jsmith@acme.com format.
- **Free-text field**: Where the field value is longer than the field length the content will be truncated.
- **Record owner**: Enter a value; otherwise, it will default to the loading data.
- **Record type fields**: Specify a value using the API Name
- **Validation rules**: Enter values for data required by validation rules. Although these might not be active during the load, it will result in a poor User experience.
- **Datetime**: Format values as required by the tool.
- **External ID fields**: Enter values if you want to store the IDs of any records as is in an external system, for example, an Account's ERP ID value.
- **Audit fields**: Specify the value it is using. We will look at Audit Fields in more detail in the section on preloading steps.

It is also worth noting that manipulating data in spreadsheets can introduce additional problems. A couple to look out for are listed as follows:

- Removal of the leading zeros on phone numbers

- Formatting and special character issues when opening in Excel and converting to CSV

In the next section, we will look at the steps involved in executing the data load.

Executing a data load

Independent of the tool, the data-loading process has similar steps. Let us look at some of the key considerations. If you are updating existing records, it is always best to take a copy of the existing data before performing the update in case there is a problem and you need to restore the original data.

Selecting the operation

Data import tools are available in a range of database operations, despite the name. The commonly available operations are as follows:

- **Insert**: Creates new records only.

- **Update**: Updates existing records only. Requires a field to use for matching.

- **Upsert**: Updates existing records and creates new records if existing ones are not available. Requires a field to use for matching.

- **Export**: Downloads data based on criteria.

- **Delete**: Deletes record. Usually only requires record IDs.

You can select one of these per data-loading operation.

Selecting the source

In this chapter, we have focused on loading data from flat files, such as spreadsheets. When loading from files, it is beneficial to have the files stored locally on the executing machine for the upload. This reduces the amount of data transferred across networks and the cloud. This is more important when large-sized files are involved.

In the next section, we will consider the data mapping and settings to think about.

Confirming settings and mapping

Depending on the tool and the loading operation you have selected, you will also have slightly different settings options. However, common settings to confirm before you load the data are date format (i.e., dd/mm/yyyy or mm/dd/yyyy), time zone (you may need to confirm whether you are currently in a daylight-saving time zone), and batch size; the maximum batch size is 200, but this can be adjusted.

You will also have options specific to the operation that you are carrying out, for example, setting the matching fields for Updates and Upserts. In third-party tools, you may have the option to select other look-up attributes to match records. They may also give you the option to trigger a workflow (i.e., processes). It is important to step through all the setting options carefully, particularly if you're new to the tool and before you commit to the data load. It is more time consuming to undo a data load than it is to double-check the settings before committing.

If the template you are using has the heading names in a format the tool can understand, it should automatically map the data to the target fields. This option reduces the potential for human error.

In the next section, we will look at what happens when you click **Start Import**.

Loading data

With any tools you are using, you are likely to get a warning when you click to upload so that you don't accidentally click the option before you are ready. This is a good time to take a moment to mentally run through whether you have mapped the fields, selected the settings, and carried out any other steps you planned to do before the load. We will explore how you plan your legacy data load in the *Planning your legacy data load* section later. This includes preloading steps, testing, and communication.

While the data is loading, the tool should provide you with a progress indicator. For large data loads, this can take some time. Most tools will show you the number of successes and failures as it goes. If you are seeing failures, you may want to abort the load so you can investigate and correct the issue.

If you are using a cloud-based tool, your job might be queued and therefore not start immediately.

In the next section, we will look at how you can view errors and some of the most common causes.

Reviewing error logs

If there are errors with the load, you will need to review the error logs. This should show you the error message the system reported. Depending on the tool and the format of the log, you may have to work out the data that caused the error from the row.

Common reasons for errors are as follows:

- Missing required data
- Duplicate Rules
- Validation Rules – if they are enabled during the load
- Multiple emails in the email field
- Special characters

In the next section, we will look at ways to validate the data.

Validating a data load

Once the data has been loaded, it is important to review the data in the system to confirm that it is as expected. If you are loading data at the request of someone else, it is important they check that the data is as they expect.

Create a report on Sales Cloud that should display the data that you have loaded and confirm the total record numbers and that the data displays as expected.

In the next section, we will explore the options if you need to undo a data load.

Undoing a data load

With a data load, there is no simple rollback option. The best way to avoid having to undo a data load is to do a test run on the settings first with only a very small sample of data. There are, however, times when you need to remove the data you've uploaded.

If you are performing an insert, there is an option to mass-delete records. This is only available to users who have the mass-delete permission. Some tools will provide a list of record IDs in the success log. This can be used to run a Delete operation in the same tool to remove records.

If you have performed an Update, Upsert or Delete, your only option will be to restore the original data from a backup you took before you made the change. If you are using a backup and restore tool, it is likely this will be the quickest way for you to restore the data.

We have now completed all the steps for loading data. Next, we will look at how to plan a legacy data load.

Planning your legacy data load

Now that you have confirmed what you are going to load, selected the tools, and determined any transformation required, it is time to plan your data load. An initial data load is typically part of an implementation, so it is essential to have a plan that can be communicated and scheduled with other implementation activities.

In the following sections, we will learn about the elements you should think about when planning your legacy data load. The first element to consider is how to transition Users from their current system to Sales Cloud while keeping data up to date and accurate. We will look at the options for business transition in the next section.

Business transition

Sales is a live and often fast-moving function. It is essential that salespeople have continuous access to their data. For this reason, it is important to plan how you transfer data from the as-is system to the to-be system. The options available will depend on the volume of data involved, the amount of preprocessing involved, and whether the data is being loaded into a brand-new or live production org.

For smaller data volumes with limited preprocessing that are being loaded into a new org, it might be possible to extract, process, and load the data and go live in one work effort. This will depend on whether all the elements can be completed during a down period such as a weekend.

For larger data volumes, an initial data load and then a delta load will be required. For the initial load, a cut of the data is taken, preprocessed, and loaded. Then, just before the system goes live, the changed data, the delta, is taken, processed, and loaded so that Users have a complete set of prepared data at go-live. The key is that the processing of the delta can be completed during a down period.

Data transitions or any system updates should always be planned to avoid any key financial milestones in the month, quarter, or year end.

To reduce the risk of delays at go-live, you may also want to consider decoupling some of the data from the initial release. For example, if you are bringing in data that would have not been available before, such as Order data, you might schedule the upload of this shortly after go-live to reduce the complexity in a single load.

In the next section, we will learn about the order data that needs to be loaded.

Loading order

The loading of data into related Objects needs to be executed in an order that creates parent records before child records. We also covered in *Chapter 3*, that each record needs an owner. This means that all the User records for record owners need to be created before records they own can be inserted. It is worth noting that each User needs a Profile so either a standard Profile must be assigned or a custom Profile must be set up in advance of the load.

The first records that need to be set up in the system are as follows:

- Setup Profiles
- Users

The following are groups of Core Sales Process records that need to be set up in order based on their parent relationship dependencies:

- Accounts – Parent then Child accounts
- Contact
- Opportunities
- Opportunity contact roles

Say you use one of the following:

- Products
- Price Books
- Price Book Entries incl Standard
- Opportunity Products

The following can be set up any time after opportunities:

- Activities
- Account Teams
- Opportunity Teams

For the Lead Generation Process, after Users are created, records need to be set up in the following order:

- Accounts: Parent then Child accounts
- Contact
- Leads
- Campaigns
- Campaign Members

To relate child records to parent records, you need an identifier. This can either be the Salesforce record ID of the parent or another identifier available in the data. If a unique identifier is already available in both the parent and child data, for example, a Product Code, this can be used. If one is not available, it might be possible to construct one by concatenating fields to create a unique string. Where a unique identifier is available, to be used to relate child records, it must be in a field on the parent of the type **External** ID type and the field must enforce uniqueness. External ID fields are available to select in data-loading tools for the upsert operation.

In practice, if no identifier is available, parent records will need to be loaded, then their record IDs need to be exported and substituted into child data using a `vlookup` type function before the child data can be loaded. If an identifier is available in an External ID, the parent records can be loaded, then the child record via an upsert operation with the fields that hold the unique identifier mapped to each other.

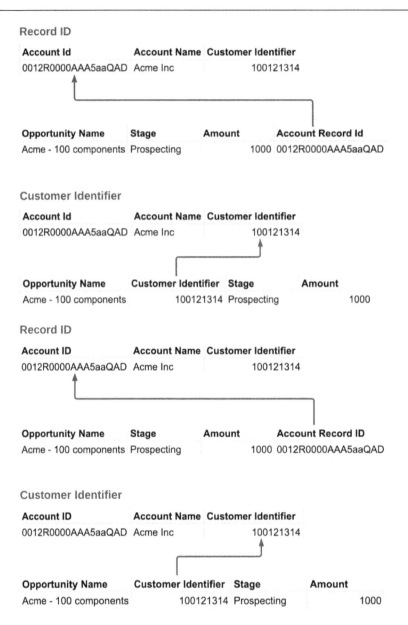

Figure 6.6 – Relating Child Records to a Parent via Record ID or unique identifier

In *Figure 6.6* you can see how the data would look if you were using the parent record ID (Account ID) as the field to match the child record or a custom unique ID, in this case Customer Identifier.

Preloading steps

Before a data load happens, there are usually a number of steps that should take place to prepare the environment. Some of the most common steps are described in the following list. Determine what preloading steps are relevant to your solution and list them in your execution plan along with who should complete them:

- Add **Set Audit Fields upon Record Creation** permission to the User
- If a mutable option has been designed, deactivate Validation, Duplication Rules and Processes
- Defer Sharing Calculations
- If record owning Users are not already Active, either activate them or add **Update Records with Inactive Owners** permission

In the next section, we will review the steps to enable the Audit Fields.

Enabling Audit Fields

To preserve the integrity of your data, Salesforce allows you to override the **Audit Fields**, **Created By**, **Create Date**, **Last Modified By**, and **Last Modified Date** records so you can enter the values of the source system. Other fields that you can also set on insert are `IsConverted`, `ConvertedDate`, `ConvertedAccountId`, `ConvertedContactId`, and `ConvertedOpportunityId`. Values can be inserted but not updated. This used to be something you had to request from **Support**, but it is now available to enable in **Setup**. To do this, go to **Setup** > **User Interface**. In the **Setup** section, check the option with **"Set Audit Fields upon Record Creation"** and **"Update Records with Inactive Owners"**, as shown in *Figure 6.7*.

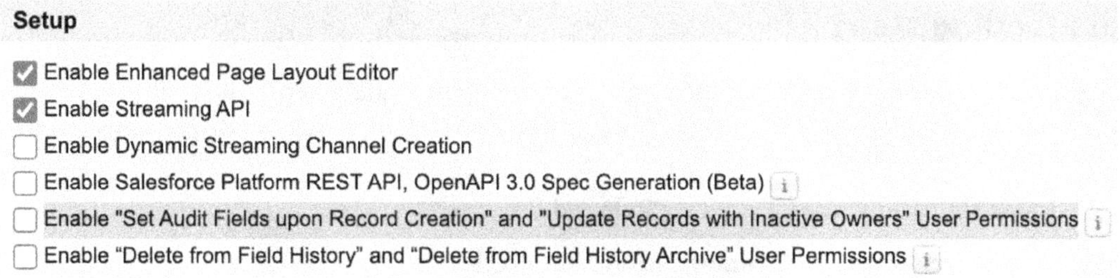

Setup

- ☑ Enable Enhanced Page Layout Editor
- ☑ Enable Streaming API
- ☐ Enable Dynamic Streaming Channel Creation
- ☐ Enable Salesforce Platform REST API, OpenAPI 3.0 Spec Generation (Beta) ⓘ
- ☐ Enable "Set Audit Fields upon Record Creation" and "Update Records with Inactive Owners" User Permissions ⓘ
- ☐ Enable "Delete from Field History" and "Delete from Field History Archive" User Permissions ⓘ

Figure 6.7 – Screenshot of Setup | User Interface

If it doesn't already exist, you will need to create a permission set that includes the **Set Audit Fields upon Record Creation** and **Update Records with Inactive Owners" User Permissions**.

To create the **Permission Set,** go to **Setup** > **Permission Sets** and click **New**. Enter a name and description and click **Save**. Add the permissions Set Audit Fields upon Record Creation and Update Records with Inactive Owners from System Permissions. This Permission Set will be available to assign to Users loading the data as a pre deployment set.

Mutable Rules & Processes

Following Salesforce Well-Architected principles, any automations including Validation Rules, Duplication Rules, Apex Triggers and Processes should be mutable by design. This means that they are designed with an option to disable them all for a User performing a mass action such as a data load. The assumption is that you have already carried out work on the data you are loading so it meets the criteria of any Validation Rules, any unwanted duplicates have already been removed and that record updates that process would perform have already been made.

As an admin, you can then make a judgment as to which automation and rules should be disabled before loading the data.

Where your system is not set up to be able to disable Validation Rules, Duplication Rules or processes you will need to review and identify a rule that will cause issues and deactivate these manually.

Deferring Sharing Calculations

It is possible to suspend **Sharing Calculations** while you are loading data. This is beneficial when you are making a large number of changes that will trigger **Sharing Rule** calculations such as adding data or changing ownership. This prevents long Sharing Rule evaluations or timeouts. It is important to remember to Resume the rules and manually trigger a **Recalculation**. **Sharing Rules** can take a long time to run and may need to run overnight or on a weekend.

The option to defer **Sharing Rules** is not automatically available in an Org,; you will need to ask **Salesforce Support** to enable the option in your Org.

Next, we will look at the steps that commonly need to be completed once a data load has been completed.

Post-loading steps

Once the data upload has taken place, there are a number of post-loading steps that are often needed:

- Turn off **Audit Fields**
- Enable **Validation Rules**, **Duplicate Rule** and **Processes**
- Setup **Sharing Rules** or **Resume rules** and **Recalculate**
- Deactivate Users that should not currently have access
- Delete all locally stored data including log files. Particular attention should be paid to files that contain PII or commercially sensitive data.

The steps that are appropriate for your solution should be added to your execution plan along with who should complete them.

In the next section, we will learn the value of rehearsing your data load.

Data load rehearsal

Rehearsing the full data load in a Sandbox provides an opportunity to identify any errors, issues, or anything that has been forgotten. It also allows you to measure how long the load will take so it can be accurately scheduled in a data load or full release plan. Data loads and deployments often take place out of hours to minimize the disruption to Users or Customers. This means that all those involved are scheduled to perform their roles at set times and need to complete them within the given deployment window. Carrying out a rehearsal reduces the risk that, on the day, it doesn't go as expected.

During out-of-hours data loads and deployments, there are a limited number of people available. It is usually out of standard office hours, which means that it can be harder to get additional assistance to resolve issues. There are also usually high expectations that the system will be ready to use, and that scheduled business Users will test the system and confirm system and data are available as expected. If the data load follows directly after a deployment, there is a further risk of complications and delays.

If you are using a tool that can save your import operation, you can confirm this works correctly during the rehearsal and then execute it with minimal modification during the actual load.

In the following section, we will review the considerations for scheduling your legacy data load.

Scheduling

The data-loading plan should have a schedule of who is performing what roles, when they are scheduled to perform the task, where they will be carrying it out, and how they can be contacted.

In addition to people carrying out the load, you will also want to schedule at least one person to validate that the data has loaded as expected. This is most likely to be a business user who has been given the authority to be the main business stakeholder.

In addition to the full load, consideration should be given to the steps required if the data update needs to be rolled back. Ideally, this will not be required, but if any additional people are required or it would have an impact because it takes longer to roll back, this should be documented in the schedule so that during the load, everything is about execution and not working out what to do.

In the next section, we will learn what communication is required around a legacy data load.

Communication

Communication is an important part of any solution design and deployment. So, it is important that every step, including loading data, is communicated. What will be communicated when and how should be agreed on as part of the plan so it can simply be executed during the load. Common communication milestones are as follows:

- Data-loading activities begin.
- Data-loading activities complete.

- Data-loading activities are validated.

- Data load completes.

- If an issue occurs during the load that is likely to have an impact on the timeline, this should also be communicated followed by status updates. The distribution and escalation list for this type of update should be agreed on in advance.

Where possible, all the people performing these tasks will be in the same location, but if this is not possible, then the communication will happen by mobile or email. The final communication should be sent to all business stakeholders.

We have now explored all the main components of a legacy data-loading plan. In the next section, we will consider some of the common ongoing data-loading activities.

Ongoing data-loading activities

Loading data is an essential part of getting your Salesforce Sales Cloud implementation up and running, but you may also find that you have an ongoing need to load data. Examples of this include loading Leads and Contacts captured from marketing activities, or adding or updating Account data from other internal or external sources.

If you are asked to load data on a regular basis, there are a few key questions you will want to ask to decide on the best approach. The first is as follows:

- The first and most important is, do we have permission to store this data?

- Then, we have the following practical questions:

- What is the volume of data?

- How regularly does this happen?

- Could this create duplicates?

This will allow you to ultimately answer the following two questions:

- What tools can we use?

- Who should do this?

Within Sales Cloud, you can give the Users permission to access the **Data Import Wizard** so they can load their own Leads and Contacts. This is possible without access to **Setup** and the **Customize Application** permission. There is a button on the **Campaign Member**s Related List for Campaigns that allows Users to access the Data Import Wizard directly. This option means that Users are not dependent on a System Administrator to load their leads into the system.

Figure 6.8 – Campaign Members related list

Figure 6.8 shows the **Campaign Member** Related List and the **Import Leads and Contacts** option.

However, giving this permission requires careful consideration. While there are productivity benefits, there are also some risks. If Users are not well informed about what they should and shouldn't load, there is the risk that the system will quickly have a large volume of poor-quality data that the organization does not have permission to store. The productivity gains can be outweighed by the effort required to identify, clean up, or remove poor data. In the worst case, it can have an impact on customer experience, reputation and can even be a risk to compliance with regulatory and statutory requirements. Forexample, people who have not given consent being contacted or incorrect people being targeted.

Ways of reducing this risk include the following:

- Specify what data can and can't be loaded, including the format.
- Define criteria that the data has to meet. Examples of required fields are last name, first name, company, email, and consent for data storage and communication.
- Allow only nominated people who have been trained in the process to load the data.
- Turn on duplicate matching rules.

Following these steps will allow data to be loaded while maintaining data quality and reinforcing that data quality is everyone's responsibility.

If the ongoing need is to load data other than Leads, Contacts, Accounts, or data in a Custom Object, then tools such as Data Loader or Dataloader.io will be required. In this situation, the person loading the data will need to be the System Administrator, or a super user trained to use the tools. Many of the elements of the initial data load will apply to a regular load of data of this type. They include mapping the data, how to match the data – an External ID can be a great help here – and turning off Flows and Validation. All ongoing data activities benefit from having a well-defined, documented process that is completed by specified Users.

Summary

In this chapter, we have learned about how to identify and evaluate sources of data in order to make a recommendation on what data to load into Sales Cloud. We explored the tools that are available to load data into Salesforce and learned about the key questions and considerations when selecting tools. We learned about the data-loading process, how to create templates, common formatting requirements, what causes errors, how to identify errors, and, if required, how to undo a load. Finally, we looked at what needs to be included in a plan to load legacy data. With this information, you should be able to plan and execute data loads in Sales Cloud.

In the next chapter, we will be learning about getting sign-off for implementation milestones, including what this means and why it is an important part of your implementation delivery.

Further reading

Salesforce Record Size

- *Salesforce Record Size Overview:* `https://help.salesforce.com/s/articleView?id=000383664&type=1`

Data Import Wizard

- *Field Mapping for Importing Leads:*

  `https://help.salesforce.com/s/articleView?id=sf.field_mapping_for_importing_leads.htm&type=5`

- *Field Mapping for Other Data Sources and Organization Import:*

  `https://help.salesforce.com/s/articleView?id=sf.field_mapping_for_other_data_sources_and_organization_import.htm&type=5`

Importing Data

- *How to Import Data into Salesforce Series:*

  `https://salesforce.vidyard.com/watch/ARIjWm2qrDkJVJxEhReFug`

Bulk API

- *Trailhead: Large Data Volumes > Load Your Data:* `https://trailhead.salesforce.com/content/learn/modules/large-data-volumes/load-your-data`

- *Trailhead: Platform API Basic > Use Bulk API 2.0:*

  `https://trailhead.salesforce.com/content/learn/modules/api_basics/api_basics_bulk`

- *Introduction to Bulk API 2.0 and Bulk API*:

  `https://developer.salesforce.com/docs/atlas.en-us.api_asynch.meta/api_asynch/asynch_api_intro.htm`

- *A comparison of Bulk API 2.0 and Bulk API*: `https://developer.salesforce.com/docs/atlas.en-us.api_asynch.meta/api_asynch/bulk_common_diff_two_versions.htm`

- *Quick Start: Connect Postman to Salesforce*:

  `https://trailhead.salesforce.com/content/learn/projects/quick-start-connect-postman-to-salesforce`

Defer sharing calculations:

- *Defer Sharing Calculations*:

  `https://help.salesforce.com/s/articleView?language=en_US&id=sf.security_sharing_defer_sharing_calculations.htm&type=5`

7

Getting Sign-Off

For a system to be considered successful, it has to provide a solution that stakeholders agree meets their needs. Keeping your stakeholders informed and aligned and managing their expectations throughout the implementation is essential for success.

In this chapter, you will learn how you can use sign-off checkpoints to keep stakeholders' understanding and expectations aligned through the different phases of your implementation.

The value and mechanics of sign-off are generally not talked about. Those who are unfamiliar don't appreciate the importance, meaning project milestones can come and go without formal (or only a passing) acknowledgment from those who are involved. They have a personal view of how the implementation is progressing, which is not challenged. This topic has a dedicated chapter to help you understand why sign-offs play an important part in ensuring the success of your Sales Cloud implementation.

We're going to cover the following main topics in this chapter:

- The what, why, who, how, and when of sign-off
- Types of sign-off

Supporting tools and information

Sign-off is a business process. Organizations need to document the sign-off process so that there is readily available evidence in case the need arises. A method of documenting sign-off is needed so evidence can be provided in the future if required. These are all typically available in business for other activities. Use the tools available to you. There is no need for a specialized tool for this purpose.

The what, why, who, how, and when of sign-off

In this section, we will look at the anatomy of sign-off: in practice, what does it mean, why is it important, who needs to be involved, how does it happen in reality, and when do we include the different types?

If your organization has a framework for signing off projects or system development work, it is important that you understand that framework and follow it, unless you have specific reasons to take an alternative approach. The content here is for those who don't have an existing framework or want to know more about sign-off on typical Sales Cloud implementations. We will refer to the work as the implementation rather than as a project, which is a much broader term.

Sign-off can be an ambiguous term that people are expected to understand but is rarely explained. That is why we break it down in this chapter.

First, we need to learn what sign-off means.

What is a sign-off?

A sign-off is an approval process. The objective is for all stakeholder parties to confirm that they agree with the outcomes from the work so far and any proposed future work. Within a Sales Cloud implementation, sign-off takes place at the milestones, where one phase of work is completed, and the next phase is about to start. It serves as a checkpoint to confirm that implementation stakeholders accept what has happened so far and agree on the next proposed actions. It provides an opportunity to confirm that stakeholders are aligned in their understanding and expectations. It means that any misalignment can be explored and resolved.

If an external supplier is involved, these checkpoints will be one of the contractual requirements. Even if the work is being carried out internally, these checkpoints are still essential for ensuring alignment with current company goals and objectives and forming a commitment that stakeholders make to each other and the business.

A sign-off usually includes the following:

- Reviewing the deliverables
- Stakeholders discussing, questioning, and challenging completed and proposed work
- Agreed future deliverables

The important characteristics of sign-off are as follows: that the process is captured and evidenced so that what was agreed can be accessed at a future date and that those with sign-off responsibility understand they are accountable for implementation success.

In another following section, *Types of sign-off*, we look at the specifics, including the components of the sign-off types corresponding with the implementation milestones. An implementation might not have every sign-off described, and we have considered that in more detail in the *When to use the different types of sign-off* section.

Next, we consider why it is important in more detail.

Why is sign-off important?

Implementations can be complex and fast-paced. Verbal and email communications are good for keeping things moving but are more prone to interpretation, and with multiple threads happening at any one time, it can be easy for an implementation to start to veer off course. Additionally, everyone comes to a project with a different frame of reference. Their expectations can be shaped by other systems they have used or previous projects. While they can be using the same words, their intended meaning or the way they interpret them can be different.

This is why it is essential to have enforced pauses, which are sign-offs where key representatives are required to review the same content, consider any implications, confirm their understanding that it is what the people they represent are expecting, and agree with any future approach.

Overlooking this can be costly, fail to identify conflict, and, ultimately, mean the solution is viewed as unsuccessful. A sign-off prevents the gap between what is expected to happen and what is actually happening from deviating too far.

The following are some situations where sign-off checkpoints are particularly important:

- **Multiple stakeholder groups are represented**, as this means there can be a wider variation of expectations
- **All or some of the work is being delivered by external suppliers**, as deviation can have a contractual impact
- **People leave and join the implementation**, meaning the history is required for review

It is also important to recognize that what is required from the implementation can change over the course of the delivery based on business changes. These might be changes to the timeline, the capability of the system, or who will be using it. These potential changes need to be reviewed and incorporated where appropriate. We consider this in more detail in the *Change sign-off* section.

We will now look into who is involved.

Who is involved?

Who is involved in the sign-off will depend on the sign-off type, the size of the implementation, who is delivering the work, and your organization's culture. Who should have sign-off responsibility and what sign-off types will be used should be agreed upon at the beginning of each project. There are no set rules. It is about striking the right balance between having a good level of business representation and minimizing project administration. Further, who you have represented at these checkpoints will influence the direction of the project.

As mentioned in the previous *What is sign-off?* section, the people who have this responsibility need to understand that they are accountable to the business and the stakeholders they represent. They may be called on to explain their decisions and report back to the people they represent on what's happening.

The people who are typically represented or directly involved in sign-off are the following:

- Project Lead

- Project Sponsor, i.e., Sales Director and CRO

- Finance

- Business function subject-matter experts, i.e., Sales Manager and Marketing Manager

- External supplier primary contact, i.e., Engagement Manager or Project Manager

Finance may not be involved in every implementation, but they will have a role when an external supplier is delivering the solution. There may be payments associated with sign-off milestones or finance sign-off to release additional budget.

The minimum involvement you would expect for a sign-off is a person representing those who have requested the work and the person responsible for delivering it. Aim to have a named contact for each of the sign-off roles and confirm with them that they understand what is required, the time commitment involved, the level of responsibility, and that they accept the responsibility. Not having named people in advance can cause delays that could otherwise be avoided.

> **Important note**
>
> It is important that those people who are involved in a sign-off know what is expected of them, and they must have the authority, be available, and have the capacity to attend any meetings or review any content at the required time. Schedule these times with them in advance to avoid delays and keep them informed of any changes to the schedule. The people involved may have a number of responsibilities and will not appreciate having to find time in their calendar at the last minute for activities that could have been anticipated. They may also have scheduled time out of the business. Every step and interaction has an impact on the overall perception of the success of the implementation.

Next, we will review how sign-off happens in practice.

How does it happen?

The sign-off activity is usually initiated by the person responsible for making sure the work is complete, which may or may not have the formal title of the Project Lead. They will gather the information that those involved need to review and circulate it, schedule any meetings (if this happens outside normal implementation meetings), and specify the timeline. If a specific project methodology is being followed or your organization already has one, you may need to populate a template with information.

The actual sign-off will be given in person via a meeting or electronically via email. In all cases, it will need to be captured in a way that can be available for review in the future.

Examples of how sign-off is captured include the following:

- Email response

- The minutes and decisions in the meeting

- Signing off a form

- Within project tooling

For small pieces of work, confirming sign-off can be relatively informal; for example, the project lead, who is also building the functionality, might email the person requesting it, describing what will and won't be done, how long it will take, and when it will be available. The person requesting it might then simply respond to the email with confirmation to go ahead. For a new implementation of Sales Cloud, more people will be involved to ensure the implementation delivers the value that was promised when Sales Cloud was purchased. *Figure 7.1* is an example of an email requesting sign-off from the person that requested the enhancement.

Figure 7.1 – Email requesting design sign-off for functionality enhancement

The email asks the requestor to view the details that have been captured about what is required, confirm that they will commit to participate in the process, attend the playback, and agree to the timescale.

Finally, in *The what, why, who, how, and when of sign-off* section, we looked at the considerations for deciding what sign-off milestones to include for your implementation.

When to use the different types of sign-off

There are different types of sign-off, which we will explore in more detail in the next section, *Types of sign-off*. They are not necessarily all used for every implementation; for example, some types of sign-off are critical if any development is being delivered by an external supplier, but it might not be as essential for a smaller-scale, internally delivered project. If an external supplier is carrying out the work, it is likely that all the sign-off types described in the next section will be required as part of the supplier's process and your contractual engagement.

If the work is carried out by internal teams, which sign-offs are included will be defined by your existing internal processes and the appetite of the stakeholders involved. I recommend an informal check-in with stakeholders at each of the described sign-off points, even if it is agreed that a formal process is not required. For all implementations, you want to get a sign-off that you can evidence for scope, testing, and implementation. We will explore each of these in the following sections.

Sign-off, even if carried out informally, is an opportunity to confirm that everyone is happy with the progress and celebrates the work that has been completed. Even though these steps might consume time, it is a false economy to miss them out. In an organization with an internal delivery team that is experienced and has a very good understanding of the business requirements, sign-offs might be quick and uneventful, but they are still important as they keep everyone on the same journey.

I also recommend using all the sign-off points when Sales Cloud is being implemented for the first time in a greenfield implementation. This will represent a significant change for the commercial business, and it is important that they are represented at each stage of the journey to confirm what is being developed is in line with their expectations.

In the next section, we will explore the types of sign-off in more detail, including the specifics of who will be involved and the common deliverables included.

Types of sign-off

In this section, we explore what each of the following types of sign-off represents, the typical deliverables included, who is usually involved, and when this type of sign-off is included. *Figure 7.2* shows the phases of an implementation and where sign-off milestones occur:

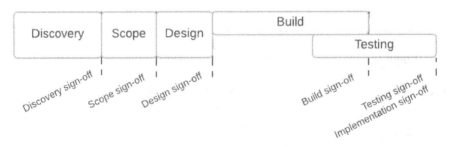

Figure 7.2 – Implementation phases with sign-off milestones

From the diagram, you can see that sign-off usually happens when one phase ends and before the next starts; however, testing activities can occur before the build phase is signed off.

We will start by exploring *Discovery sign-off*.

Discovery sign-off

A **discovery** is a piece of work that investigates and documents the **as-is** situation in a business, typically including an assessment of its systems. It allows for the gap between where they are and where they want to be to be more accurately understood. This is commonly carried out when an external supplier is building the solution, as they do not have the implicit knowledge that employees have about the way a specific business operates. It allows for a more accurate estimate of the transformation required.

If a discovery is taking place, it is important that internal stakeholders thoroughly review the findings, as this will form the basis of the estimates for implementing Sales Cloud.

The deliverables commonly associated with Discovery sign-off are as follows:

- A summary of the as-is situation, including diagrams and narrative
- A summary of the business challenges and impacts
- A blueprint of the to-be solution, which will resolve the business challenges

It may also include the following:

- Recommendations on how to address the business challenges
- What function and business areas are out of scope

The people involved in Discovery sign-off are (typically) the following:

- The business leaders of the functions included in the work
- The subject matter experts (SMEs) of the functions included in the work
- Finance (if carried out by an external supplier)
- The overall business sponsor

The Discovery sign-off ensures all the stakeholders involved have the same understanding of the current situation, the target situation, and the level of change required to get there.

Scope sign-off

The **scope** is the definition of the work that is being carried out. It is the first milestone to be signed off for a lot of implementation work, particularly if they are delivered internally.

Throughout the duration of the implementation, it is important to manage the scope of the work. Stakeholders' expectations can easily expand to features, functions, and capabilities that were not in the original plan. This often happens as people become more familiar with Sales Cloud capability and imagine how it can help them. It is also common for those working on the implementation to want to add extras they think will help users and improve the end solution, even though they are outside the gathered requirements.

For these reasons, defining, communicating, and getting sign-off on the scope of the work is essential and arguably the most critical type of sign-off for ensuring implementation success, as it defines what everyone is working towards.

If the implementation work is being carried out by an external supplier, the scope will be formally captured in a **statement of work**. They will require the statement of work and, by extension, the Scope, to be signed off before any work on the implementation starts. This is in the best interests of both parties. The external company will want to tightly manage the scope, always coming back to what was agreed.

As part of the Scope, it is as important to document what is not being done as it is. This avoids ambiguity and interpretation. Stating what is not included can identify differences in expectations early so they can be discussed and resolved. You always want to avoid a situation where some capability that is not in the Scope is expected because the person or team will realize it at some point and will be disappointed. It is always best to address this as early as possible rather than just hope it will go away.

The deliverables commonly associated with Scope sign-off are the following:

- A description of the scope of the work, including what is out of scope
- A set of deliverables

It may also include the following:

- A set of implementation objectives
- A set of success criteria
- A business case
- A set of high-level or detailed requirements

The full set of detailed requirements might be available to include in the scope sign-off if a Discovery has been carried out. If not, then this should be the first piece of work carried out and would become a deliverable for the Design sign-off that we review in the next section, *Design sign-off*.

The people typically involved in Scope sign-off are the same or very similar to the Discovery sign-off.

Design sign-off

The **Design sign-off** is where business stakeholders review documentation that describes the design of the Sales Cloud solution that will be built. A high-level or detailed version of this may have already been provided as a deliverable of the Discovery phase. This is essential when Sales Cloud is being implemented for the first time, or the work is being carried out by an external supplier. It may not necessarily be a formal sign-off if the work is incremental and carried out internally.

The Deliverables commonly associated with Design sign-off are the following:

- Solution design, describing how the to-be state will be achieved.

They may also include the following:

- Detailed requirements
- A Prototype
- Development plan
- Environment strategy.

The Solution design describes the proposed solution, including diagrams and a narrative. It will document the included business processes and the Sales Cloud functionality that will be used, i.e., objects and functions. A typical challenge at this point is that the design will inevitably include descriptions of Sales Cloud functionality; however, business SMEs may have limited exposure to Sales Cloud functionality and, therefore, make inaccurate assumptions based on their historical frame of reference. A prototype can be a great way of getting everyone to a shared understanding and avoiding differences in expectations.

The people involved in Build sign-off typically include the following:

- The Project Lead (may not have the formal title)
- The Business leaders of the functions included in the work
- The Subject matter experts (SMEs) of the functions included in the work

Note that functions such as Finance and the overall business sponsor can be less interested in the technical details. *Figure 7.3* is an example of an email informing project stakeholders that design sign-off has been achieved:

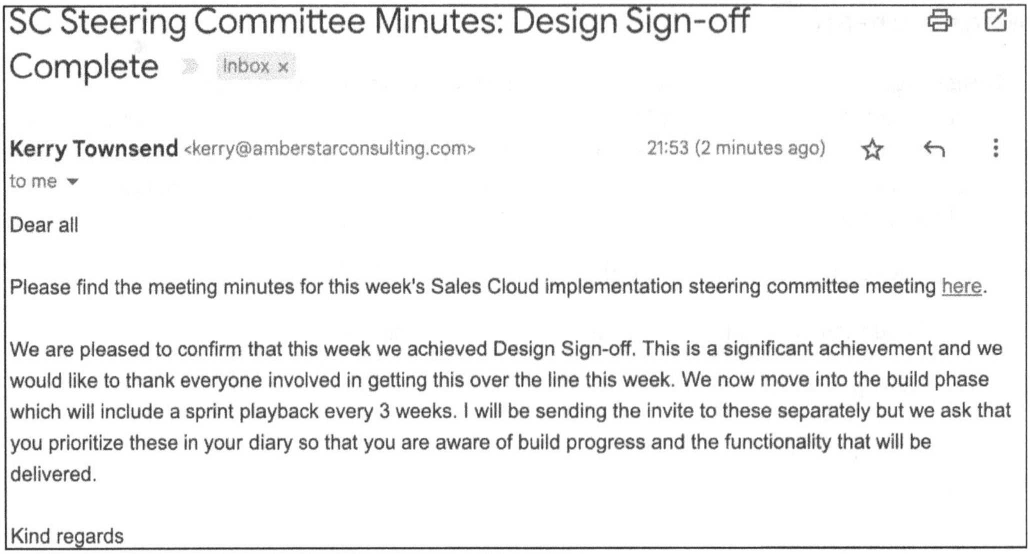

SC Steering Committee Minutes: Design Sign-off Complete Inbox ×

Kerry Townsend <kerry@amberstarconsulting.com> 21:53 (2 minutes ago)
to me

Dear all

Please find the meeting minutes for this week's Sales Cloud implementation steering committee meeting here.

We are pleased to confirm that this week we achieved Design Sign-off. This is a significant achievement and we would like to thank everyone involved in getting this over the line this week. We now move into the build phase which will include a sprint playback every 3 weeks. I will be sending the invite to these separately but we ask that you prioritize these in your diary so that you are aware of build progress and the functionality that will be delivered.

Kind regards

Figure 7.3 – An example of an email sharing that design sign-off was achieved

The example email communicates the sign-off, celebrates the milestone, thanks those involved, and highlights the key involvement that is required moving forward.

Next, we will look at *Build sign-off*.

Build sign-off

The **Build sign-off** signifies the end of the build phase, where all the focused build work is complete. This is a significant milestone and usually means that some or all of the technically skilled team members involved move on to other work. This sign-off is usually carried out within the team which is carrying out the build.

The Deliverables commonly associated with the Build sign-off, in addition to deliverables in other sign-offs, are the following:

- A configured solution in a development environment that has been unit-tested

It may also include the following:

- Build Tracking documentation
- Solution playbacks to business users
- Solution documentation

The people involved in Build sign-off are typically the following:

- The Project Lead (may not have the formal title)
- The Build Team Leads

If an external supplier is delivering the build, it is most likely that this sign-off will be carried out by their team, and your organization will be notified that it has happened. The opportunity to confirm that the Sales Cloud solution delivers the capability expected is during user acceptance testing (UAT), which we will talk about in the next sign-off milestone.

Immediately after the build phase, the solution needs to be independently tested. In the following section, we explore what is required for the *Testing sign-off*.

Testing sign-off

The **Testing sign-off** represents the formal end of all testing and, therefore, confirms that the solution is complete and works as designed and as users expect. It means it is in a state ready to deploy.

We explore how to execute the testing phases in more detail in the next chapter, *Chapter 8, Executing Testing*.

If an external supplier is delivering the build, it is most likely that the sign-off of the **quality assurance (QA)** and **system integration (SIT)** phases will be carried out by their team. You will have the opportunity to confirm that the Sales Cloud solution works as you expect during **user acceptance testing (UAT)**. Your business representatives sign this off.

If the work is incremental and carried out internally, signing off UAT may be as simple as the person delivering the solution getting on a call with the person who requested it and getting them to step through key actions to confirm it is what they need.

The Deliverables commonly associated with Testing sign-off, in addition to deliverables in other sign-offs, are the following:

- Completed test phases

  - Quality Assurance, (QA)
  - System integration testing (SIT) (if there is integration)
  - User acceptance testing (UAT)

It may also include the following:

- Testing tracking documentation

The people involved in testing sign-off are typically the following:

- The Project Lead

- The business users via user acceptance testing (UAT)

- The Test Lead

Testing sign-off usually represents the end of most of the build and testing teams' involvement. The same number may be involved with deployment. It is a significant milestone to achieve for an implementation.

Implementation sign-off

Implementation sign-off may be considered the same as project sign-off, depending on the terminology you use. This is the final stage of the implementation project. It signifies that the work of the implementation team is complete and that all stakeholders accept the deliverables and outcomes.

Depending on the size of the piece of work, implementation sign-off might be the only project milestone that is formally recognized. It is an essential milestone for all projects.

The Deliverables commonly associated with implementation sign-off, in addition to the deliverables in other sign-offs, are the following:

- Live capability and seeing the implementation in use in a production environment

It may also include the following:

- Project effort cost summary

- Completed user training (if included)

- Solution Documentation

- Handover to the current owner

- Lessons learned

This should include all the deliverables that were promised in the Scope.

The people involved in the implementation sign-off are typically all of those involved in the Scope sign-off.

Finally, we will explore the type of sign-off used when changes are required to the scope or effort.

Change sign-off

It is common for both internal and external implementation circumstances to change during the course of an implementation. An external factor might be a business process change, and an internal factor might be a functionality limitation or additional time required to complete a phase. The likelihood is that a change increases with the complexity of the solution and the overall time estimate. These changes to the scope of the implementation need to be formally managed, as they have an impact on effort, time scales, and/or cost.

A common term used to refer to this is **change request** (**CR**), although other terms might be used, such as **request for change** (**RFC**). It is important that all of those who are invested in the implementation are aware of and understand the reasons for the change. Even if there is no effort, timescales and/ or cost impacts may still require sign-offs if the change affects the terms of the agreement of an external supplier.

The deliverables commonly associated with change request sign-off are the following:

- A summary of the change

- A summary of the impact, i.e., cost and time.

It may also include the following:

- A completed change request form (if the organization or supplier has one)

The people involved in the change sign-off are typically all of those involved in the Scope sign-off. The Project Lead might have the discretion to approve certain types of changes, particularly if they don't have a cost impact. It is likely that if there is a cost impact, finance will need to be involved. No one on the project should assume they have the authority to approve a change unless it has been expressly confirmed.

Now that we have reviewed all the types of sign-off, we will review what we have learned in this chapter.

Summary

In this chapter, we have learned what is meant by sign-off, why it is important for ensuring that stakeholder's expectations are kept in alignment, who is involved, and how it happens. We have learned that there are different types of sign-off and that a formal version is not required for all implementations. However, it is recommended that they are all included when Sales Cloud is implemented for the first time or when work is delivered by an external supplier. When all the types of sign-off are not included, it is still essential to include the scope and final implementation sign-offs, and if a formal sign-off is not planned for any of the milestones, it is recommended that an informal check-in be carried out with the key stakeholders to confirm their expectations are still aligned, and their sentiment is positive.

In the next chapter, we expand on the testing approach that we introduced in *Chapter 2, Preparing for Success*. You will learn how to execute testing for your Sales Cloud implementation.

8

Executing Testing

Ensuring quality in your Sales Cloud solution is an essential component for success. Users must trust that the system will consistently deliver what they need so that they adopt it. In *Chapter 2, Defining the Approach*, we considered why testing is an essential part of the Application Lifecycle, and we learned how the Development Methodology, Environment Strategy, and DevOps methodology influence and constrain the options and flexibility you have when structuring testing. We also learned about the types of testing that are commonly used in Salesforce projects and the role that the **Testing Strategy**, **Test Plans**, and **Test Cases** have in enabling you to deliver effective testing for your Sales Cloud implementation.

This chapter gives you the information you need to put your test approach into action. We will learn about the considerations and what is included in a Test Plan for the most common test phases included in Sales Cloud implementations. We will also learn how to translate Users' Stories into Test Cases. We start by exploring some of the practical overarching considerations when planning your testing execution.

We're going to cover the following main topics in this chapter:

- Testing in practice
- Creating and executing Test Plans
- Translating Users' Stories into Test Cases
- Other testing

Supporting tools and information

To carry out testing, you will require access to the Salesforce Org designated for this type of testing. This will be defined by the environment strategy. If you are carrying out system integration testing, an equivalent-level environment will need to be connected to the Salesforce environment you are testing in.

To document the testing, you will need access to a spreadsheet tool or, if your organization already uses one, a dedicated testing management platform. Test scripts are often captured in spreadsheets, as they are easy to share between team members and any external service providers.

Testing in practice

It is worth noting that the way testing is executed during each project depends on a number of factors, including the complexity of the solution, an organization's Salesforce maturity, as well as the time, budget, and skills available. As with a software solution design, there is no single perfect way to deliver testing. Your primary goal is to take the best approach based on your solution with the time, skills, and budget available.

There are some common principles and best practices to keep in mind when planning and delivering your test phases.

- **Test as early as possible**: Aim to confirm the quality of the development and suitability of the functionality as early in the process as possible. Also, aim to identify differences between the solution and the User's expectations so that these can be resolved as soon as possible. Testing early in the development cycle is also referred to as shifting left.

- **Do enough testing for your situation**: The level of testing needs to be appropriate – not over-engineered. It is important to understand the intent of the functionality to ensure the tests are appropriate. The further along in the testing phases, the more business context testers you require. The earlier you can bring this understanding into the process the better, as it identifies issues earlier.

- **Every implementation should have a Test Plan**: This allows everyone to understand what is going to happen and what is expected. It brings consistency into the process.

- **Documenting defects fully, saves time**: If any issues are identified, it is essential that the steps to recreate the issues are recorded, including the data used. Screenshots and links to records can be a great way to capture the specifics of an issue.

- **Test failures should be triaged**: Reported defects need to be reviewed to determine whether a fix is required, the solution is as designed, or the report is for a change to the original requirement. Not every issue recorded as a defect will require a build change.

- **Build or other project delays create pressure to reduce testing**: If there are any delays or overruns in the activities upstream of testing, there is always some pressure to reduce the time scheduled for testing so that the deployment is not delayed.

- **Test should be carried out with non-system administrator permissions**: Typically, Users involved in the build process have System Administrator profiles. It is essential to carry out testing with Users that have the exact Profiles and Permission Sets as target Users. Test Users also need to have the appropriate roles in the Role Hierarchy to test Sharing Rules on data that should be restricted.

- **Size of regression testing increases over time**: Every time new functionality is released, the quantity of regression testing increases. Manual regression is time-consuming, and as the rate of Salesforce development is high, this volume can create a challenge.

The considerations and best practices described here apply to implementations of all shapes and sizes. Keep these in mind as you approach and execute testing and factor them into your plan.

Creating test plans and executing testing

In this section, we will deep dive into the most common functional test phases used in the Sales Cloud implementation projects. In *Chapter 2, Defining the Approach*, we learned how a mature organization might have an overall Test Strategy and Test Plan per project or testing phase, whereas organizations new to application development might have a single Test Plan that they create for their project, combining the information from the Strategy and the Plan.

In this section, we considered the most detailed scenario and reviewed the information that would be included in a Test Plan for each phase, as well as practical execution considerations. *Figure 8.1* shows the four types of testing we explore here, how they relate to each other, and how they can either be considered as part of the build or testing phase.

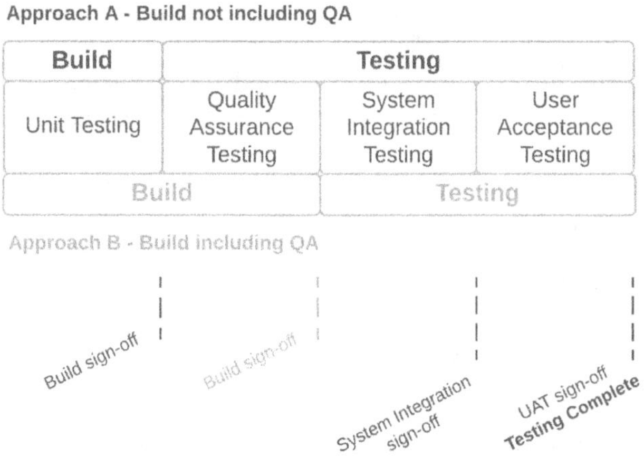

Approach A - Build not including QA

Build	Testing		
Unit Testing	Quality Assurance Testing	System Integration Testing	User Acceptance Testing
Build		Testing	

Approach B - Build including QA

Build sign-off   Build sign-off   System Integration sign-off   UAT sign-off   Testing Complete

Figure 8.1 – Testing phases with different build approaches

From the figure, you can see the order in which the test phases are carried out and two different ways they can be incorporated into the overall development phases. Unit Testing is always part of the build phase; however, Quality Assurance can also be incorporated into the build phase in order to carry out testing as early as possible, to shift left.

For each of the four testing phases, we will look in more detail at the following:

- The Objective
- The Scope
- The Schedule – when it should happen
- Resources – who should be involved
- Environment
- Datasets
- Defect Process
- Artifacts
- Sign-off

We will review these in the order they are executed, starting with Unit Testing.

Unit Testing

The purpose of Unit Testing is to confirm that the built solution, works functionally as per the requirement specified. Unit Testing is carried out as part of the build by the person developing the functionality. Unit Tests should be carried out to confirm that the built functionality performs not only all the expected actions as defined but also all the User Story Acceptance Criteria In the Agile methodology, a User Story is not delivered until it has been verified that it works; Unit Testing is part of the definition of it being done.

Unlike all the other types of testing, Unit Testing is fully integrated into the build sprint or phase, as it is carried out by the developer. The Build is not started on a new User Story or requirement until the current User Story is complete, including testing. This means the time needed for Unit Testing has to be factored into the built estimate or Agile story points.

Where appropriate, it can also be beneficial for developers to include negative test scenarios to confirm unintentional functions or vulnerabilities aren't introduced. This further reduces the number of defects that come back when Users carry out testing.

Where functionality is dependent on an integration, Test Classes should be provided to mock responses.

In the following section, we provide example headings and content for a Test Plan for this phase.

An example Unit Test Plan

A Test Plan is likely to have the following content, although the headings might vary:

- **Objective**: The objective of Unit Testing is to confirm that the solution built delivers the functions specified by the requirement or User Story.

- **Scope**: The scope of Unit Testing is to verify that each unit or element of a solution, in isolation, performs as specified by the requirement. All the required functions shall be divided into testable units, and it will be varied that the solution delivers these. Where appropriate, developers should carry out negative Unit Tests to confirm that unintentional functions have not been introduced.

- **Schedule**: Unit Tests will be fully integrated into the build. For Agile projects, Unit Testing is carried out within each built sprint. For projects with a build phase, Unit Testing is completed within the phase, which will have projected start and end dates.

- **Resources**: Team members in developer roles will carry out Unit Testing.

- **Environment**: Unit Testing will be carried out in the developer's build environment. It is recommended that each developer works in a separate environment – either a developer or scratch org.

- **Datasets**: Data used for Unit Testing will be created by the developer (or a Sandbox seeding solution) in their individual build environment. The data should be representative of real-world data and be sufficient to confirm each unit of testing.

- **Defect process**: Any required rework will be carried out as soon as a defect is identified by the developer. No formal defect logging and categorizing process is required.

- **Artifacts**: As part of Unit Testing, the following artifacts will be generated:

  - Salesforce Test Classes – for solutions that generate code.

  - Formal Test Cases are not typically created for Unit Testing; however, it is expected that all the Acceptance Criteria are tested along with any obvious negative tests. The level of documentation for Unit Testing is often at the discretion of the developer or specified in the strategy or plan. It is common for tests of low-code (declarative) features not to be documented, particularly simple configuration such as creating fields. Functionality delivered by Apex code requires Test Classes to deliver a minimum of 1% test coverage per Apex Class and an aggregated 75% in the Production Org, in order for deployment. For complex low-code solutions, it is recommended that Test Cases are documented. A complex Screen Flow that automates the creation of complex Opportunities is one such example.

- **Communication**: Developers confirm that they have completed build and Unit Testing by setting the requirement or user story as done.

- **Sign-off**: A Unit Testing sign-off is assumed as part of the build sign-off.

> **Execution notes**
>
> It is in the developer's interest to test their solutions well so that the user story or requirement is not returned at a later stage when they have moved on to other work.
>
> When the build is being carried out by developers offsite, it is important that they have as much context about the requirement as possible so that they can carry out realistic tests on the solution they create. Appropriate, high-quality testing removes defeats at the earliest and is cost-effective.

Unit Testing is an essential component of development and the earliest opportunity to ensure quality by removing defects. The time invested by developers at this point saves a lot of time later in the implementation.

Quality Assurance testing

The aim of **Quality Assurance** (**QA**) testing is to independently confirm that what has been built performs as is functionally specified in the requirements. It should also check that the customization is consistent with any UI, development, or coding standards. For example, include consistent methods for triggering automations, field naming, help text, Validation Rule error placement, and text. Testing of standard Salesforce functionality should not be included – for example, the ability to navigate to different objects in Sales Cloud. This will have been tested by Salesforce before release.

QA testing is carried out by someone other than the person who developed the solution. It can be conducted as soon as the developer confirms the user story is complete. In practice, this can happen in the same sprint, a following sprint, or in a separate phase that happens once the build is complete. In the Agile methodology, testers can be part of the sprint team. They work very closely with developers and create Test Cases while the build is taking place. The tester takes ownership of the story once the developer has completed Unit Testing, and the story is not delivered until the functionality has passed QA testing.

When regression testing is carried out, it takes place during QA testing. The amount of existing customization determines the volume of regression testing that can be conducted. If QA with regression testing is conducted as a separate phase, there is flexibility to set a duration that would allow for manual regression testing. If an Agile methodology is used, the duration for QA testing is limited to a sprint duration. This can make manual regression testing, in addition to testing new functionality, unrealistic unless a large number of testers are available. In this scenario, automated regression testing is commonly used. If Continuous Integration or Continuous Deployment is used, then automated regression tests can be triggered to run as soon as the code is checked in. When automated regression testing is used, the automation scripts for the new functionality are built.

All QA and regression testing must be documented so that progress can be measured and signed off.

In the following section, we will look at the information that would be included in a Test Plan for this phase.

An example QA Test Plan

A Test Plan is likely to have the following content, although the headings might vary:

- **Objective**: The objective of QA Testing is to independently confirm that the solution built delivers the functions specified by the requirement or User Story. It also ensures a consistent level of quality across the solution.

- **Scope**: The scope of QA Testing is to independently verify that the solution performs as specified by the requirement. Each User Story or individual requirement in the project scope will have at least one Test Case written and verified by a tester. Where appropriate, negative Test Cases should be used to confirm unintentional functions have not been introduced.

- **Schedule**: QA Testing will be carried out directly after the build. For Agile projects, QA Testing will be carried out during the sprint that the functionality is built in or the following sprint, depending on the approach. In both cases, developers need to respond to testers' questions and fix defects in the same timeframe that they are working on new stories. Time for defect resolution should be factored into capacity.

  For a phased approach, QA Testing will be carried out in a phase that follows the build phase. Developers must be available to resolve defects so that testing can continue to a conclusion.

  For all approaches, Test Cases can be prepared while the build is taking place.

- **Resources**: Team members in tester roles will carry out QA Testing. Testers must have access to the requirement developer for clarification.

- **Environment**: QA testing will be carried out in a dedicated environment where no changes take place, as this can interrupt and invalidate tests. It is essential that the QA environment is built and ready for testing when QA is scheduled to start.

- **Datasets**: Data used for QA testing will be created by the tester (or a Sandbox seeding solution) in the dedicated QA environment. The data should be representative of real-world data, including picklist options and data combinations that trigger Validation Rules. It should be sufficient to confirm each Test Case.

- **Defect process**: The outcome of a test is captured against the Test Case, and where there are failures, supporting information should also be captured. Failed Test Cases will be prioritized and reviewed with developers to confirm there is a defect. Additional clarification or information will be provided until the developer accepts the defect for rework. Any required rework is carried out within the sprint or phase in which the defect is identified. Test Cases will be retested and reworked until the Test Case is passed or there is an agreed outcome.

- **Artifacts**: As part of QA testing, the following artifacts will be generated:

  - Tests Cases with outcomes recorded

  - Automated Testing Logs if automated regression is carried out

- **Communication**: Testers will communicate testing progress with the development team during stand-ups and status meetings.

- **Sign-off**: The Test Lead or test owner confirms sign-off. For sign-off to occur, all stories must be tested with an agreed outcome.

Execution notes

Agile testers should attend sprint planning, user story refinement, and playback sessions so that they know what is expected from each user story.

It is worth noting that when working in Agile, for developers, the need to switch between building functionality and responding to questions about and resolving defects can be challenging, as both are intensive work that is best suited to limited disruption. The time consumed by this type of switching should be factored into capacity.

Ideally testers will be familiar with Sales Cloud and the expected functionality, so they can work through the user stories and develop Test Cases with minimal additional training. High attention to detail is a beneficial characteristic of testers as well as industry and/or process knowledge, as this increases their productivity.

For small projects, it is common for there to be only one tester. Where there is a team of testers, it is typical that each tester will pick up the next Test Case on the list when they become available.

System integration testing

The purpose of **System Integration Testing (SIT)** is to confirm that an end-to-end solution delivers the functionality specified by the requirement, even when Salesforce is connected to another system – for example, a back-office system that is responsible for generating orders and invoices. SIT is carried out by one or more people who understand the systems and the integrations developed.

It is conducted after QA is completed, as it is important to confirm the functionality performs in a single domain first. In practice, this can happen in a following sprint or in a separate phase that happens once QA is complete. This type of testing takes more planning and coordination, particularly if the other systems are owned or developed by an independent team. In addition to collaborating on the details of Test Cases, coordination is required to set up and connect the appropriate test environments.

Initial Test Cases usually focus on simply confirming that the connection between systems is successful, sometimes referred to as pipe cleaning. At a basic level, the aim is to confirm that the message from one system reaches the other and is correctly formatted. Test Cases should then build in complexity until the full extent of the required functionality is validated. The Test Cases will mirror those performed for QA, but in this environment, the responses do not need to be mocked. Negative testing should also be performed to confirm that you get a handleable (i.e., understandable) error or exception handling.

Ideally, SIT testing would be carried out in a dedicated testing environment; however, if this is not possible, then SIT testing and User Acceptance Testing can be carried out in the same environment but ideally at different times.

In the following section, we will look at the information that would be included in a Test Plan for this phase.

An example SIT plan

A test plan is likely to have the following content, although the headings might vary.

- **Objective**: The objective of SIT is to confirm that the end-to-end solution delivers the functions specified by the requirement or User Story.

- **Scope**: The scope of SIT is to verify that the elements of the solution that cross-system domains perform as specified by the requirement. Each User Story or individual requirement in the project scope that requires actions that cross system domains will have at least one Test Case written and verified by a tester. Where appropriate, negative Test Cases should be used to confirm unintentional functions have not been introduced.

- **Schedule**: SIT will be carried out directly after the build. For Agile projects, SIT will be carried out in the sprint following QA. Developers need to respond to testers' questions and fix defects in the same timeframe that they are working on new stories, or before they have moved on to other projects. Time for defect resolution must be factored into capacity.

  Test Cases can be prepared and agreed upon by representatives from all domains before the SIT phase starts.

- **Resources**: This includes team members with testing experience who have the knowledge and access to all the domains in scope for the Test Cases.

- **Environment**: SIT will be carried out in a dedicated environment where no changes take place, as this can interrupt and invalidate tests. The SIT environment should be built and connected ready for testing when SIT is scheduled to start.

- **Datasets**: Data used for SIT testing will be created by the tester (or a Sandbox seeding solution) in the dedicated SIT environments. The data should be representative of real-world data and be sufficient to confirm each test case, including confirming that restricted options, such as picklist, are respected in all systems.

- **Defect process**: The outcome of tests is captured by the testers against the Test Case. Where there are failures, supporting information should also be captured. Failed Test Cases will be prioritized and reviewed with developers to confirm there is a defect. Additional clarification or information will be provided until the developer accepts the defect for rework. Any required rework is carried out within the sprint or phase in which the defect is identified. Test Cases will be retested and reworked until the Test Case is passed.

- **Artifacts**: As part of system integration testing the following artifacts will be generated:

  - Test Cases with outcomes recorded

- **Communication**: Testers will communicate the testing progress with the development team during stand-ups and status meetings.

- **Sign-off**: The Test Lead or test owner confirms sign-off. For sign-off to occur, all stories must be tested with an agreed outcome.

When Sales Cloud is integrated with other systems, SIT is a very important type of testing to include. If defects make it into production, it will become very complicated and time-consuming to fix them.

User Acceptance Testing

The purpose of **User Acceptance Testing (UAT)** is for system users to confirm that a solution delivers the functions specified by the requirement or User Story, as well as testing non-functional elements such as usability and performance. UAT is carried out by business stakeholders that have been selected to represent their fellow users. This is the first time that stakeholders, who are not members of the implementation team, get hands-on access to the functionality. It is the opportunity for users to supply feedback and confirm that their solution delivers as per their requirements. These users are likely to require a level of training and orientation in the system to be able to carry out the training in a meaningful way. Without any training, the questions and defects that these users will raise are more likely to be about their lack of understanding rather than system defects.

UAT is the last type of functional testing that is performed. It will either be after SIT, if that is conducted, or after QA.

Unlike QA and SIT, which are performed in a very uniform manner by people whose primary role is usually testing, UAT requires business users to dedicate time from their schedules. For this reason, it is essential that senior leaders understand the importance of UAT and enable the selected representatives to dedicate the time required. Failure to fully participate in UAT results in a Sales Cloud solution that users do not fully accept.

UAT should be designed to suit the business users carrying out the testing. It should take into account their availability, their existing understanding of the UAT process, and their prior knowledge of the Sales Cloud solution.

UAT can be conducted in groups, at an individual's own pace, or a combination of the two. There are pros and cons for both approaches, which are summarized as follows:

- **In-person groups**:

  - **Pro**: Dedicated, focused time with limited distractions

  - **Pro**: Creates a sense of togetherness and excitement

- **Pro**: Completed at a given time

- **Con**: Time-intensive for participants

- **Con**: It's harder to schedule time due to time commitment

- **Individually paced**:

  - **Pro**: Less disruptive for the participants

  - **Con**: A delayed response to user's questions and blockers

  - **Con**: Takes longer to complete

  - **Con**: Can be seen as a lower priority

Running UAT in groups is particularly beneficial when business stakeholders are new to Sales Cloud, the new functionality is complex, or the implementation project is run by an external supplier.

In the following section, we will look at the information that would be included in a Test Plan for this phase.

An example UAT plan

A test plan is likely to have the following content, although the headings might vary:

- **Objective**: The objective of UAT is for system users to confirm that the solution built delivers the functions specified by the requirement or User Story. As users are knowledgeable about the business processes and the current system, as they perform tests, they will also assess the solution for usability and performance.

- **Scope**: The scope of UAT is to verify that the solution performs as functions, as specified by the requirement, and also that non-functional elements such as usability and performance are delivered. Where appropriate, negative Test Cases should be used to confirm unintentional functions have not been introduced, and exploratory testing can be used to challenge the solution.

- **Schedule**: UAT will be carried out as the last phase of testing, either after SIT, if that is being conducted, or after QA. For both Agile and projects with phases, UAT will be carried out as a separate phase, as it needs to accommodate business stakeholder schedules. Developers need to respond to testers' questions and fix defects during this timeframe, even when they are working on new stories or have moved on to other projects. Time for defect triage and resolution must be factored into capacity.

  Test Cases should be prepared and a schedule of what will be tested and when before the UAT phase starts.

- **Resources**: Business stakeholders that have been selected as representatives from all stakeholder groups. A mix of representatives should be considered, including experienced process users, plus new process users for a different perspective and insight into the ease of adoption. Availability should be confirmed in good time before the testing phase starts.

- **Environment**: UAT will be carried out in a dedicated environment where no changes take place, as this can interrupt and invalidate tests. However, if this is not possible, then UAT and SIT can be carried out in the same environment, but this must be at different times. It is essential that the UAT environment is built and ready for testing when UAT is scheduled to start. When the environment holds replicated production data, the environment must be secured to the same level as production environments.

- **Datasets**: Data used for UAT will be a copy of or representative of current production. Whenever possible, a copy of production data should be used, although personal data should be obfuscated. If available, a Sandbox seeding solution should be used. The data should be representative of real-world data and be sufficient to confirm each test case. Users should be encouraged to test the full range of data combinations.

- **Defect process**: The outcome of tests is captured by the testers against the Test Case. Where there are failures, supporting information should also be captured. Failed Test Cases will be triaged to confirm whether there is a defect, as per design or a change. All confirmed defects will be prioritized and communicated to developers. Additional clarification or information will be provided until the developer understands the defect and the rework required. Any required rework is carried out within the phase. Test Cases will be retested and reworked until the Test Case is passed.

- **Artifacts**: As part of SIT, the following artifacts will be generated:

  - Tests Cases with outcomes recorded

  - Artifacts communicating the value of the project, the role, the importance, and the process of UAT

  - Sales Cloud training or orientation artifacts

  - A schedule for UAT that documents what stakeholders are testing when

- **Communication**: The Test Lead will communicate testing progress to the development team during stand-ups and status meetings. The status will also be communicated to all involved business stakeholders, including any User Stories that are ready for retesting.

- **Sign-off**: The Test Lead or test owner works with the business stakeholder representative to confirm sign-off. For sign-off to occur, all stories must be tested with an agreed outcome.

In the following section, consider how you create detailed test cases from your User Stories.

Translating Users' Stories into Test Cases

A fundamental part of any structured testing is Test Cases, also referred to as Test Scripts. In *Chapter 2 – Defining the Approach* we learned about how a Test Strategy, Test Plan(s), and Test Cases provide the framework and structure of how testing is approached and delivered. In this section, we are going to explore in more detail how User Stories are translated into Test Cases.

The following diagram shows how Users' Stories, Acceptance Criteria, and Test Cases relate to each other.

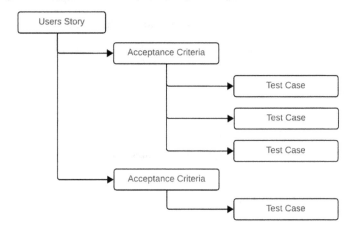

Figure 8.2 – The relationship between the User Story, Acceptance Criteria, and Test Cases

The diagram illustrates that a User Story can have multiple Acceptance Criteria and that Acceptance Criteria can have multiple Test Cases. When preparing Test Cases, there must be at least one Test Case for each Acceptance Criteria.

Test Cases require the following:

- A Test Case reference
- The requirement or User Story
- Acceptance Criteria
- Test Scenario
- Test Steps
- Actual Result
- Pass/ Fail
- Notes

- Status (Open, In Triage, In Fix, Ready to Retest, Change, As Designed)
- Assigned Tester

Testers may use their discretion to create a test case for an anticipated scenario even if it has not been explicitly documented in the Acceptance Criteria. For example, if the requirement is for something to be "enabled" or "set to true," the test is to confirm that it can be "disabled" to "set to false."

Within Agile, it is quick and easy for a tester to confirm whether an anticipated scenario is valid.

Ideally, Test Cases will be written and signed off before the test phase begins.

In the next section, you will explore other types of testing that may be appropriate for your use case.

Other testing

Some types of testing are only appropriate in certain situations; an example of this is Performance Testing. This is only relevant when there is a significant increase in the scale of the solution – for example, in Users or data volumes. We will explore Performance Testing, as there is a specific approach to this on the Salesforce Customer 360 Platform.

Performance Testing

The purpose of Performance Testing is to confirm that a system performs in a useable manner as it scales in terms of the number of Users, data volumes, or requests per second. It should be considered when there is a significant increase in these factors.

At this scale, you are likely to have a technical team and possibly a Salesforce Architect overseeing the design of your solution, who will advise and guide you through this type of testing. Performance Testing has a number of considerations, depending on the complexity of your functionality, the integrations you have, and the tools that have been used to implement it. To test fully, it is recommended that you have an identical configuration to the way you use your Production Org, in terms of the browser, network settings, geographical location, and hardware.

As this is both a broad and deep topic, we will only touch on it at a very high level in this this book. Salesforce also provides detailed information on how to do this. It provides a guided path on how to understand, approach, and execute Performance Testing on the Salesforce Customer 360 platform, called Performance Assistant. The Performance Assistant is found in Setup > Performance > Performance Testing > Performance Assistant.

The following are some of the higher-level considerations for you to be aware of as you approach this testing:

- **Environment**: Performance Testing is not permitted in Production Orgs, as it is a multitenant platform. Therefore, it must be carried out in a Full Copy Sandbox, which is available at an additional cost.

- **Measurement**: Salesforces use a measure called **Experience Page Time** (**EPT**), as mentioned on the Salesforce **Help** page: "*Experienced Page Time (EPT) is a performance metric Salesforce uses in Lightning to measure page load time. EPT measures how long it takes for a page to load into a state that a user can meaningfully interact with.*" You can see the EPT for a Lightning page load by appending `?eptVisible=1` to the page URL (`https://help.salesforce.com/s/articleView?id=sf.technical_requirements_ept.htm&type=5`).

- **Test Plan**: As with all testing types, this requires a Test Plan. Salesforce provides instructions on what is required in the Test Plan in Performance Assistant. Performance Tests must be submitted for approval two weeks in advance of the preferred testing date. This is done by submitting a Support Case. All Performance Tests must be approved.

- **Platform limits**: Platform limits (i.e., governor limits) exist to ensure fair usage of resources on the Salesforce multitenant platform. You should familiarize yourself with your Salesforce Developer limits. Exceeding these limits may mean that a throttle is applied to your system.

- **Resources**: You will need to collect and interpret results, as Salesforce doesn't do this for you. The person who does this will need technical knowledge of the platform or be willing to review this topic thoroughly. If you don't have or are not sure you have the expertise in-house to plan, execute, and interpret this type of testing, you should consider engaging an external supplier.

Therefore, we can say that there are many things to consider when approaching Performance Testing; the Lightning architecture requires some additional considerations, including metrics. There is a specific way of carrying out Performance Testing on the Salesforce Customer 360 platform that requires you to use the Performance Assistant. Salesforce Help provides detailed information about how to approach and execute Performance Testing; you can find this information by searching for Technical Requirements and Performance Best Practices on the Help page. Links have been provided in the Further information section.

Summary

In this chapter, we learned about the considerations and best practices when delivering testing in practice. We reviewed all the commonly used functional testing types used in Sales Cloud solution implementations, including capturing the information typically included in a Test Plan for each phase. Finally, we learned how Test Cases are generated from User Stories.

In the next chapter, we will build on the Change Management and training planning we explored in *Chapter 2 – Defining the Approach* and learn how to execute training in practice.

Further reading

- *Shift Left Testing*: https://en.wikipedia.org/wiki/Shift-left_testing
- *Sandbox Seeding*: https://trailhead.salesforce.com/content/learn/modules/sandbox-seeding-with-ownbackup/brush-up-on-sandbox-seeding-basics
- *Introduction to Performance Testing*: https://developer.salesforce.com/blogs/2020/09/introduction-to-performance-testing
- *Performance Testing on the Lightning Platform*: https://developer.salesforce.com/blogs/2020/09/performance-testing-on-the-lightning-platform
- *What is EPT?*: https://help.salesforce.com/s/articleView?id=sf.technical_requirements_ept.htm&type=5

Executing Training

Enabling your stakeholders with the skills and knowledge they need to get the most from Sales Cloud is an essential component for success. A high level of adoption is always the goal.

In *Chapter 2, Defining the Approach*, we learned about the pillars of organizational change management and how training is a component of that. We learned about the types of testing that are commonly used in Salesforce projects, along with the importance of developing a Training Plan and the different types of training that you might choose to include in it.

This chapter gives you the information you need to create a Training Plan for your implementation and the practical considerations for creating and delivering the training. We start by exploring some of the practical considerations when planning and executing your training.

We're going to cover the following main topics in this chapter:

- Training in practice
- Developing your Training Plan
- Creating training materials
- Delivering training

Supporting tools and information

To execute training, you will require access to the Salesforce environment designated for creating and delivering training. This will be defined by your environment strategy. Depending on the training materials you are creating you may need a word processing tool, a tool to create screenshots, and a tool to capture, edit, and caption voiceover videos. If training is being delivered virtually you will require an online meeting tool such as Zoom or Google Meet. If you are using Trailhead as part of your training mix you will need to register for a free Trailhead account.

Your organization might have a Learning Management Tool or e-learning tool that you are planning to use as part of your training. If so, you will need access to these tools to create content.

Training in practice

The mix of training that is planned and executed for each implementation depends on a number of factors, including the complexity of the solution, the organization's Salesforce maturity, and the time, budget, and skills available. As with a software solution design, there is no single perfect way to deliver training. You are looking to take the best approach based on your solution, the audience you are training, and the time, skills, and resources available.

There are some common principles and best practices to keep in mind throughout the process of planning and delivering your training program:

- **Involve content creators early** – The people creating the materials should be involved as early as possible. This allows the materials to be created in parallel with other implementation activities and keeps timelines tight, as training can be completed shortly after system changes have been completed.

- **Creating quality materials takes time** – Often the simplest-looking and well-structured materials take the longest to create. Creating concise, targeted materials requires a deep understanding of trainees' requirements. The time required to document every step in a process can be deceptively long, particularly if screenshots with representative data are included for most steps. The same can be said of video recording and editing.

- **Training should be scheduled around sales milestones** – It is important to understand the key dates your training audience has and avoid these in your training schedule. Sales teams will be completely focused on customers at month-, quarter-, and year-end, depending on how they are targeted. You will not have their attention or attendance at these times. Also, avoid scheduling training before seasonal or religious holidays if attendees will not be able to use the live system before the holiday.

- **Process steps are as important as system steps** – It can be tempting to only include instructions on Sales Cloud in the training. However, attendees will have questions about the business processes the system enables. A good approach can be to frame any instructions in the context of the business process by naming and giving an overview of it. If the person delivering the training is not an expert on the processes, it is also good to have a plan on how to answer questions on them. This can be done by having a business leader in the session or by capturing the questions and committing to getting them answered within a certain time frame.

- **Executive buy-in is essential** – It is important that your company executives support the training efforts. System users will need to take time out of their day-to-day jobs to attend training and it is essential that the managers support them in this. They will also be looking to understand how important it is for them to adopt this new system. Executives illustrate the importance by attending training themselves or introducing sessions and reiterating their importance.

- **Training affects Adoption** – The quality, mix, and timeliness of training will impact adoption. It is likely that time will have to be invested to understand the specific requirements and accordingly customize Sales Cloud. That time may end up being wasted if stakeholders don't know how to use it. Good training avoids this.

- **Train the trainer is a common approach** – Designing and developing a system and designing and developing training separate skills are likely to be carried out by separate people. It is common for the build team, particularly if it is external, to train training creators to then create the plan and content for end users. This makes the best use of people's skills, and if the development is being carried out by an external provider, it keeps costs down.

In the next section, we will explore how to build out a Training Plan for your Sales Cloud Implementation.

Developing your Training Plan

In *Chapter 2*, *Preparing for Success*, we learned about the role of a Training Plan and what it would typically include. In this session, we are going to explore how to create a plan for your specific user case. Your organization may have a process or template they use for planning training. If so, you should consider adopting those. If not, you can use the planning approach covered here.

As we learned in *Chapter 2*, although the format of Training Plans may vary, they contain a core set of information that describes what they aim to achieve and how they are going to achieve it. The initial steps to create a plan are as follows:

1. Define and agree on the objectives.
2. Gather information to confirm training needs.
3. Design the training program.
4. Identify resources.
5. Create the materials.
6. Communicate the plan.
7. Prepare to deliver.
8. Monitor progress.

To develop your plan, you will need to gather information. The following are examples of the sort of questions you will want to ask, grouped by the area in the Training Plan they influence:

- **Scope**

  - Are you replacing an existing system with Sales Cloud or updating it? Is this a transformational or incremental change?

  - What processes are in scope for the training?

- **Objectives**
- **Learning outcome**
  - What functional tasks should trainees be able to complete?
- **Audience**
  - Are the system's users office- or field-based?
  - If they are field-based, is there a budget to get everyone together for training?
  - What teams or roles will require training?
  - How much time can users dedicate to training?
  - Where are users located?
- **Types and methods**
  - What methods and types of training does your organization already use?
  - What content will people want to revisit?
  - What needs to be continually reinforced?
- **Curriculum and materials**
  - Are there any topics or concepts that users might find difficult to understand? What topics will need detailed explanations?
  - What do you anticipate will be the most commonly asked questions?
- **Timeline**
  - When are the busiest sales periods?
  - How much time do you have to prepare materials?
  - Are there any public holidays scheduled around the release time?
- **Resources**
  - What content creation skills are available?
- **Content creation**
  - What tools are available?

- **Measures**

  - How have other training programs been measured in your organization?

- **Deliverables**

If this information is not known within the development team, you can ask your audience what types and methods of training they find most useful.

Figure 9.1 is an example of the content you might find in a Training Plan for an initial implementation of Sales Cloud. A full plan would include all the details of a plan and document everything in scope. Depending on the scale of your training program, you might not include all of these sections as there might be repetition.

Example Training Plan

Scope

The Training Plan outlined in this document is to support the rollout of the Salesforce Sales Cloud to all members of the commercial team. The initial implementation of Sales Cloud will support the following processes:

- Lead Management from website collection to Sales Ready Lead
- Opportunity Management from Sales Ready Lead to Close
- Sales Forecasting

Objectives

This Training Program has the following Objectives:

- For all Sales Cloud Users to have completed at least one form of training within one week of system go-live.
- For all Sales Cloud Users to consider themselves able to complete the tasks expected of them within one month of go-live. Confirmation via User surveys – post-training.

Learning outcomes

- This program has the following high-level learning outcomes. Further detailed outcomes are expected to be developed once there is a detailed understanding of the functionality being delivered. The following knowledge and skills will be learned.
- Training Participants will be able to:
- Progress a Lead from the point of collection on the website to Sales Ready when it is handed over to an Account Executive.
- Explain how Leads, Contacts, Accounts and Opportunities related to each other.

- Understand the information required and process for qualifying a Lead.

- Explain the information required and when to Convert a Lead.

- Understand when it is appropriate to create an Opportunity.

- Create an Opportunity in Sales Cloud either via Lead Conversion or as a new record.

- Identify and merge duplicate Leads.

Audience

The training audience will be:

- Marketing Team Sales Cloud Users

- Sales Team Sales Cloud Users

Types and methods

A blended training approach will be used to take into account different people's learning styles.

It will include the following types and methods:

- Instructor-led Training course so that Users can learn in a group and offer each other peer support. All Users will be asked to attend in person, but a virtual option will be provided for those who are not able.

- Bite-Size training videos will be created with a duration of between 2-5 minutes. These will be signposted and available after the instructor-led training. They will be available on demand so that Users can recap how to complete the most common tasks in Sales Cloud.

- A Frequently Asked Questions (FAQs) document will be created and available for Users to view on-demand from the internal knowledge management system.

- A dedicated Sales Cloud Channel will be created in the internal collaboration platform where Users can ask questions or request support. If an internal collaboration platform is not used, a Chatter channel will be created.

- A series of drop-in 'Office Hours' sessions will be scheduled after the Sales Cloud go-live for Users to be able to drop in and ask any questions or get support with any issues.

Curriculum & materials

Instructor-led training: Three training sessions will be delivered 1-2 weeks before go-live on the following topics:

- Managing Leads from web collection to Sales Ready

- Managing sales Opportunities from Sales Read Lead to Closure

- Sales Forecasting in Sales Cloud

A set of hands-on exercises is expected for each instructor-led session. It is expected that instructor-led training will have a duration of 2-4 hours.

Bite-size training: A minimum of 10 bite-size video shorts will be created that demonstrate the key concepts and tasks that Users need to understand. It is expected that videos will have a duration of 2-5 minutes.

The content creator has the discretion to define the video content depending on the solution playbacks and the required Learning Outcomes.

- A set of FAQs will be created based on the questions asked during the solution playback sessions and instructor-led training, also informed by questions asked in the collaboration channel.

Timeline

The training program will run for 2 weeks prior to go-live and continue for an additional 2 months after go-live.

Content creation will begin during the build phase, starting from the first build solution playback. The content creator will be expected to attend all build solution playbacks to understand the content that needs to be taught. They will design the individual materials based on playback content. Preparation of the training slide decks can start once the course agenda has been confirmed. Creation of hands-on exercises and video content can start as soon as a stable environment is available to perform the tasks in.

Resources

A member of the organization's training team will create the training materials and deliver the instructor-led training. They will need to be available to participate in solution playback sessions to understand the functionality that is being released. The person will have the following skills:

- Creation of instruction-led training slide decks and hands-on exercises
- Creation of bite-size training videos
- Design and execution of User Training Surveys

The project sponsor will attend the start of each instructor-led training course and introduce the training, including describing the benefits of Sales Cloud to the trainee audience.

A Sales Manager will help facilitate each of the training sessions and answer any questions about the sales process.

Content creation

3 x instructor-led training courses

- 10 short bite-sized videos of approximately 2-5 minutes each on the most common lead and sales management actions.

An FAQ document

The content creator has the discretion on the final content depending on areas that get the most feedback during solution playbacks.

Measures – KPIs

- The following KPIs will be used to measure the success of the training:
- Total number of Users trained within one week of go-live
- Total number of Users trained within one month of go-live

Deliverables

- 3 x Instructor-led Training courses each with a Training Presentation Deck, hands-on exercises, and instructor notes
- 10 short bite-sized videos of approximately 2-5 minutes each on the most common lead and sales management actions
- The text for an FAQ document
- A Sales Cloud channel on the internal collaboration platform
- A schedule of Office Hour sessions with at least one nominated super *user to answer questions*

Figure 9.1 – An example Training Plan for a Sales Cloud Implementation

As you can see from the example Training Plan, they can contain a reasonable level of detail. The detail and length will vary depending on the use case.

The types and methods of training that you will commonly find on Sales Cloud Implementations are as follows:

- Instructor-led Training that covers all the key functions
- A guide describing the steps for completing important or common actions such as creating and managing an Opportunity
- An FAQ document or internal web page
- A chat channel to ask questions – this could be Slack or Chatter
- Video demos of key actions
- Post go-live drop-in session where users can ask questions, sometimes referred to as Office Hours

For more inspiration on the different types and methods of training, please see *Chapter 2 – Preparing for Success*.

Next, we will look at some of the considerations for creating training materials.

Creating training materials

Creating well-structured, concise, high-quality training materials is a skill in itself. It is easy to leave the creation of training materials until the very end and underestimate the time it requires. Tasks such as creating screenshots and editing errors out of video recordings can take a deceptively long time.

The following are some tips on creating content:

- Content creators need a good understanding of the functionality; along with access to developers to ask for clarification on the functionality.

- Content creators need an environment with representative data to take screenshots or record videos.

- Screenshots and training should not display any sensitive data, particularly customer names and contact details such as emails or phone numbers.

- People learn when they are enjoying themselves and having fun; so including icebreakers and quizzes helps to reinforce learning.

- It is more time-consuming to edit video content than rehearse and record it with the right steps and pauses.

The time it takes to create good-quality training materials is often underestimated but following the previous tips helps keep the time required to a minimum.

Delivering training

There are a number of things to consider when delivering training. The considerations differ depending on the method of delivery. We will consider these in turn, starting with **instructor-led training**.

Instructor-led

When delivering instructor-led training, you need to consider the following:

- **Breaks**: It is important to have regular breaks. It will help keep attendees focused if they know in advance when the breaks are as they will know when they can make calls and check emails.

- **Ground rules**: Sharing ground rules for the training at the start lets everyone know what is expected of them. This might include attendees shutting down email or silencing devices.

- **No or silent devices**: This will be influenced by your organizational culture, but you may consider asking attendees to hand over their phones at the beginning of the session. At a minimum, you will want to ask people to put their phones on silent.

- **Parking lot**: Explain the concept of a parking lot where questions that can't be answered or are not appropriate for the session are captured and followed up after the session.

Let's now look at the additional considerations for in-person and virtual delivery.

In-person delivery

In addition to the Instructor-led points, you should also consider the following when the training is delivered in person:

- **Check the room setup**: Check the configuration and temperature of the room to make sure attendees can see the instructor and screens and that they will be comfortable during the session.

- **Consider bringing snacks**: Having some snacks available can make sure no one is preoccupied because they are hungry. It also keeps energy levels up in the room.

Virtual delivery

In addition to the Instructor-led points, you will also want to consider the following when the training is delivered virtually:

- **Recommend two screens**: If people are attending online, it is beneficial for them to have two screens as this gives them a better view, allowing them to follow the course materials, the online meeting controls, and the instructor's video at the same time.

- **Attend from a quiet space**: It is important that the instructor and attendees join the session from a quiet space where they will not be interrupted. Maintaining concentration for online training can be hard for prolonged periods. It is important to not introduce any further distractions.

We will next briefly look at the considerations for self-paced training.

Self-paced

Self-paced training is training that people take individually, at times that are convenient for them. This could be while in the office or when they are traveling; for example, at an airport. You may want to consider the following for this kind of training:

- **Caption videos**: Caption any video content so that it can be watched without sound

- **Bite-sized:x`** Divide on-demand training into short digestible chunks so that each module can easily be completed during downtime and will not be intimidating.

Well-planned and executed bite-sized videos can be a great addition to a suite of training materials that Users really value.

Summary

In this chapter, we learned about the considerations and best practices when planning and delivering training. We explored some of the common considerations when approaching the development of a training program before considering the types of questions to ask to gather information to create a detailed plan. Finally, we looked at creating training material and delivering training. With this information, you will be able to create and deliver an effective training plan for your Sales Cloud implementation.

In the next chapter, you will learn how to plan the deployment of your Sales Cloud Implementation.

Further reading

Salesforce training:

- *Trailhead: User Training and Enablement*

  `https://trailhead.salesforce.com/content/learn/modules/user-training-and-motivation`

10

Deployment Planning

In this chapter, we will learn about **release planning**, also known as **deployment planning**. The term **release planning** can also be used to refer to the planning of the whole release cycle but, in the context of this book, we are referring to the planning and execution of moving the new configuration into the production environment and how and when to make it live for users. We will also review the importance of the post go-live period, as this transition period is when users form their opinions about the system.

We're going to cover the following main topics in this chapter:

- Deciding how and when to deploy
- Creating a deployment plan
- Going live
- Post go-live support

Supporting tools and information

A release or deployment plan is a business process that has a technical deployment component. The business process component can be captured by standard business tools. Use the tools available to you; no special tools are needed for this purpose. A deployment checklist is most typically captured on a spreadsheet.

The deployment itself will use technical tools, the same tools that were used to deploy the functionality between test environments. The people carrying out the deployment will need skill and access to these tools. They will also need System Administrator access to the Production environment. This may have been restricted until this point.

Deciding how and when to deploy

How and when to roll out your new implementation, or update your implementation, depends on the scale of the change. The obvious answer is as soon as testing and pre-go-live training is complete. This may be the case if your new implementation or updates impact a single set of stakeholders, for example, a single sales division. If your implementation impacts a large number of users or involves multiple teams or locations, you might want to consider rolling out access in phases. The benefit of enabling the functionality or access for a small number of users first is that any issues can be identified and resolved with a limited impact on users. Once in a live environment, any issues that were either not identified in testing or are the result of the deployment can have an impact on live data, which will need to be corrected. This is easier to do if it impacts a limited dataset.

If you are considering a phased approach, the first point to determine is if your changes can be rolled out in phases. Can the functionality that is used by one team be decoupled from that of another, or does it break the process or have a negative impact on the customer experience? You are looking to identify ways you can divide users into groups that can use the functionality independently of each other. This might be by team, territory, or geographical location. It will also depend on whether you are integrating with other systems and if that functionality can be limited to regions or teams.

A phased approach will also have an impact on data migration. The data relevant to each team or region will have to be loaded just before they are about to use the system. This will need to be carefully planned to ensure that enough time is scheduled to load the full set of data or the change in the data (the delta). We explored how to plan your initial data load in *Chapter 6, Bringing Data into Sales Cloud*. In this chapter, we talk about rehearsing data loads to get an accurate estimation of their duration.

While a phased approach has many benefits, it also means that you will have some live users while you are deploying new functionality or updating data. The complexity of your deployment will be significantly impacted by whether you are deploying your functionality in a new Production Org, a greenfield implementation, or a production environment that already has live users. If it is a greenfield implementation, then all the functionality and system changes can be made prior to any users having access. Then bringing users onto the platform, either all at once or in phases, only involves activating the users and bringing in the latest data.

If you are deploying new functionality to an existing Production Org with live users, then there is additional complexity. In this case, you have to consider the impact of the deployment on existing users, as well as any new users, if there are any. The impact can be minimized if the deployment takes place out of working hours. However, this has additional considerations:

- **Additional costs**: Those working on the deployment may need to be paid overtime.

- **Commercial support unavailable**: Out-of-hours support teams for commercial tools might be unavailable. Examples include support for your dev ops tools and any platforms you are integrating with. If you are using tools that you might need support with, check the support level you have in advance in case you need to change it.

- **Key resources unavailable**: Key business sources are also not readily available; however, with agreement, they can be used for escalation. This might be in a situation where there is a problem and agreement is required on whether to increase the time users are out of the system or abort the deployment.

Where integrations are involved, you will also want to consider whether you conduct them in phases.

For the most complex types of deployment, where you are adding new functionality and users to an existing Production Org that already has live users, you will want to work through the following:

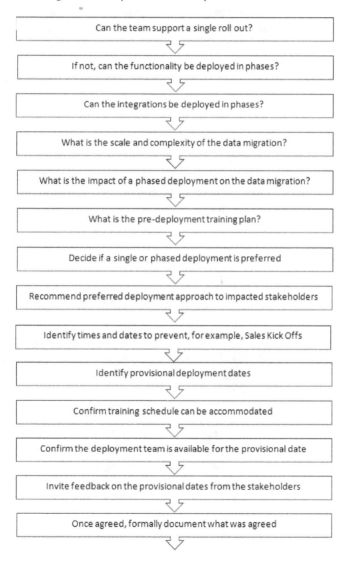

Figure 10.1 – Flow for determining your deployment date

The figure shows an example of the questions to ask to gather the information you need to determine the best way and time to deploy. It also shows the checks and agreements it is important to do and to get. Your implementation may have some additional considerations, but following the outline list should catch all of the major considerations.

Creating a deployment plan

It is very important that your deployment goes smoothly because delays and issues in this final step can overshadow all the great work that has been done up to this point. This is particularly important if the time you have to deploy is limited, that is, out of office working hours. The best way to achieve this is to have a detailed plan that everyone involved agrees with. This means that the deployment window is simply about executing tasks, not about working out what the tasks are. You will also want to agree what happens if something doesn't go according to plan. This includes who gets notified, what additional expertise might be brought in, and what happens if the problem can't be resolved during the deployment window.

As with all the plans we've created during the implementation, the deployment plan includes what you're trying to achieve, how you're going to approach it, who's going to be involved, the schedule, any artifacts that will be created, and any communication that will happen. In addition, this plan will include what happens if anything doesn't go to plan and the lines of escalation. With the deployment, it is typical that one person is responsible for overseeing it and all those involved regularly update that person.

You would expect to see the following in the deployment or release plan:

- **Objectives**: A typical objective might be: To successfully deploy and onboard Users of the Q4 2023 Sales Cloud update with minimal disruption to existing Users.

- **Approach**: This documents the approach that we talked through defining in the previous section when deciding how and when to deploy. It should include the approach agreed and the reasoning. It should include details of any phases, including the order that groups of users will be brought onto Sales Cloud. It should also include the details of any integration deployments, data migration, and the timing of training.

- **Dependencies**: A deployment is a series of activities that are dependent on each other. This is one of the reasons why it can be complex. In the dependencies section, you want to capture all the elements that need to be in place in order for you to go ahead with the deployment. Examples include the availability of the web team or other integrated systems to escalate issues or no other known active Sales Cloud issues.

- **Schedule**: This is the schedule of the deployment, ideally in the form of a diagram, such as a Gantt chart. This should include all the activities that need to happen in advance of the deployment date and all the on-the-day activities. For the on-the-day activities, it should not include every single step but blocks of time for the key components, for example, kick off, pre-deployment, deployment, and data migration.

- **Deployment method**: This should capture the method and tools used for the deployment, for example, Change Sets, DevOps tools, Deployment Scripts, or a combination of them all.

- **Resources**: The resources typically involved in a deployment include a Deployment Lead, who is the person responsible for overseeing and delivering the deployment. One or more members of the development team are responsible for executing the deployment. A nominated business representative is for escalations and business-impacting decisions. One or more team members carry out the data migration. Where integrations are involved, one or more team members carry out their deployment steps.

- **Artifacts**: The artifacts typical for deployment are a deployment checklist, a list of names and contact details of everyone involved in the deployment, and names and contact details of people to escalate to.

- **Communication**: There are typically two types of communication: communication with the deployment team, and communication with the wider business. A plan for both of these types of communication can be defined in advance. We explore this in more detail in a future section called *Deployment communication plan*. Communications with the wider business are typically sent out by the person responsible for the deployment.

The exact structure of this document may vary from organization to organization, but they should always have this type of content. In the next section, we will look at the deployment checklist artifact in more detail and explore what it should include.

Deployment checklist

A common practice to ensure that a deployment is effective is to have a checklist that is defined in advance. With the deployment, the aim is to automate as much as possible. However, it is rarely possible to automate everything. This means there will be manual steps. There are usually manual steps before and after any deployment automation. These are called pre-deployment and post-deployment steps. An example of these steps is freezing and unfreezing users' access to sales cloud. This means the checklist is usually broken down into three parts: pre-deployment steps, deployment, and post-deployment steps. There are some pre-deployment steps that can be carried out before deployment day and some that can only be carried out on the day. The checklist should also include the person responsible for the step and its status, so the status can be updated as the activity is performed.

The following are examples of the types of steps that you would expect to see in a deployment checklist. They are divided into the deployment stage and when they should happen:

Pre-deployment: Pre-deployment Day

Typically, manual steps…

- Create any deployment packages. For example, if you are using change sets to deploy configuration you should create them in advance, upload them to production, and validate them to confirm there are no errors.
- Check the audit trail in the Production Org to identify any changes since the creation of the development sandboxes.
- Confirm all the manual settings changes that will be required on the day and update the On the day checklist.
- Take a backup copy of the existing metadata.
- Make the go/no-go decision on the deployment.

Pre-deployment: On the day

Manual steps:

1. Communicate that deployment has begun.
2. Freeze all user access.
3. Take a data backup of affected objects to be in a position to roll back.
4. Disable email deliverability.
5. Defer sharing rules if you're loading large volumes of data.
6. Install any required managed packages.

Deployment checklist: On the day

Typically, starting an automation…

1. Start automated deployment.
2. Confirm automated deployment has been completed successfully.

Post-deployment: On the day

Typically, manual steps.

1. Make any destructed changes that could not be applied by the automated deployment, such as deactivating validation rules or flows.
2. Apply appropriate permission set licenses and permission sets to users.

3. Confirm any data migration can begin.

4. Enable email deliverability.

5. Unfreeze users.

6. Communicate that the deployment is complete.

This example deployment checklist has many of the steps you would expect to have in a Sales Cloud deployment. However, each deployment is different, and the checklist must be specific to your build. It is likely you will have additions for your deployment.

It is worth noting that the number of steps in the deployment plan is an indicator of how long users will need to be out of the system. However, the length of these steps does depend on your specific customization.

Deployment communication plan

Communication is an essential part of a deployment. This includes communication with those who are involved in the deployment activities and the users who will be using Sales Cloud as it will change their working practices.

For communication with the development team, the following are key communication milestones:

Communication	Content
Kick off	Letting stakeholders know activities relating to deployment have begun.
Deployment Started	Technical deployment activities have begun.
Deployment Complete	Technical deployment activities are complete.
Smoke (Sanity) Testing Started	Nominated users check the system functionality.
Smoke (Sanity) Testing Complete	Post-deployment functionality tests are complete.
Data Migration/Transformation Started	Data migration activities have begun.
Data Migration/Transformation Complete	Data migration activities are complete.

Table 10.1 – List of communications for the deployment team

For communication with existing or future users, the following are key communication milestones:

Communication	Content
Users' Access Disabled	Informing users their access has been temporarily removed.
Deployment Started	Technical deployment activities have begun.
Deployment and Data Migration Complete	Technical deployment and data migration activities are complete.
User Access Re-enabled	Users can log back in.

Table 10.2 – List of communications for business stakeholders

In addition to this minimum level of communication, you might also expect that a communication is sent out if there are any delays experienced. The content of the communications can be written in advance with options to add additional information. This can reduce delays in sending them. As described in the previous section, creating a deployment plan and communications with the wider business are usually sent by one person, the deployment lead.

In the next section, we will look at what happens during the go-live.

Going live

In this section, we look at what happens during the actual go-live and the considerations. The aim is to carry out all the detailed planning and get agreement from all involved in advance, as we have discussed. This means that the go-live is just about executing a plan.

The following are some additional practical points that you may want to consider to ensure your deployment goes well:

- **Shared artifacts**: It is essential that all members of the deployment team have access to the deployment checklist and other artifacts, so they are clear on the actions. Ideally, the deployment checklist will be a shared file that team members can update in real time.

- **Location**: It is beneficial if you can get everyone involved in the deployment in the same room. This ensures that communication is as efficient as possible. It also creates a sense of team.

- **Remove distractions**: If the deployment is happening during the day, it is essential that all of those involved are 100% focused on the deployment. The deployment team should be instructed to excuse themselves from any meetings and turn off any distractions.

- **Provide substance**: Ideally, food and drink will be supplied for the deployment team, particularly if this is out of hours, so they can stay solely focused on the deployment.

- **Introduce the team**: A group of people works better together if they know each other. Where possible, arrange a meeting in advance of the go-live for team members to introduce themselves and understand everyone's role in the deployment.

These are some simple practical steps that can be taken to help a go-live go smoothly.

Another area where you want to have a clear approach is what happens when things don't go to plan. In this case, you should have clear routes of escalation. On the day, the Deployment Lead should be made aware of any issues immediately. They can then decide if an escalation is required. It is likely that the team will be encouraged to work together to find a resolution to any issue; however, this will not always be possible.

After the deployment is complete and users are activated, the final step is to congratulate and thank the deployment team for their work. At all stages of an implementation, it is important to celebrate the successes.

In the next section, we will look at the benefits and considerations of post-go-live support.

Post-go-live support

It is tempting to think that once the deployment is complete and the system is live, that is the end of the work. However, the post-go-live period is critical. Users are forming their opinions about the system that will have a lasting impact. It is recommended that you plan how the system will be supported directly after go-live rather than working out a course of action once you get there.

> **Note**
>
> The aim is always that that there will be no issues post-go-live but, in reality, issues do occur for a number of reasons. Users use the system in a way that wasn't tested, data anomalies occur that cause errors, and things get missed in the deployment and data migration.

There are a couple of elements that you will want to have in place. You will need a communicated method of capturing, triaging, and resolving system defects. This includes agreement about the environment defects will be resolved in and the frequency with which they will be deployed. These are often referred to as hot-fixes. It is important that this fix process is separate from any ongoing development process that is happening for future iterations because speed is often important for issues identified immediately after go-live. It is important for users of a new system to see that the issues they raise are acknowledged and investigated, and that a proposed plan of action is decided.

This phase, typically up to a month after go-live, is a mini version of the testing and defect resolution phase that happens in testing. It often needs to happen in an accelerated timeframe as the issues identified are blocking or limiting users' ability to do their jobs. Support during this time is sometimes referred to as hyper-care.

In practice

In practice, much of what was put in place for the previous testing phase can be applied here. Next is a summary of what should be considered and an example of what happens in practice:

- **Timescale**: For one month post-go-live.

- **Reporting channel**: A chat, email, or phone channel that users can use to report any issues.

- **Reporting method**: Users are asked to provide screenshots of the issue they experience, links to the records, and a description of the steps they took to produce the issue. They are also asked not to delete the records so they can be used to investigate the issue.

- **Resource**: A person to monitor reported issues and at least one representative of the development team and the business to be able to triage and classify the issue. A member of the development team should be there to fix any issues that are confirmed as urgent defects.

- **Issue management**: Once an issue is reported, it needs to be documented in a consistent way that is accessible to those who are delivering hyper-care. This might be in a spreadsheet or the defect management system that was used during testing. It then needs to be triaged and classified by someone from the business, and someone from the development team. The first level of classification determines whether further action is required and is typically as follows: defect, as designed, not repeatable, and future development.

  Those that are classified as defects need to be prioritized and sized, and their progress also needs to be tracked. The status for these issues might be something like this: to fix, in progress, ready for retest, and complete. The statuses you use should be consistent with the status you used in your testing phase. Once an issue has been identified for fixing, it should be allocated to a member of the development team. It is beneficial if this is the same person who built the functionality, but this is not always possible, in which case it should be someone with comparable skills. The aim of this phase is to get the defects fixed as quickly as possible. The developer may need to contact the reporter directly for more information or ask them to test that the issue is resolved.

- **Communication**: You should communicate with each issue reporter the status of their issue. As a bare minimum, you can notify them once the system becomes accessible for verifying resolution. It is also beneficial to widely communicate when fixes have been made because news of problems spreads and others may have seen an issue but not taken the time to report it.

By planning for and following the points outlined, you will be able to put in place the process and resources you need to run a successful post-go-live support phase.

Summary

In this chapter, we have learned about the importance of planning your go-live in order to support users, including how to approach the activities associated with deploying the functionality and plan how to support users during the time immediately after go-live. All of these benefit from careful planning to ensure minimal disruption to the users of the live system. For post-go-live support, we learned that this is a smaller-scale version of the testing function that was carried out before. Additionally, a lot of the processes and planning that can be applied on a smaller scale.

In the next chapter, we will move beyond the foundation and explore Sales Territories. This functionality enables sales functions that have more complex territory assignment requirements to create a model based on their needs and assignment rules.

Further reading

- Change Set Deployment:

  Change Sets: Create, Add Components, Validate, Deploy

  `https://youtube.com/playlist?list=PLFNbZmUNjID5Wej5SE0ron`
  `nj5m61cJjS2&si=xD4ZTZELykNx09bq`

- Salesforce Certification: Development Lifecycle and Deployment Architect:

  Architect Journey: Development Lifecycle and Deployment

  `https://trailhead.salesforce.com/users/strailhead/trailmixes/`
  `architect-dev-lifecycle-and-deployment`

Part 3:
Beyond the Fundamentals

In this section, we will cover the following chapters.

11
Territory Management

Dividing up sales territories effectively can be the difference between a happy and harmonious commercial operation that exceeds the needs of its customers and a situation where commercial teams are competing with each other at the expense of those customers. Modeling and managing sales territories can be complex and labor-intensive if all changes have to be made manually.

By the end of this chapter, you will understand why organizations divide their areas of commercial business into sales territories, and why they actively manage these. You will look at the information you need to gather to understand how your organization manages territories. You will then learn what Sales Cloud Sales Territories is, its capabilities, and when to use it. You will look at how to translate your business needs into a design, and finally, you will learn the steps to enable and set up Sales Territories. This will allow you to determine whether you should use Sales Territories , and if so, set it up for your implementation.

In this chapter, we're going to cover the following main topics:

- What are sales territories?
- Understanding your Organisation's Territory Strategy
- What is Sales Cloud Sales Territories ?
- When to use Sales Cloud Sales Territories
- Translating Territory Requirements into a Design
- Setting up Sales Territories

Supporting tools and information

For this chapter, you will need access to a sandbox to set up, assess, and test your proposed Sales Territories configuration.

Please note that Territory Management is not available in Professional Edition.

What are sales territories?

Let's start with some of the fundamentals. A **sales territory** is an area or a grouping of existing and potential customers, that an individual or team is responsible for targeting. Sales territory management is the process of defining or mapping, and then managing those territories. Sales territory mapping is the process of deciding how the territories are defined, who is allocated to them, and the sales and revenue they are expected to deliver. Management is the ongoing monitoring, allocation, and adjusting of territories to ensure they support business objectives.

A very common way of defining territories is by geographical areas. This takes into account language, cultural differences, and physical proximity, ensuring that someone with the appropriate knowledge can serve the relevant customers. It doesn't necessarily evenly balance customer needs and possible revenue in each territory. For example, small businesses have different requirements and budgets than global enterprises, and some types of companies can be found in geographical clusters, such as financial services.

In terms of management, some organizations keep the same territories year after year, while others rebalance and reallocate theirs every year. The latter requires an efficient territory mapping process and an easy way of reallocating customers and prospects.

The complexity of an organization's territory strategy depends on the organization's maturity, the volume of sales, and how much effort is required for each sale. Technology has made it much easier to understand and classify customers by their characteristics and needs.

Geographical technology such as Salesforce Maps makes it easier to balance territories by selected attributes. Salesforce Maps and Territory Management are add-on licenses to the standard Sales Cloud so we will not be exploring them further in this book.

Why manage sales territories?

By dividing territories wisely, organizations can ensure that their sales efforts do not overlap and that every potential customer is adequately covered.

Balancing territories across the sales teams promotes better resource utilization, reduces internal competition, and often leads to higher customer satisfaction as sales representatives can focus more on customer needs and local market conditions.

Territories need to be monitored and adjusted to ensure they continue to support changing organization objectives and activities, such as a move into a new geographical region or a new product release. Salespeople also join and leave, but customers expect a consistent level of attention. Business conditions change. The ability to respond to these quickly by adjusting and reallocating territories can be a competitive advantage.

When done well, good territory management practices can enable an organization to reach customers, maintain a happy and harmonious sales team, and achieve their business goals.

Next, we will explore how you can learn more about your organization's territory strategy.

Understanding your organization's territory strategy

You can pick up a basic understanding of how your organization approaches sales territories by understanding how the sales team is divided up and their geographical locations. For example, if there are salespeople who focus on specific product lines or businesses depending on their sizes, these could also be used as types of territory in addition to the geographical ones.

How organizations divide up sales territories is a strategic question and varies in complexity depending on the scale of the organization. The territory strategy is defined at a senior level of the organization by the Head of Sales, Sales Director, or Chief Revenue Office. It supports the organization's overall objectives and will be based on a combination of insight from data and the sales leader's judgment.

To gather detailed requirements, you would ideally speak to or gather information from the person who defines the strategy and the person responsible for managing it operationally. These could be the same person. You will want to understand what they do now and must be able to do, as well as anything they would like to be able to do but can't at present.

The following includes some of the key information you would want to gather:

- How do they divide geographical regions into territories?
- Do they have more forecast types than just geographical? (For example, by product line.)
- Are there different brands within the business and if so, do they divide territories in the same way?
- What customer attributes do they use to allocate territories? (For example, number of employees, country, zip code, product interest, and so on.)
- Do salespeople have multiple territories or forecasts?
- How regularly are changes required and what volume of change is required? For example, how often do people leave, or are territories reassigned every year?
- What can't they do now that they would like to be able to do?
- Do they already have a system that manages their territory planning and allocation and if so, is this to be integrated with Sales Cloud or replaced?
- Are the people who own each of the forecasts defined and is it documented somewhere?
- What types of reports or forecasts are required?

This is not an exhaustive list but will allow you to start the conversation to get the information you need. Understanding the matrix of territories your organization requires will allow you to design the requisite types and hierarchy as you implement Sales Territories. We will discuss when to use Sales Territories and how to translate requirements into a design in later sections. Next, you will learn about the capabilities of Sales Cloud Sales Territories.

What is Sales Cloud Sales Territories?

Sales Territories in Salesforce Sales Cloud, also referred to as Territory Management, is the capability designed to allocate Accounts to sales territories and individuals based on various criteria. The functionality allows you to specify types of territories, define your territories and their hierarchy in a model, and then automatically assign Accounts to territories based on rules. It provides the flexibility to assign Accounts to multiple territories and increases the flexibility in reporting with additional ways to filter data in both reports and Collaborative Forecasting.

As already mentioned in the *What are sales territories?* section, this capability is not explicitly designed to enable territory mapping. Salesforce does have a product to map territories, called Salesforce Maps or Territory Planning. We will not be looking at this in this book as it is not available in the Salesforce Enterprise edition without an additional fee.

Next, we will look at the capabilities in more detail.

The capabilities of Sales Territories

Sales Territories has the following key capabilities:

- **Model complex territories**: Using Territory Types and creating a Territory Model with territories in a hierarchy allows the creation of a flexible matrix structure

- **Assign Accounts to more than one Territory**: Accounts can be assigned to multiple Territories

- **Automatically allocate Accounts to Territories**: Assignment Rules can be created for each territory and applied to the territory and all those below it to automatically assign Accounts

- **Open up view and edit access to Accounts based on Territories**: Territory Default Access Levels and individual Territory Access Levels provide a way of opening up view and edit Access Levels for Accounts, Opportunities, and Cases so changes to the Org Sharing Model are not required

- **Forecasting based on the Territory Hierarchy**: Once enabled, Collaborative Forecasting uses the Territory Hierarchy rather than the Role Hierarchy for more flexibility in forecasting

- **Additional filter options in Reporting and List Views**: The Report and List View Filter options for **My territories' accounts** and **My territory team's accounts** become available so users can find the records they need

- **Build and test a new Territory Model without impacting the live Model**: A new Territory Model can be set up and enabled without impacting the currently active model

Now we will take a look at the data that supports the ETM functionality.

Sales Territories data model

When Sales Territories is enabled, you will see that some new Objects become available in the Object Manager: Territory Model, Territory, User Territory Association, and Object Territory Assignment Rule. It is worth noting that there is a limit to how these can be customized. The options are predominantly adding fields, Triggers, Validation Rules, and modifying page layouts.

The Entity Relationship Diagram in *Figure 11.1* shows all the Objects that power Sales Territories. Note that there are more available than are visible in the Object Manager in Setup, as it is not possible to customize most of them.

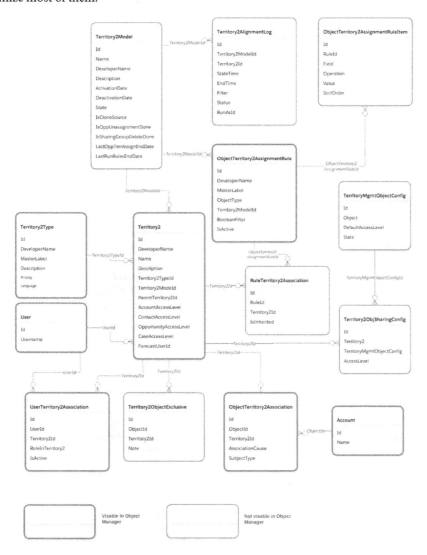

Figure 11.1 – An overview of the Territory Management Entity Relationship Diagram

Figure 11.1 is the second version of Sales Cloud's Territory Management, which is why there is a **2** in all the names in the Objects on the diagram. Object Territory Associations is a junction object between Accounts and Territories and User Territory Associations is a junction object between Users and Territories. It is important to be aware of all parts of the model if you have complex requirements or if you need to integrate with these objects. To view *Figure 11.1* in greater detail, you can download a hi-res version of this image from `https://packt.link/gbp/9781804619643`.

Next, we will introduce some of the key terminology and concepts.

Key concepts

Let's explore some of the key terms and concepts of Territory Management, as it is important to understand them to be able to design your solution. We will start with the model.

Territory Models

The **Territory Model** is simply the hierarchy of Territories. You create the model by creating Territories in a hierarchy in much the same way as you create roles in the Role Hierarchy. A model has a status, so you can have multiple models and specify which one is active at any one time. This means that you can have one model live in the `Active` status while working on a new model with a status of `Planning`, ready to switch on when required. A model that you are no longer using can be set to `Archived`. However, it is important to note that once a model is set to `Archived` it can't be moved back to `Active`. Models can also be cloned.

Territory Types

Territory Types are a way of segmenting the Territory Model. Each Territory must have a Territory Type, and you will need to define and create these before you can start building your Territories and model. Territory Types provide the extra dimensions that allow you to create the matrix element of your territory allocation. Territory Types require a Priority. You can set up Territory Types for strategy areas that are being targeted.

Territories

Territories are groups of Accounts that users are assigned to work with. Territories are where you specify much of how your model is set up. Here you provide a name and description, what users are assigned to the territory, the rules used to assign accounts, who the Forecasting Manager is, and the Access-Level permissions for the specific territory.

Assignment Rules

Assignment Rules are the rules that determine how Accounts are allocated. The configuration options are the same as those for Lead Assignment Rules. However, only Account fields are available to use in the filter criteria. These can be activated and deactivated. It is possible to specify that rules should be applied to child territories. Where there is more than one rule that applies to a territory, they are applied together with AND logic rather than OR.

Limits

It is important to be aware that there are some limits in ETM. The following are the key limits to be aware of:

- Number of Territory Models by edition:

  - Enterprise – 2

  - Developer, Performance, Unlimited – 4

- Only one active Territory Model at one time

- All editions – 1,000 Territories per Territory Model

- Up to 1,950 Users per Territory but expect slower performance when there are more than 300

- 15 assignment rules per territory

- The Assigned Territories Related list is read-only on Mobile

Now that we have an understanding of the functionality, let's see how to decide whether you should use it.

When to use Sales Cloud Territory Management

As part of your implementation, you need to decide whether you are going to use the Sales Territories functionality. It is important to note that just because your organization has sales territories it doesn't automatically mean that you should implement Sales Cloud Sales Territories. You will still want to carry out an assessment of whether to use it. ETM provides much-needed functionality for organizations whose territories are complex or change regularly. However, if an organization's requirements can be met by using the standard role hierarchy and reporting, you should just use that as enabling Territory Management will increase the complexity and maintenance required.

There are some key questions that will help you decide:

- Are you going to forecast in Sales Cloud?
- If yes, are you using Collaborative Forecasting and does it meet your needs by using the Role Hierarchy, or do people need to submit forecasts to multiple managers?

If salespeople need to submit forecasts to multiple managers, then ETM is a good fit. Also, if Accounts need to exist in multiple territories, you will also want to confirm that the criteria used to allocate Accounts is based on Account attributes or there is a way of specifying these at the Account level. Collaborative Forecasting must be enabled for ETM to be enabled.

You will also want to consider using ETM if you are not forecasting in SF, but you need Accounts to be allocated to territories so the data can be pulled into an external source of truth for forecasting.

It is useful to know that this feature can be disabled if business needs change, unlike some others. All testing and feasibility assessments should be carried out in a Sandbox and not Production.

> **Tip**
>
> *If you do not have a clear and compelling use case for Sales Territories, then you could consider planning it for a second or later release of functionality.*
>
> The standard Role Hierarchy provides a structure for you to build a baseline of Dashboards and Reports and also set up Forecasting if that is part of your implementation. Sales Cloud is likely to offer different and new ways of working – sometimes once stakeholders are in the new system, they realize there is a previously unknown way of achieving something they need.
>
> The benefit of assessing and implementing Sales Territories when Sales Cloud is operational is that you can evaluate the setup against current data and play it back to users who understand what it is like to use the system day to day.
>
> Any assessment and setup should be carried out in a Sandbox, not the Production Org.

In the next section, we consider how to translate your requirements into a design.

Translating Territory requirements into a design

Before you can build your Territory Model, you need to define your types and hierarchy. Your hierarchy will typically have a geographical component and your types will likely represent the other dimension in your forecasting matrix, such as the industry vertical or customer size. You should aim to draw out your hierarchy before you start to build.

You also need to decide how you structure your assignment rules. You are likely to have geographically based criteria, perhaps by country, or for countries as large as the US, it might be by state or zip code. For this, you need to make sure that the data you are using is standardized and complete. If you have not done so already you should consider implementing the **State and Country/Territory Picklists** functionality. This will ensure you have a consistent set of data to use in the criteria. In addition to the geographical criteria, you will also have criteria that specify the other dimensions, such as the industry. It is likely that you will define one type of these rules at the top of the hierarchy and specify that the child territories inherit them while specifying the rules for the other dimension for each child.

Once the Territory Hierarchy becomes the basis for the forecast, you don't need to maintain your Role Hierarchy for that purpose as this results in unnecessary duplication. The Role Hierarchy is good for modeling management where one person reports to only one other. The Territory hierarchy offers a matrix structure where a person might report to more than one manager. Once set up you may want to consider simplifying your Role Hierarchy to only include roles that are required for reporting rollups, approval, and hierarchical workflows.

Defining Territories from an external source

If your organization has a complex territory structure, there might already be a system that manages the territory hierarchies. Depending on the information available and the options for extracting the data or integrating the system with Salesforce, you may want to continue to use the existing source as the "source of truth". If the other system only defines the territory hierarchy and its functions can be replaced by the functionality in Sales Cloud, then you might want to consider bringing the capability over to Sales Cloud and retiring the existing system. If the system performs other functions, then you might want to continue using it as the source of truth and allow data to be transferred between the two systems by creating External IDs in Sales Cloud to map data to. It is worth noting that if you create a unique External ID on a Territory Object, it does mean the Clone options on Territory Models will no longer work. If this is a requirement, you should do a detailed mapping of data between the systems.

Key considerations

Salesforce recommends applying inherited rules to child territories to keep the number of rule evaluations to a minimum for performance reasons. You can define each territory branch as its own tree to isolate the number of rules that are evaluated. This approach makes the branch mutually exclusive from the sibling branches at the same level.

Good practice for rule design is to base criteria on number fields where possible, rather than string fields. Always try to avoid criteria where numbers are expressed in string fields as this slows performance. Also, try to make your criteria as restrictive as possible: OR statements can also have a performance impact and this usually results in a higher number of Accounts being assigned to a territory.

Salesforce also provides some recommendations on the number of User and Accounts to assign to a single territory. The general rule is three Users to one territory. Make sure to keep the number of Accounts to less than 10,000 to avoid performance issues.

In situations where you need the account assignment to stay the same over a period of time, for example, across a fiscal year, you can create custom field equivalents of the attributes you use in your assignment rules, and then only update these at the time interval you want the assignment to change.

> **Tips**
> When making changes to a model that is active, update the rules at the lowest-level territories first to avoid any re-evaluation that could occur. Models that are inactive don't have an impact on performance.

Changing territories can be painful for sales reps so when planning any change, it is important to give them time to prepare, and when the time comes, make any changes quickly without further disruption. Make sure you identify any opportunities that may be there in the later stages so that if a transition is required, it is carried out thoughtfully.

Now we will look at the steps for setting up ETM.

Setting up Sales Territories

Before setting up ETM you should be aware that the following is required:

- Customizable forecasting must be turned on
- Users need Manage Territories and View Setup and Configuration to view the active territory and the Accounts assigned to it

The main steps for setting up ETM are as follows:

1. **Enable Territory Management**: First, ensure that Territory Management is enabled in your Salesforce setup. This can be done from the **Setup** menu.
2. **Define Default Access Levels**: Select the Access Levels that Territory Users have to Accounts, Opportunities, and Cases.
3. **Define Territory Types**: Establish different types of territories based on your business needs, such as geographical areas, customer size, or product lines.
4. **Create Territory Model (hierarchy)**: Build a hierarchical structure of territories. This involves setting up parent and child territories, reflecting how your organization's sales territories are structured.
5. **Set Up Assignment Rules**: Define rules for account assignment to territories. These rules determine how accounts are allocated to different territories based on predefined criteria.
6. **Assign Territories to Users**: Allocate these territories to individual sales representatives or teams. This includes roles within each territory.

7. **Activate the Model**: Set your completed model to live.

8. **Monitor and Adjust**: Regularly review and adjust your territory settings to reflect changes in your sales strategy or market conditions.

Sales Territories

To enable Sales Territories, enter `Territory Settings` in the **Quick Find** search or go to **Setup > Feature Settings > Sales > Territories > Territory Settings**. You will see a **Territory Settings** page that outlines the steps to activate your model, as shown in *Figure 11.2*.

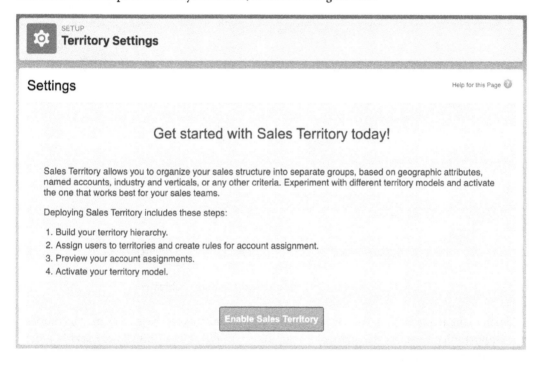

Figure 11.2 – Territory Settings page pre-feature enablement

To enable the feature, click on **Enable Sales Territories**. It is possible to disable Territory Management, unlike some Salesforce features such as Person Accounts. This can be done on the **Settings** screen. In the menu, you will now see that **Territory Models** and **Territory Types** have been added under **Territories**.

When enabled, Territory Objects become available in the **Object Manager**. The Assigned Territories Related List becomes available to add to the **Account Page Layout**. Territory filters become available on Reports and List Views.

Territory-wide access defaults

On the **Settings** page, you can set the record access settings. These offer a way for you to specify the Access Level for the Accounts, Opportunities, and Cases that are part of territories, above and beyond your **Organization-Wide Sharing (OWD)** rules. These are the defaults, but you can also set these on the individual territory level. You can see the options in *Figure 11.3*.

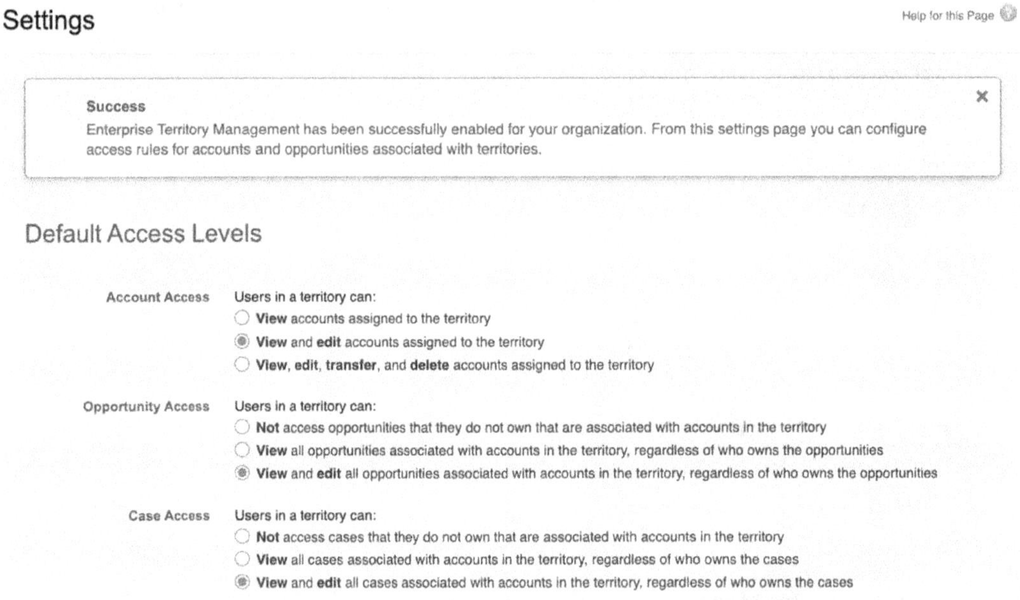

Settings   Help for this Page ⓘ

> **Success**   ✕
> Enterprise Territory Management has been successfully enabled for your organization. From this settings page you can configure access rules for accounts and opportunities associated with territories.

Default Access Levels

Account Access   Users in a territory can:
    ○ **View** accounts assigned to the territory
    ◉ **View** and **edit** accounts assigned to the territory
    ○ **View, edit, transfer,** and **delete** accounts assigned to the territory

Opportunity Access Users in a territory can:
    ○ **Not** access opportunities that they do not own that are associated with accounts in the territory
    ○ **View** all opportunities associated with accounts in the territory, regardless of who owns the opportunities
    ◉ **View** and **edit** all opportunities associated with accounts in the territory, regardless of who owns the opportunities

Case Access   Users in a territory can:
    ○ **Not** access cases that they do not own that are associated with accounts in the territory
    ○ **View** all cases associated with accounts in the territory, regardless of who owns the cases
    ◉ **View** and **edit** all cases associated with accounts in the territory, regardless of who owns the cases

Figure 11.3 – Territory Settings page post-feature enablement

In addition to the access defaults, you can also specify **Opportunity Access** based on parent territories in the **Opportunity Territory Assignment** section shown in *Figure 11.4* This allows **Users in a the parent territory** to be given access to Opportunities.

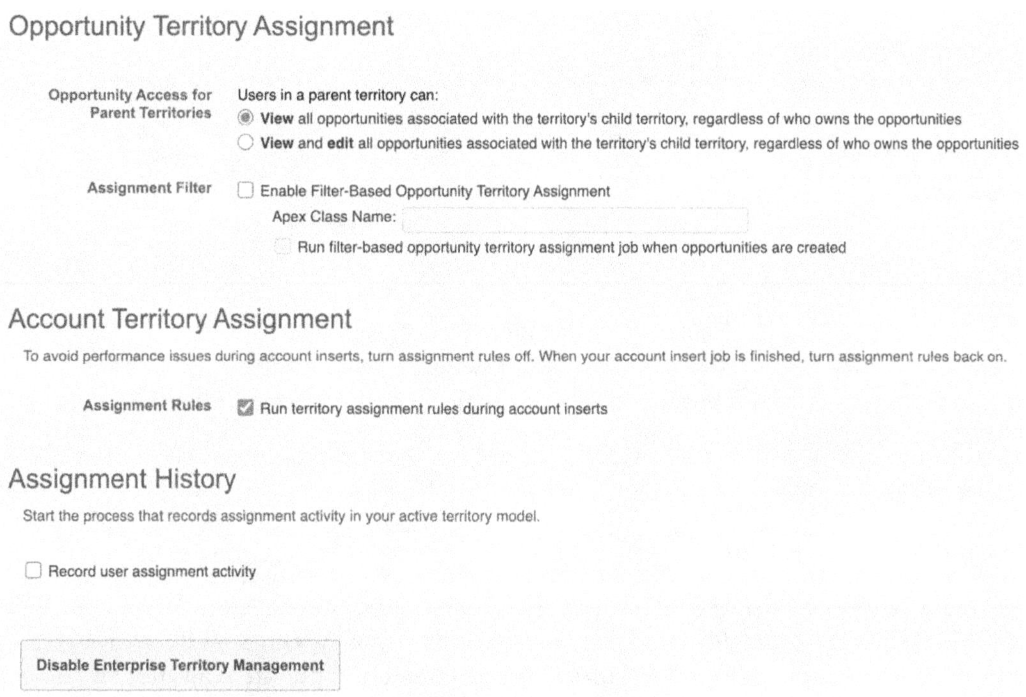

Opportunity Territory Assignment

Opportunity Access for Parent Territories   Users in a parent territory can:
- ● **View** all opportunities associated with the territory's child territory, regardless of who owns the opportunities
- ○ **View** and **edit** all opportunities associated with the territory's child territory, regardless of who owns the opportunities

Assignment Filter   ☐ Enable Filter-Based Opportunity Territory Assignment
Apex Class Name: [   ]
☐ Run filter-based opportunity territory assignment job when opportunities are created

Account Territory Assignment

To avoid performance issues during account inserts, turn assignment rules off. When your account insert job is finished, turn assignment rules back on.

Assignment Rules   ☑ Run territory assignment rules during account inserts

Assignment History

Start the process that records assignment activity in your active territory model.

☐ Record user assignment activity

[Disable Enterprise Territory Management]

Figure 11.4 – Territory Settings page

On the **Opportunity Territory Assignment** page, there is also the option to set the **Assignment Filter** if you want Opportunities to automatically be assigned to Territories. This can be done with an APEX class that can be specified on the **Settings** page or via Flow, as long as the criteria are not too complex. The latter is easier for low-code developers to maintain. Salesforce does provide some example APEX code that you can use or modify to meet your requirements: the class is called `OppTerrAssignDefaultLogicFilter`, which you can find more about on `developer.salesforce.com`. A link to the page is provided in the *Further reading* section.

Defining Territory Types

Before you can create your Territory Model, you need to set up your Territories. To define these, enter `Territory Types` in the **Quick Find** search or go to **Setup** > **Feature Settings** > **Sales** > **Territories** > **Territory Types**. Territory Types have a limited number of fields. These are shown in *Figure 11.5*. Note that **Label**, **Name**, and **Priority** are required.

Figure 11.5 – Example of a Territory Type

The scale for priority is defined by each organization so that you can determine whether the highest or lowest number is the highest priority.

Next, we will get into creating the Territory Model.

Creating a Territory Model

You create a Territory Model by creating Territories in a hierarchy. You can see in *Figure 11.6* part of an example model. To find this, enter `Territory Models` in the **Quick Find** search or go to **Setup** > **Feature Settings** > **Sales** > **Territories** > **Territory Models**. You create a child territory from the parent node in much the same way as you create roles in the Role Hierarchy. You also have options to edit, delete, and run the assignment rules from the model hierarchy view.

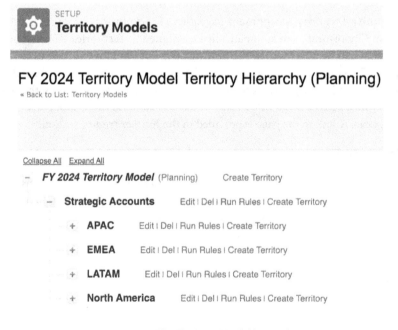

Figure 11.6 – The Territory Model hierarchy

The majority of the work for setting up the model is in creating the territories, so we will look at that next.

Creating Territories

To create a territory, click **Create Territory** next to the Territory you want to be the parent. Here you can set **Label**, **Name**, **Territory Type**, the parent, and **Description** values. The Access Level can also be set for the individual territory. Once it has been created, you can set **Forecast Manager**, **Assignment Rules** can be created, users can be assigned, Accounts can be manually assigned, and it is also possible to create child territories. *Figure 11.7* shows a Territory record and its related lists.

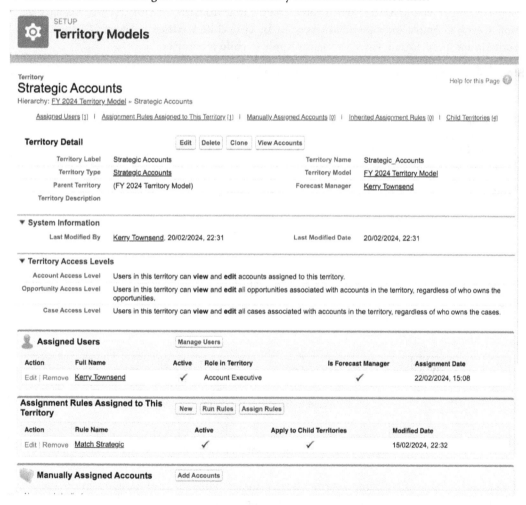

Figure 11.7 – A Territory record

You can create fields on the Territory Object and add them to the page layout. An example is adding an Account Owner field to be used as a reference for a Flow to set the Account Owner. We will explore this in more detail in the later *Further Automation* section.

Set up Assignment Rules

You can set up Assignment Rules based on Account attributes. You will need to give the Rule a name and you can then set up your filter criteria, which might be based on the geographical location, the industry, or an Account type. When you create an Assignment Rule from the Territory Model, you have the option to set it to **Active**. When you create the Rule from the Territory record, you have the option to set it to **Active** and you can also specify **Apply to child territories**. *Figure 11.8* shows how the criteria are specified and where you select **Apply to child territories**.

Step 2: Enter the selection criteria for this rule

Base your rule on object characteristics such as:

- Industry
- Annual revenue
- Number of employees
- Region

Field	Operator	Value	
--None--	--None--		AND
--None--	--None--		AND
--None--	--None--		AND
--None--	--None--		AND
--None--	--None--		

Add Filter Logic...

Step 3 (optional): Apply to child territories

Apply to child territories   ☐ Applies the rule to **Strategic Accounts** territory and its descendants

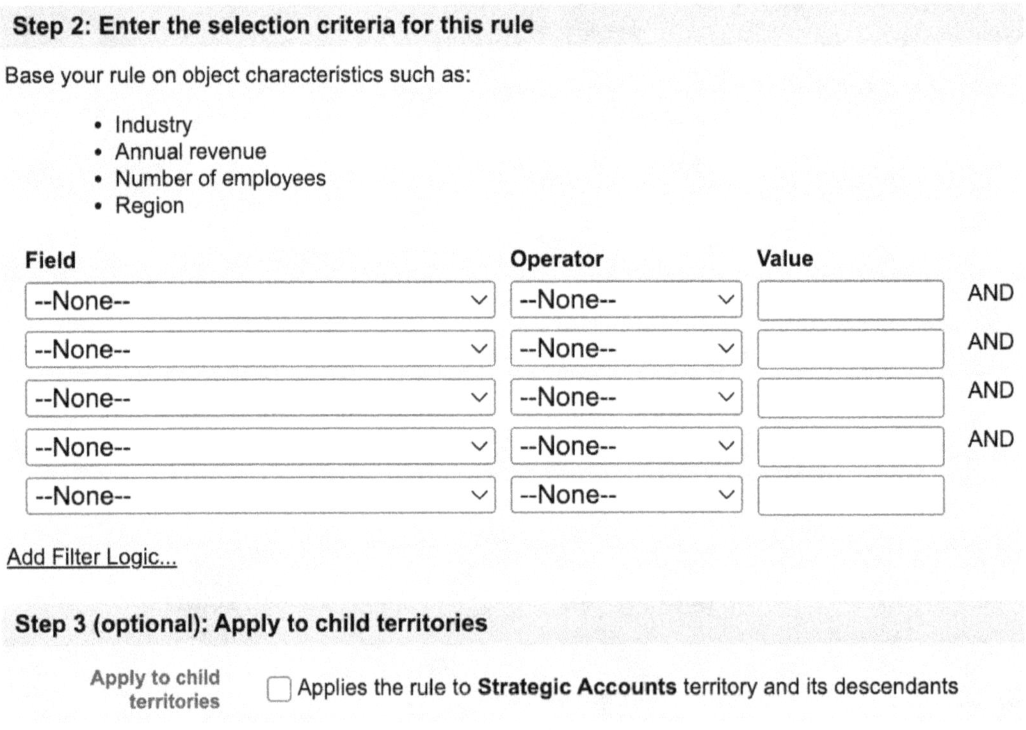

Figure 11.8 – The Assignment Rules setup page

The way you set criteria for assignment rules is very similar to that for Lead Assignment rules; if you are familiar with those. You can apply AND and OR logic by clicking on **Add Filter Logic**.

Once set up, you can run rules from multiple locations including the Territory Model page and the territory record. These rules can also be set to run automatically when an Account is created. This is set on the **Territory Settings** page. If enabled, you will want to turn it off went you are loading data in bulk.

If a Territory doesn't have any inherited or Territory-specific assignment rules, then it only has Accounts if they are assigned manually. If an Account matches multiple rules in the same branch of the hierarchy, it is added to the lowest match. When there are multiple territory-specific rules, an Account has to match everything to be assigned.

Plan your rule strategy before you start building. If you have more than one rule applied to a Territory, then test early on that they work together as you expect, rather than building it all out and only then realizing the approach doesn't work as you expected.

Finally, we will activate the model.

Activate the Model

To activate your Territory Model, go to **Setup** > **Feature Settings** > **Sales** > **Territories** > **Territory Models** and open the model you would like to activate. Then, click on the **Activate** button as shown in *Figure 11.9*.

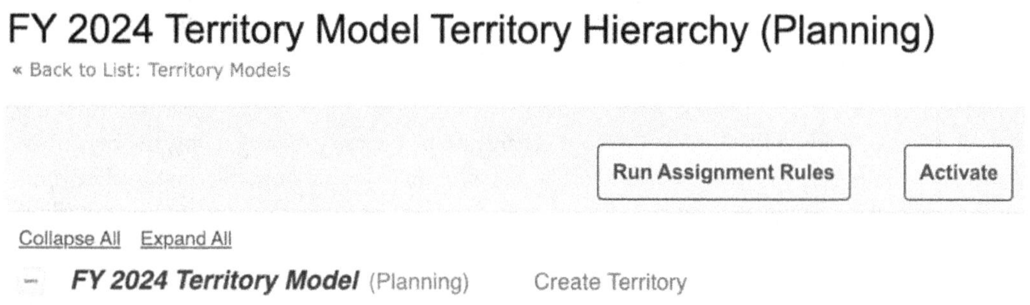

FY 2024 Territory Model Territory Hierarchy (Planning)

« Back to List: Territory Models

	Run Assignment Rules	Activate

Collapse All   Expand All

– **FY 2024 Territory Model** (Planning)   Create Territory

Figure 11.9 – Activation from the Territory Model page

Your model is now live and you can use all your assignment rules to allocate your Accounts. It is recommended that you do this out of office hours as it can require a lot of processing.

Including Territories in Forecasts

To see a rolled-up forecast in **Collaborative Forecasts**, each territory must have a **Forecast Manager** even if there isn't a person in a manager role for the territory. When a Forecast Manager is assigned, the manager can view and adjust the forecast. If a Forecast Manager is not assigned but individual Users are enabled for Forecasting, then they can view and adjust their *own* forecasts, but not others, even those in their territory. When a territory model is enabled, the Territory Forecast becomes available in the **Forecast Type** picklist. When selected, the forecast is totaled by Territory Types.

Further automation

ETM doesn't have the functionality to change the Account Owner based on territory. This is because there is a lot of flexibility in terms of functionality: the Account can exist in more than one territory and there can be multiple users assigned to a territory, so who the owner should be isn't straightforward. It is possible to set the Account Owner using Flow if you have a consistent set of rules for what happens when an Account has multiple territories. You can create a custom field on Territories that defines the owner and use that for your allocation in Flow.

We have now learned how to set up ETM, so we will recap what we have covered in this chapter.

Summary

Salesforce Sales Cloud Territory Management is a powerful tool designed to optimize the allocation of Accounts to sales territories, ensuring efficient resource distribution and enhanced sales performance. By organizing sales efforts according to specific territories and assigning them to the appropriate teams or individuals, companies can improve their sales strategies and customer relationships. Territory Management provides the tools that simplify the maintenance of territories for organizations that have complex requirements.

In this chapter, we learned how to identify your organization's territory requirements, the capability of Sales Cloud Sales Territories, and when to use it. We went on to look at how you can translate your organization's requirements into a design and then stepped through how you can set up this functionality.

In the next chapter, we will explore how you can model processes other than the Sales and lead generation processes. This includes looking at the other capability that Sales Cloud offers and how you model a process that Sales Cloud doesn't have support for out of the box.

Further reading

- *How Do Permissions for Territories Affect Feature and Data Access?*

  `https://help.salesforce.com/s/articleView?id=sf.tm2_how_access_ permissions_work.htm&type=5`

- *Sales Territories Allocations*

  `https://help.salesforce.com/s/articleView?id=sf.tm2_allocations. htm&type=5`

- *Territory Design and Management*

  `https://help.salesforce.com/s/articleView?id=sf.tm2_territory_ design_and_management.htm&type=5`

- *Trailhead: Sales Territories and Forecasting*

  https://trailhead.salesforce.com/content/learn/modules/sales-territories-and-forecasting

- *Trailhead: Advanced Territory Management*

  https://trailhead.salesforce.com/content/learn/modules/advanced-territory-management

- *How do permissions for Territories affect feature and data access?*

  https://help.salesforce.com/s/articleView?id=sf.tm2_how_access_permissions_work.htm&type=5

- *OpportunityTerritory2AssignmentFilter Global Interface*

  https://developer.salesforce.com/docs/atlas.en-us.248.0.apexref.meta/apexref/apex_interface_TerritoryMgmt_OpportunityTerritory2AssignmentFilter.htm

12

Modeling Additional Processes with Sales Cloud

You have been, or you are, setting up Sales Cloud to manage your core sales process or lead generation process. This unlocks the benefits of allowing multiple stakeholders to collaborate to better serve your customers. Now that you have this core information centrally available, you might want to continue to bring processes that support or follow on from closing a deal onto the platform.

This chapter gives you the understanding and the practical knowledge to determine whether it is appropriate to implement some of the additional functionality in Sales Cloud that captures and sends Quotes, captures Orders, and captures Contracts between you and your customers. You will also learn how you can use Custom Objects and Fields to build the capability to record and manage processes where there isn't out-of-the-box functionality or your organization's processes are bespoke.

In this chapter, we're going to cover the following main topics:

- Additional process requirements
- Additional Sales Cloud functionality
- Quotes and Quote Line Items
- Contracts
- Orders and Order Line Items
- Custom Objects

Supporting tools and information

For this chapter, you will require access to a Sandbox or Dev Org to be able to explore and prototype the functionality we describe in this chapter.

You will also want to review the requirements that were collected as part of the requirements gathered for your core sales process to determine whether any of those are met by the functionality we describe here. You may also need access to the tools that were used to capture requirements and document processes in case any additions or modifications are identified.

Additional process requirements

During the requirement gathering carried out for the core sales process that we learned about in *Chapter 3 – Design and Build: The Core Sales Process*, it is highly likely that you captured requirements that went beyond that single process and the capability we reviewed in that chapter. It is very common to identify requirements or at least requests for functionality that enables everything a salesperson might have to do – for example, providing a potential customer with different prices based on a time-bound discount or for different product mixes.

These might have been excluded from the scope of an initial implementation but if they are in scope, it is as important to understand and capture the requirements on these as it is for the core process. Common things that you will want to listen out for and ask for more detail about are whether they need to send a quote document to the customer, whether they typically provide multiple prices, whether they need to capture who was involved in the contract signing process, or whether salespeople need to see the status of orders post-sale. All of these are more common if Sales Cloud is being used alongside Service Cloud, as it means that a wider group of stakeholders can benefit from accessing this information to serve the customer.

What you might expect to see is a process like that shown in *Figure 12.1*:

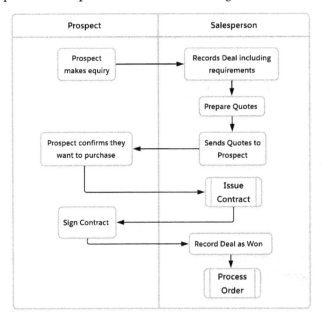

Figure 12.1 – Simple sales inquiry to process order process diagram

In *Figure 12.1*, you can see a very simplified process diagram of how a deal can be taken from inquiry to order. Notice in the diagram that the contract and order steps are processes in their own right as they can be quite involved and involve different stakeholders and systems. The first step is to determine whether capturing these processes is in the scope of the implementation and if so, to what scale. The next step is to understand them in detail and determine whether Sales Cloud will be the source of truth for this information or whether it will be another system. That will determine whether the processes should be initiated in Sales Cloud or whether the requirement is only for the data to be visible to Users in Sales Cloud, in which case a visual integration might be a better alternative. We'll learn about integration layers in the next chapter, *Common System Integrations*.

If you identify a requirement to capture data or to manage a process that doesn't appear to naturally fit with the out-of-the-box functionality, you have the flexibility to build Objects and automation that support this.

Next, we will look at the out-of-the-box functionality in Sales Cloud that we have not already covered in *Chapters 3* and *4*.

Additional Sales Cloud functionality

In this section, we explore the Objects in Sales Cloud that are in addition to those that enable the management of the core sales process such as Opportunities, Opportunity Products, Accounts, and Contacts. These Objects provide out-of-the-box options that provide a solution for organizations that have relatively lightweight requirements. Like the majority of Sales Cloud functionality, they can be customized and extended to your organization's needs. If your organization has requirements that can't be met by this functionality out of the box, you may also want to investigate the capability of Salesforce CPQ or other **Configure, Price, Quote** (**CPQ**) solutions available from the AppExchange before investing significant time in building a bespoke solution. You may still decide that customizing the standard functionality is your best option, but it is important to understand what third-party tools are available as part of coming to that decision.

Sales Cloud data model

It is important to understand the out-of-the-box data model so you can map your organization's requirements to it and determine whether you need additional Objects and Fields for your process.

The entity relationship diagram shown in *Figure 12.2* shows the Objects that we learn about in this chapter and how they relate to each other and the core Sales Cloud Objects such as Opportunities, Opportunity Products, Accounts, and Contacts:

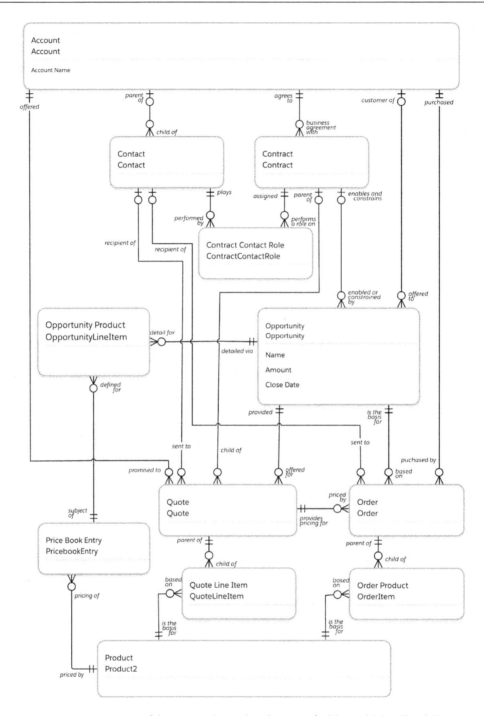

Figure 12.2 – A overview of the entity relationship diagram of additional Sales Cloud Objects

As you can see from the diagram, the Quote and Order Objects have very similar relationships to the Opportunity and Opportunity Products and those are all tightly related. You will see that the Order Object has a required relationship with the Contract Object, which means there has to be a Contract before an Order can be created. To view *Figure 12.2* in greater detail, you can visit this link: `https://packt.link/gbp/9781804619643`.

The Objects in the relationship diagram are listed in *Table 12.1*, along with their API name and their intended use:

Object Name	Object API Name	Usage
Quote	Quote	Used to store headline data about the Quote such as who it is for, the total, and the status.
Quote	Quote Line Item	Used to store data about the specific product and services that are included in the Quote, such as name, quantity, and cost.
Contract	Contract	Used to store data about contracts that customers agree to.
Contract Contact Role	ContractContactRole	Used to capture the role a person has in the contracting process. This Object is not available to view in the Object Manager. See the Contract Contact Roles section for more information.
Order	Order	Used to store headline data about orders that customers have made, such as the status of the order.
Order	Order Line Item	Used to store data about the specific products and services that are included in the Order, such as name, quantity, and cost.

Table 12.1 – Table describing the additional Sales Cloud Objects

In addition to the Objects in *Figure 12.2*, you will note that there are four other Objects on the Sales Cloud ERD in *Chapter 3 – Design and Build: The Core Sales Process* that we do not explore in detail in this book. These are Asset, Case, Partner, and Partner Role. An Asset is used to capture the specific details of the product a client has purchased. Examples of the data that might be collected are purchase date, serial number, and installation date. Cases are designed to capture and manage customer support issues. This is a primary Object for Service Cloud. There is a limited feature version available in Sales Cloud. Some organizations use these when they don't already have a customer service or asset management solution. These two business functions are not typically the responsibility of the commercial team, which is why we do not cover them in this book.

Partners and Partner Roles are not visible by default in Sales Cloud but become available in Orgs where Partners are enabled. They allow organizations to record Partners, which are business accounts that channel managers use to manage partner relationships. Partner management and the functionality that Salesforce provides in its **partner relationship management** product are a significant topic and beyond the scope of this book.

Next, we will take a deeper look at the Quote objects and the associated functionality.

Quotes and Quote Line Items

In this section, we will look at the capabilities of Sales Cloud for creating, managing, and sending quotes to customers as well as highlight some practical considerations.

Sales Cloud capabilities

In the Customer 360 platform, potential and completed sales are captured as Opportunities. However, during the course of the sales process, multiple product and service solutions might be discussed or recommended as the overall need is understood or requirements change. The information captured on the Opportunity needs to represent the salesperson's current understanding of what will be purchased for forecasting purposes. While it is possible for the person to change the Opportunity Products to get different price combinations, this approach means there is no record of the different combinations discussed, and there will be additional manual work if the product combination needs to be reverted.

The Quotes functionality allows multiple Quotes to be created against an Opportunity and for the Opportunity Products to be updated on the Opportunity by simply clicking the **Sync** button from the synced Quote. A pdf Quote can be generated for the Quote record, saved on the record, and sent directly to a Contact. This can save a lot of time for salespeople, particularly if they have had to prepare these manually.

Quote

The Quotes Object captures the headline information about a Quote that is being offered to a potential customer. It captures information such as the company and person the quote is for, and its current state using the Status and Expiration Date fields.

Table 12.2 summarizes key information about the Quote Object and its fields:

Key Information	
API Name	Quote
Required Fields	Quote Name (Name)
Standard Relationships*	Opportunity (Master-Detail to Opportunity)
	Account Name (Lookup to Account)
	Contact Name (Lookup to Contact)
	Contract (Lookup to Contract)
Other Key Fields	Syncing (Checkbox)
	Status (Picklist)
	Expiration Date (Date)
	Total Price (Roll-Up Summary (SUM Quote Line))
	Discount (Percent)

Table 12.2 – Key information about the Quote Object

*Lookup relationships to the User Object for Owner, Created By, and Modified By have not been included as they exist on all Objects.

Now we will learn how to set up the functionality.

Enable Quote

This feature is enabled by searching for Quotes in the **Quick Find** search or going to **Setup** > **Feature Settings** > **Sales** > **Quotes** > **Quotes Settings**. This feature can be disabled; however, the sync between any existing Quotes and Opportunities must be stopped and customization that references Quotes must be removed first. *Figure 12.3* shows where you enable Quotes; this is also the place where you can specify that you want to **Create a Quote without a Related Opportunity**:

Quote Settings

Help for this Page

Enable or disable quotes for your organization. This feature allows users to create a quote and email a PDF of the quote to customers.

☐ Enable Quotes

☐ Create Quotes Without a Related Opportunity

Save   Cancel

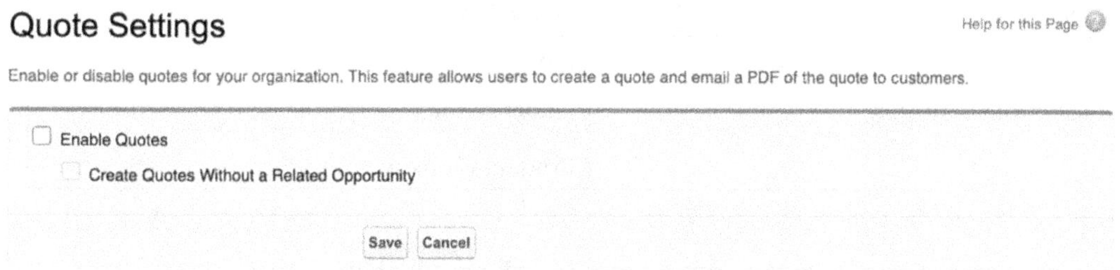

Figure 12.3 – Quote Settings page

Immediately after enabling Quotes, you will be prompted to select the **Opportunity Page Layouts** you would like to add the **Quote Related List** to. Once enabled, you will see a new menu option, **Quote Templates**. We will explore Quote Templates in a later section of that name.

Syncing Quotes

It is possible to select and sync the Quote Line Item on a Quote with an Opportunity with the click of a button. This functionality is unique to Quotes. It means that a salesperson can create a number of Quotes for a potential customer to give them different price points and options and when the potential customer confirms, the salesperson can update the Opportunity by simply selecting to sync the selected Quote by clicking the **Start Sync** button.

Quote Templates

You set up Quote Templates by searching for `Quote Templates` in the **Quick Find** search or going to **Setup > Feature Settings > Sales > Quotes > Quote Templates**. From this page, you can click **New** to create a new template by specifying a **Template Name**. You also have the option to base a new template on an existing one, which can be a timesaver. The template editor is very similar to the original Page Layout editor. You can include fields from the Quote, Account, Opportunity, Contact, User, and your Organization. You can add your company logo, typically in the header. If your company name is in a specific font, you will need to add that as an image.

It is not possible to add conditional logic into the template so if you need variations, you will need to create a template for each type.

Finally, you need to activate the templates that you want to be available to Users.

Quote Line Item

The Quote Line Item Object captures the detailed information for a specific Quote, including the product being quoted for, quantities involved, discounts, and a line price. This information is then aggregated to the related Quote.

Table 12.3 summarizes key information about the Quote Line Item Object and its fields:

Key Information	
API Name	Quote Line Item
Required Fields	Line Item Number (Auto Number)
Standard Relationships*	Quote Name (Master-Detail to Opportunity)
	Product (Lookup to Product)

Key Information	
API Name	Quote Line Item
Other Key Fields	Quantity (Checkbox)
	Line Item Description (Text)
	List Price (Currency)
	Sales Price (Currency)
	Total Price (Currency)
	Discount (Percentage)

Table 12.3 – Key information about the Quote Object

*Lookup relationships to the User Object for Owner, Created By, and
Modified By have not been included as they exist on all Objects.

Note that these are very similar to the Opportunity Line Item fields, and it is this Object that Quote Line Items sync with.

Key considerations

The syncing functionality means that variations in Product combinations are created at the Quote level rather than changing the Product on the Opportunity. Some Users can find this counterintuitive so training and a means of guiding Users on this feature is very helpful. Users might need some time to really get used to how it works, particularly if they have used Opportunities and Opportunity Products without Quotes first.

It is common for some type of approval to be required on discounts of a certain size. Quotes don't have an Approval Process already built in so you will need to design and build this if it is a requirement.

In practice

It can be beneficial to adopt a naming convention for quotes so they can be easily identified from each other.

Contracts

In this section, we will look at the capabilities of Sales Cloud for capturing a record of the contracts that have been agreed upon and the people who were involved. Then, we explore some key considerations and what happens in practice.

This functionality is not to be confused with Service Contracts and Contract Line Items, which are part of Service Cloud, or Salesforce Contracts, which is an add-on license for CPQ+.

A full list of Sales Cloud add-on products can be found here: `https://www.salesforce.com/content/dam/web/en_us/www/documents/pricing/all-add-ons.pdf`

Sales Cloud capabilities

This lightweight object is based on a single object that allows the capture of key information related to a contract. It is not designed to manage a contract generation and signing process with multiple participants. If your requirements involve managing the full process, you will also want to consider third-party tools. We'll learn about how you can extend your solution with third-party tools from the AppExchange in *Extending with the AppExchange*.

Contract

The Contract Object captures details about the contracts that have been agreed upon and the people who have been involved in agreeing to them.

Table 12.4 summarizes key information about the Contract Object and its fields:

Key Information	
API Name	Contract
Required Fields	Contract Number (Auto Number)
	Account Name (Lookup to Account)
	Status (Picklist)
	Contract Start Date (Date)
	Contract Term (months) (Number)
Standard Relationships*	Account Name (Lookup to Account)
	Customer Signed By (Lookup to Contact)
	Company Signed By (Lookup to User)
	Activated By (Lookup to User)
	Price Book (Lookup to Price Book)
	Ship To Contact (Lookup to Contact)
Other Key Fields	Contract End Date

Table 12.4 – Key information about the Contract Object

```
*Lookup relationships to the User Object for Owner, Created By, and
Modified By have not been included as they exist on all Objects.
```

This is a single Object and unlike Quotes, it doesn't have a companion Object that captures the products or services involved. This is part of the functionality for the Service Contracts and Contract Line Items that are part of Service Cloud, which we will not be covering in this book.

Contract Settings

This feature is enabled by searching for `Contract Settings` in the **Quick Find** search or going to **Setup > Feature Settings > Sales > Contract Settings**:

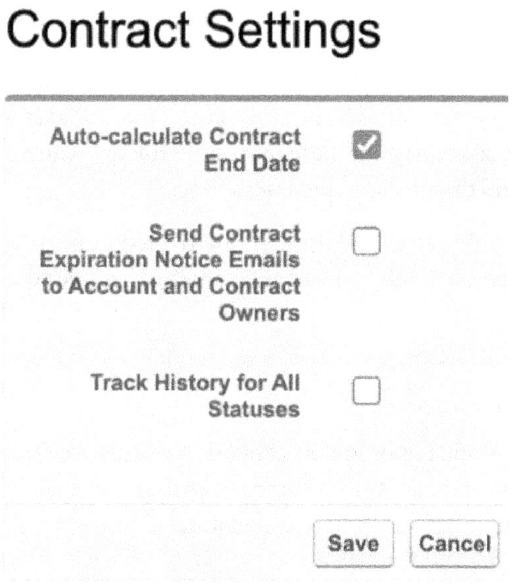

Contract Settings

Auto-calculate Contract End Date	✅
Send Contract Expiration Notice Emails to Account and Contract Owners	☐
Track History for All Statuses	☐

Save   Cancel

Figure 12.4 – Contract Settings

When enabled, there are three other settings that become available. **Auto-calculate Contract End Date**, when enabled, means that the Contract Start Date and Contract Term (months) are used to calculate the Contract End Date. The **Send Contract Expiration Notice Emails to Account and Contract Owners** setting means that Account and Contract owners will be sent an email. With Contracts, history tracking is automatically carried out on the Status field for In Approval Process and Activated statuses. If you would like all statuses tracked, you need to check the **Track History for All Statuses** setting.

Contract Contact Roles

Like Opportunity Contact Roles, it is possible to capture the roles that Contacts have in the contracting process. This is captured in a Related List just like Opportunity Contact Roles, but in this case, the Related List is called Contract Contact Roles. Unlike Opportunity Contact Roles, which is an Object that you find in Object Manager, the only configuration possible with Contract Contact Roles is customizing the Roles picklist. This is done from a page in the **Settings** menu. Enter `Contact Roles on Contracts` in the Quick Find search or go to **Setup** > **Feature Settings** > **Sales** > **Contact Roles on Contracts**.

Key considerations

If you decide to use the Contract Object, you will want to decide whether you want to create Contracts as part of the pre-sales process – for example, in the contracting stage – or whether the records will be created retrospectively, once everything is done and signed. You will also want to consider whether you want to automate the initial creation of these records with Flow, which will reduce errors, reduce the training requirements, and directly save the User's time.

Out-of-the-box Contracts only have a relationship with Account, so you might want to add a relationship with Opportunity, particularly if you are planning to trigger the creation of these records from Opportunities.

In practice

In practice, if you have any specific requirements about the creation, tracking, and digital signature of contracts, it is likely that you will benefit from using the well-established contract management tool. These typically include document generation and signature.

Orders and Order Line Items

In this section, we will look at the capabilities of Sales Cloud for capturing placed orders and managing them through a process. Then, we'll explore some key considerations and what happens in practice.

These objects are commonly used as an integration point between front- and back-office systems, such as to connect your Sales Cloud instance with an **enterprise resource planning** (**ERP**) tool that is hosted elsewhere.

Sales Cloud capabilities

These Objects have the same parent-child structure that we see with Opportunity and Opportunity Products and Quotes and Quote Line Items, with a header parent record and child records that capture the individual products and services.

Order

The Order Object captures the headline details of what a customer has purchased. If Opportunity Products are also used, then Order Line Items can be set up to enable a corresponding set of Order Line Items to be created. In this case, the Order record acts as a header.

Table 12.5 summarizes key information about the Order Object and its Fields:

Key Information	
API Name	Order
Required Fields	Account Name (Lookup to Account)
	Order Start Date (Date)
	Contract Number (Lookup to Contract)
	Status (Picklist)
Standard Relationships*	Account Name (Lookup to Account)
	Bill To Contact (Lookup to Contact)
	Contract Number (Lookup to Contract)
	Opportunity (Lookup to Opportunity)
	Original Order (Lookup to Order)
	Price Book (Lookup to Price Book)
	Ship To Contact (Lookup to Contact)
	Quote (Lookup to Quote)
Other Key Fields	

Table 12.5 – Key information about the Order Object

*Lookup relationships to the User Object for Owner, Created By, and Modified By have not been included as they exist on all Objects.

You will notice that this Object has a lot of relationships with the other Objects we have explored in this book as it is the culmination of the sales effort.

Order Product

The Order Product Object captures details about the products and services included in an order. If Opportunity Products are also used, then Order Line Items can also be set up to enable a corresponding set of Order Line Items to be created. This captures data such as the Product Name, the Sale Price that was agreed upon, the quantity, and any specific dates.

Table 12.6 summarizes key information about the Order Product Object and its fields:

Key Information	
API Name	OrderItem
Required Fields	Account Name (Name)
	Order Start Date (Date)
	Contract Number (Lookup to Contract)
	Status (Picklist)
Standard Relationships*	Order (Lookup to Order)
	Original Order Product (Lookup to Order Product)
	Product (Lookup to Product)
Other Key Fields	List Price (Currency)
	Quantity (Number)

Table 12.6 – Key information about the Order Product Object

```
*Lookup relationships to the User Object for Owner, Created By, and
Modified By have not been included as they exist on all Objects.
```

You will notice that these fields are also very similar to those that you would see on the Opportunity Product, and like Opportunity Product, the values such as Price and Quantity are rolled up and summed on the Order.

Enabling Orders

In much the same way as Quotes, Orders also need to be enabled in your Org before the functionality is available. This is done by entering Order Settings in the **Quick Find** search or going to **Setup > Feature Settings > Sales > Order > Order Settings**. Immediately after enabling Orders, you will be prompted to select the Page Layouts you would like to add the Order Related List to.

You can set whether a Contract is required to create an Order by making the field require an Order. If you are using Contracts, the Order's, Start Date must fall within the Contract Start and End Dates.

Order Settings

Orders can also be negative, or zero, which might be used in a subscription-style model. There are a number of setting options with Orders, depending on how much management you want your Users to be able to do. The following settings enable you to make Org-wide decisions on whether Users can create these types of Orders. The settings are **Enable Reduction Orders**, **Enable Negative Quantity**, and **Enable Zero Quantity**. These are not enabled by default and act as guidelines to ensure that the User can enter data that is likely to require additional process steps, such as issuing credit notes or refunds, without realizing. If these records are created and updated via an integration, these settings do not need to be enabled for negative and reduction Orders to be created.

Key considerations

A key consideration for Order data is whether Salesforce should be the system of record or whether that should be another system and the data should be viewable in Salesforce. Orders are typically mastered in a different system and created in Sales Cloud by an integration. We'll consider this in more detail in the next chapter, *Common System Integrations*.

If enabled, you should consider whether all Users should be able to create negative Orders and add Approval Processes and validation rules where appropriate.

In practice

For organizations that don't already have a system that manages Orders, this Object can provide a system of record. If your organization already has Order data mastered in another system, you may consider a visual layer integration to allow Sales Cloud Users to see the information rather than storing the data in the Customer 360 platform.

Custom Objects

In this section, we explore the Custom Object functionality in the Salesforce Core platform, which allows you to create entities in the database to capture data that Sales Cloud doesn't have an out-of-the-box Object for. This flexibility allows you to model and manage additional processes that your salespeople are required to follow all in one system. Examples might include a key account management process, an onboarding process, or in some industries, a Know Your Customer process.

It is assumed that you are familiar with the overall concepts of the Salesforce Core platform, which include the potential for low-code development with Custom Objects. It is not possible to cover all scenarios of how to build custom processes in this book. The Salesforce Trailhead Academy offers a full five-day course on declarative development on the Salesforce platform called **Declarative Development for Platform App Builders in Lightning Experience (DEX403)**, for those who need a detailed understanding. In this book, we will review some of the key components that are available and some of the things you should consider when building Custom Objects to enable a process.

Custom Object elements

Table 12.7 lists some of the key elements that you will want to define when carrying out declarative development on the Salesforce Core platform; it is worth noting that the majority of these customization options are also available on Standard Objects:

Objects	Objects allow for a new classification of data to be stored. Junction Objects allow for many-to-many relationships to be modeled. It is important to separate data that relates to different entities, but you don't want to keep the number of Objects to a minimum of useability.
Relationships	Master-Detail and Lookup relationships are available. Master-Detail means that the child inherits the Ownership of the parent.
Fields	Fields are where the individual pieces of data are stored. There are a range of types that give a lot of flexibility and allow different types of data manipulation.
Tabs	A Tab gives a defined place that the User can navigate to see all records of an Object. Alternatively, they have to navigate the parent record each time.
List Views	List Views are only available if the Object has a Tab. Setting up views of the data that Users commonly need to see can be a real timesaver.
Apps	Apps allow Tabs to be grouped together and restrict who can access the Apps, allowing types of work to be segmented for the people who need to perform them.
Sharing and Visibility	When any new Object is created, it is very important to specify who should be able to see and edit the data. This can be defined using a selection of tools such as Permission Sets, Sharing Rules, Role Hierarchy, and so on.

Table 12.7 – Summary of Custom Object key components

The previous table provides a brief overview of the elements you will expect to use if you need to set up functionality to manage a bespoke process.

Key considerations

The biggest consideration before starting to develop bespoke functionality is buy versus build, and the build and maintenance cost versus a subscription cost. Always familiarize yourself with the tools from the AppExchange first, as these will help you understand what you do and don't need, even if you ultimately decide to build it yourself.

In practice

Having more Objects requires more admin on the User side to create and navigate them. You will want to automate any of the creation of propagation of data that you can. If you have a receptive User base, it can be beneficial to have a subset of Users pilot the functionality with limited automation to see what they really need when they use it in a real-life setting. Then, have time scheduled afterward to enhance the functionality quickly to ensure they get what they need.

It is now possible to create Custom Objects and their fields from a spreadsheet. This feature is accessed from **Setup > Object Manager**. From here, you can find **Create Object from Spreadsheet** in the pull-down arrow next to **Create**.

Summary

In this chapter, we learned about the out-of-the-box functionality available to generate and manage Quotes, capture Contracts, and track Orders in Sales Cloud. With Quotes, we learned about the unique relationship they have with Opportunities and their ability to generate and send pdf Quotes to customers. For Contracts, we learned about how you can capture the roles that people have in process but that it doesn't provide the functionality to manage the full creation process. With Orders, we learned that this Object, along with Order Line Items, is typically an integration point with other systems. Where Orders are managed in Sales Cloud, there are Org-wide settings that allow you to control the type of Orders that Users can create – for example, reduction Orders.

We also learned about Custom Objects that allow you to capture data to support processes that are not included in Sales Cloud as standard or that are unique to your business.

In the next chapter, we will learn about common integrations with Sales Cloud and what you should think about when deciding whether and how to integrate an application with Sales Cloud.

Further reading

- Trailhead: *Salesforce Contracts Foundations*

  https://trailhead.salesforce.com/content/learn/modules/salesforce-contracts-foundations

- Trailhead: *Products, Quotes, & Contracts*

    ```
    https://trailhead.salesforce.com/content/learn/modules/sales_
    admin_products_quotes_contracts
    ```

- Help: *Contracts*

    ```
    https://help.salesforce.com/s/articleView?id=sf.contract_def.
    htm&type=5
    ```

Quotes and Orders

- *Trailhead: Manage Products, Prices, Quotes, and Orders*

    ```
    https://trailhead.salesforce.com/content/learn/projects/manage-
    products-prices-quotes-orders
    ```

- *Help: Quotes*

    ```
    https://help.salesforce.com/s/articleView?id=sf.quotes_overview.
    htm&type=5
    ```

Custom Objects

- *Trailhead: Customize a Salesforce Object*

    ```
    https://trailhead.salesforce.com/content/learn/projects/customize-
    a-salesforce-object
    ```

13

Common System Integrations

Sales Cloud is a very powerful tool that enables the commercial function of a business. Salesforce offers further tools that are functionally rich tools for other business functions, such as support and marketing. However, these are not the only functions that need tools to enable their processes – for example, finance. Further, organizations already have tools that they want to continue using. Because of this, it is a common request to connect these systems so that data flows from one to the other without manual intervention. This allows information to be visible to Users where and when they need it, and enables an action in one team to trigger processes that are managed by another team. This increases organizational efficiency and can result in a better overall customer experience.

In this chapter, we are going to discuss some of the common integrations with external systems that you may want to implement to enhance your Sales Cloud solution, along with some of the key considerations you need to be aware of when implementing such integrations.

We will cover the following topics:

- Why do we integrate systems with Sales Cloud?
- Common integrations
- System integrations overview
- Who should be involved?

Supporting tools and information

For this chapter, you will require access to a Sandbox or Dev Org to be able to explore the integration options we'll describe in this chapter. You will also want to visit the AppExchange at `appexchange.salesforce.com`, something we'll review in detail in *Chapter 14 – Extending with the AppExchange.*

You will also want to review the requirements that were collected as part of the requirements that were gathered for your core sales process to determine if any of those relate to having access to information so that you can trigger processes for other functional teams. You may also need access to the tools that were used to capture requirements and document processes in case you identify that an integration is required and need to document more detail.

Why do we integrate systems with Sales Cloud?

One of the common challenges for organizations is to move from siloed ways of working, where a team only has awareness of what happens in their team, to a connected, collaborative way of working where they focus on the customer and what they need. Sales Cloud offers this shared visibility and central source of information for the commercial team but without connected processes and systems, it is still possible that the commercial team can operate in their silo.

Connecting processes and systems across functional boundaries breaks down these siloed ways of working, improving both the employee and customer experience. No salesperson wants to call or meet with a customer to talk about repeat business only to find out there is an outstanding support or finance issue that they could have known about or even resolved in advance. If this information was available to the salesperson on-demand in the single system they work in, they would be able to focus their time on actions that add value, such as identifying opportunities to generate more revenue or highlighting the impact a customer's issue is having. *Figure 13.1* shows an example **system landscape** diagram that illustrates how business applications, which hold data that the sales team might need to know about, can be connected to remove data silos:

Salesforce System Landscape

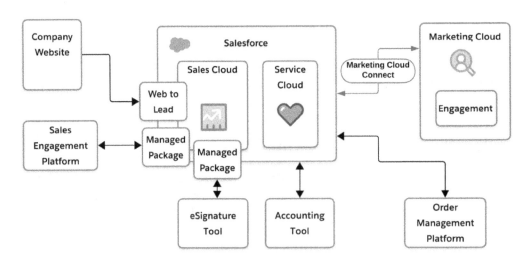

Figure 13.1 – Example system landscape diagram

In *Figure 13.1*, you can see that Salesforce is at the center, with data flowing from other business applications. We'll explore the benefits of integrating these applications in the *Common integrations* section and the types of integration approaches in the *Types of integrations* section. You'll learn how to set up Web to Lead in *Chapter 4 – Design and Build: The Lead Generation Process*.

Some of the key benefits of integration systems are as follows:

- **Streamlining operations**: Having data automatically flow through systems so that it is available to those that need it, when they need it, reduces the time to service each customer. For example, a salesperson can see all the open support cases a customer has without having to call the support team or request a report. This saves time for both teams.

- **Improved customer experience**: Overall, the customers' experience is better when they can get their queries resolved on their preferred channel. For example, it is a better experience if a customer can also ask if they have any outstanding invoices while on a call with their account executive rather than requiring them to make a separate call to finance.

- **Improved internal alignment**: When information is shared across teams, it creates a shared understanding of what is required across teams. For example, if the sales and support teams have visibility of the marketing campaigns that are currently taking place, they can respond to and even build on the requests that will come from customers. For example, if a sales promotion is sent out for free access to a product for customers that meet specific criteria, sales or support might give or not give access to the right customers if they can't see who should have it.

- **Increased revenue and profitability**: Both revenue and profitability can be increased as deeper, customized insights allow timely identification of additional opportunities and allow them to be acted on with fewer resources. For example, if product usage is available to salespeople, they can identify customers who are just about to require more or reengage those who look like they might stop purchasing.

- **Scalability**: It can be much easier to scale business operations if manual operations are removed, which can be achieved with integrations. For example, if sales are either manually entered into a finance or order system, the size of the business will depend on the number of people available to enter the information. If this is automated via an integration, the cost and time to hire more people is no longer a barrier to growing the business.

Based on some of the examples given here, you can see that integrations can be particularly impactful for **front-office** systems – those that support front-office functions such as sales, support, and marketing. These are typically the revenue generation functions, and the teams that interact with customers and access to up-to-date information can make a difference. Integrations with **back office** systems, such as finance and order management, are also beneficial as it means these functions don't also need to have a customer-face operation. It is worth noting that systems and integrations on their own won't deliver the full benefit, processes need to be cross-functional to get the maximum benefit.

Next, we will review some of the most common functions that are integrated with Sales Cloud.

Common integrations

In this section, we will look at some common types of integration with Sales Cloud and some notes and considerations for each, including how these are typically integrated. In the *System integrations overview* section, we'll explore the ways systems can be integrated with Sales Cloud.

Sales solutions

There's a broad range of sales solutions that can be integrated/added to Sales Cloud to increase its capability. Many of the capabilities covered here can be provided by add-on tools that Salesforce offers; they can either be added for an add-on cost or become available in the Unlimited edition of Sales Cloud. Some third-party providers offer all these capabilities. If you need to connect third-party tools, work will be needed to connected them. If you purchase the tools from Salesforce, you need to configure the tools but there is no integration effort. Some examples of the types of tools that are typically connected are as follows:

- **Sales engagement platforms (SEPs):** SEPs are solutions that are designed to streamline and optimize the interactions between sales teams and potential customers. Examples include SalesLoft and Outreach. They integrate various communication channels, automate sales workflows, and provide analytics to enhance sales productivity and effectiveness. Salesforce's product for this is called **Sales Engagement**.

- **Email integration tools:** These tools automate the process of syncing email communications with Sales Cloud, ensuring all interactions are logged and accessible within the system for a comprehensive view of customer interactions. In addition to Einstein Activity Capture, which we reviewed in *Chapter 3 – Design and Build: The Core Sales Process*, Salesforce also offers **Salesforce Inbox**.

- **Telephony integration platform:** Telephony integration is usually more common with Service Cloud, but these tools mean that calls are automatically recorded in the system as activity records. These tools also typically offer the option to record and analyze the content. If you have a phone system that has a connector, you may want to consider it. It is worth noting that this logging, recording, and analysis of calls and meetings are common capabilities of sales engagement platforms, which also cover further capabilities.

As these tools are some of the commonly used pairs with CRM systems such as Sales Cloud, there are usually connectors that are either built by the platform provider or a third party. Data storage is a consideration with these tools as they generate a lot of activity-type records.

Marketing solutions

While Salesforce offers industry-leading marketing solutions through its Marketing Cloud product set, it is very common for organizations to have a separate marketing suite, whether it's simply email marketing or a more connected multi-channel system, which they will want to connect with Salesforce.

Salesforce offers three tools that offer email marketing, now under the Marketing Cloud banner:

- **Marketing Cloud Growth**: This is the newest tool that started a global phased rollout in February 2024. At the time of writing, a limited amount was known about the new offering, except that at the time of release, it was aimed at allowing small to medium businesses to connect data from multiple sources via Data Cloud and then quickly create email campaigns and content with AI assistance. Marketing Cloud Growth also enables the creation of forms to capture leads and events, as well as send SMS messages. Marketing Cloud Growth connects via Data Cloud but it isn't known how it connects directly to Sales Cloud. However, it is accessible via the Salesforce platform.

- **Marketing Cloud Engagement**: This is an enterprise-scale digital marketing tool that can also be set up to send transactional messages. it offers a suite of tools that enable marketers to craft personalized customer journeys across various channels, including email, social media, mobile, and the web. This connects to Sales Cloud via a native connector. We'll learn more about native connector integrations in the *Types of integrations* section.

- **Marketing Cloud Account Engagement**: This tool, previously known as **Pardot**, is typically, but not exclusively, used for B2B marketing. It helps organizations streamline lead qualification, automate engagement based on customer behavior, and personalize communication across various channels to nurture leads until they are sales-ready. This platform is particularly focused on account-based marketing strategies, enabling marketers to create targeted campaigns that resonate with specific accounts or customer segments, thus enhancing lead generation, conversion rates, and ROI on marketing efforts. This is built on the Salesforce platform, so no connector is required.

Most popular marketing solutions have a native pre-built connector on the Salesforce AppExchange. This should be your first option when you're looking to integrate a marketing platform with Salesforce. If your solution of choice does not have a native integration, it would be wise to consider whether another that does might be a better fit, as well as review the available and recommended integration setup from that vendor.

Although integration through either a custom build or middleware such as Zapier is possible, based on experience, the use of a pre-built connector that is native to Salesforce will enable you to truly get the benefits of integrating your sales and marketing systems for more personalized customer experiences. Connecting via middleware tools requires you to have a detailed understanding of your near and medium-term requirements, and time to investigate if those requirements can be achieved with the middleware.

Additionally, data storage and contact management should be a key consideration. In many situations, storing large volumes of data, particularly email sends, can result in your org's data storage being depleted. To report on such information and display it within Salesforce, consider whether you can obtain the reporting you need from the marketing solution itself and if there is an appropriate age for the data, at which point you can archive.

Customer Support systems

Integrating your Customer Support system with Sales Cloud means that your sales teams can check if there are open issues a customer has logged before each interaction. They can also see the volume of support issues raised to get some insight into how the customer is getting on with the product or service. Opportunities could be identified here for additional products or services.

If your organization is, or elects to, use **Service Cloud**, no integration is required – only configuration of visibility. If you are integrating with a third party, then you will want to be specific about exactly what information will help sales activities. You will likely want to make some aggregate data available to view and possibly issues that are open or of a specific severity level. It is unlikely you will want to replicate all the data you have in your support system in Sales Cloud. This will take up quite a lot of data storage for little to no value.

Finance and accounting systems

Integrating your finance and accounting system with your CRM can dramatically improve your organization's ability to invoice customers and improve client management by removing the manual handover from the sales team to the finance team. There are several solutions available on the AppExchange, both fully Salesforce native or integrating with an external solution, that will allow you to auto-generate invoices based on your closed won opportunities with accurate data from Sales Cloud. Tools that are commonly integrated with Sales Cloud include *Xero* and *QuickBooks*.

For this integration, data cleanliness and quality are key to ensure that customers are correctly invoiced and that the appropriate information is utilized in generating the invoice amount. Additionally, you should consider the need for appropriate change management and user training as Salesforce is different from many accounting platforms concerning its user interface and functionality. From experience, finance teams are very detail-focused and will want to ensure that their processing is enhanced, and reporting is simplified, with many trained on (and in some instances still utilizing) spreadsheets as their primary tool.

> Tip
>
> With appropriate engagement and training, implementing a Salesforce-based finance system or integration can dramatically improve an organization's ability to manage its cash flow and will be seen as an all-around net positive.

Document generation

For many sales cycles, lots of documents will be generated, such as quotes, proposals, responses for information, and contracts. Sales Cloud can be integrated with several document generation tools that make the process of creating documents using pre-built templates populated with data from Salesforce quick and easy. Commonly used providers are Conga, DocuSign DocGen, and Nintex.

When choosing a solution, it is key that time is spent planning what documents need to be generated and the level of dynamism required within the templates. Do you need to use parent and child records? What type of file formats need to be produced? How do you want to share the files? Considering these and other questions will help you ensure that the solution meets your needs and that process improvements can be suggested to the sales and other teams who will be using the solution.

eSignature

Once a sale has occurred, commonly, a contract needs to be signed to officially complete a deal. Salesforce has several integrations with different eSignature providers that can allow you to take the documents that have been agreed upon and generated by a document generation tool or provided as a template and share them with external parties for electronic signature. Commonly used providers are DocuSign and Abobe Sign, but many other tools now have this functionality built in.

Many solutions also allow for documents to be stored and saved within Salesforce against records, as well as use data from Salesforce for the document to be signed. When implementing such a solution, you should work closely with the relevant legal teams within the business to agree on document formats and contents, as well as with the sales team to find opportunities for improvement within the sales cycle. You will also want to consider if other sensitive data is held in the eSignature tool, such as work contracts. This might have implications for how you connect the tools with Sales Cloud.

Data enrichment

Several data enrichment tools can provide information that accelerates sales activities. Some of these are provided by other integrations that we have reviewed here, for example, email engagement from marketing solutions or customer satisfaction levels inferred from custom support solutions. Common integrations include services that provide firmographic data, which offer information about company size, revenue, industry, and the number of employees, and credit information, which might be relevant when you're deciding to proceed with a customer.

If your organization already uses these services, you will want to check if there is a native connector. Services such as Dun & Bradstreet have a native connector. If you are selecting a service, you will want to make sure you understand the regions the data is available for, how it is sourced, and how current it is.

Customer Data Platforms

Organizations that have multiple customer touchpoints find themselves in a situation where each customer is in each of their systems, but they can't see all interactions in a single place. To solve this, they invest in a **CDP**. A CDP is a system that collects, unifies, and stores customer data from multiple sources at scale. Once how the data models from different systems relate to each other has been defined, organizations can relate the actions that happen in one system to another and specify actions that should happen. Sales Cloud can be connected to many commercially available CDPs.

Salesforce Data Cloud builds on the original Salesforce CDP product and now collects data across the whole platform, including Sales, Service, Commerce, and Marketing. This makes Salesforce Data Cloud another integration for Sales Cloud that will continue to increase, particularly since, at the time of writing, Salesforce offers a certain number of Data Service credits to Enterprise Edition customers at no additional cost. Data Cloud has prebuilt connectors to cloud storage, including Amazon S3, Azure, and Google Storage. If you have a requirement to unify your data across systems, you should explore Data Cloud further.

In this section, we reviewed several common integrations that can be thought of as the next steps to extend and enhance your Sales Cloud implementation to drive greater value and return on investment. In the next section, we look at how systems can be integrated in more detail, including some of the key things you will want to consider.

Systems integrations overview

Most organizations today utilize several different systems for managing their data and processes. Historically, in the world of on-premise software, integrations were primarily managed through the use of either a shared filesystem with files at a specific location in a pre-agreed format or via a highly structured integration platform operating across the internal network. In many instances, organizations would typically buy all their systems from a single vendor to make data integration easier, or manual copying was undertaken in some instances.

As more systems moved to be based on the cloud as SaaS solutions, there has become an increasing need for these systems to interoperate and communicate with each other in a way that is both performant and more standardized. This book will not go into detail about the various technologies underpinning integrations, such as REST, SOAP, and others, but you need to be aware that most SaaS applications you will look to integrate with will have a REST-based API, and are likely to have a pre-built connector with Salesforce you can utilize.

> **AppExchange – buy versus build integration**
>
> Wherever possible, when deploying Salesforce, you should review all your systems and determine whether an AppExchange solution may be a better fit than an existing solution with an integration. Many of the integrations we will be discussing here have AppExchange packages to make the integration simpler, but in those instances where a custom integration is required, it may be more cost-effective to replace the existing solution with an AppExchange package, especially if this solution is homegrown or on-premise.

First, we will learn about the ways tools can integrate with Sales Cloud and the Salesforce Core platform.

Types of integrations

Broadly speaking, three main types of integration can occur with Sales Cloud, which is built on the Salesforce core platform:

- A native integration, whereby the application vendor or a partner has an AppExchange solution (package) they provide or can recommend that manages the integration for you. Examples include DocuSign App Launcher, Campaign Monitor for Salesforce, and Breadwinner for Xero. We learn how to install packages in *Chapter 14 – Extending with the AppExchange*. These are also known as **managed packages** and can be found in `Setup > Packaging > Installed Packages`.

- An externally native integration hosted on the application vendor manages the integration with Salesforce by having you authenticate with Salesforce to retrieve an authorization token that can be used to make requests into Salesforce. An example of one is FormAssembly.

- A custom integration built and maintained by yourselves. This can either be done using a middleware platform such as Zapier or MuleSoft, or through custom development. This may be necessary for bespoke systems, or where an existing option from type 1 or 2 doesn't meet the requirements.

Wherever possible, we want to utilize an integration from type 1 or 2 for a variety of reasons, including the following:

- These integrations have been developed and are maintained by a third-party team, so they will be updated for the latest features and security releases

- Integrations of this type will typically scale better as the data volumes between the systems grow

- Some of the considerations we will cover have already been reviewed and solved by the developers, such as master data management

- The developer will typically support the application as part of the cost of the license

In some instances, a custom integration will be required that will need development. In this case, a declarative development approach should be investigated first to see if it is a viable approach before jumping straight to a pro-code solution as this is likely to have a lower maintenance overhead.

Salesforce has invested heavily in supporting common API specifications to make outbound integrations much simpler. If the integration you are undertaking is outbound only and the external solution has a REST API that is available in the OpenAPI 2.0 or 3.0 format, then you can utilize a feature called **External Services** to implement these endpoints and create actions you can utilize from Flow, which we covered in *Chapter 5 – Design and Build: Sales User Productivity*. We will not go into the specific details of how to set up an integration with External Services, but more information can be found in the *Further reading* section.

It is beyond the scope of this book to explore every aspect of integration in detail. The Salesforce platform is constantly evolving. For occasions when a bespoke integration is required, Salesforce now provides **Decision Guides** to help those responsible for delivering an integration select the most appropriate approach. These can be found at `architect.salesforce.com`.

> **Architecture Decision Guides**
>
> As the core Salesforce Platform evolves, the tools available to enable integrations change and improve. It can be difficult to keep up to date on which tools are the most appropriate for different use cases. Salesforce now provides Decision Guides to help your organization select the most appropriate tools. If you are planning a custom integration, the person who designs the integrations should use these to inform their approach and design. There are currently guides for data integration and Event-Driven Architecture. Links to these have been provided in the *Further reading* section.

As with any integration, there are a few key considerations and decisions we must make to ensure that the integration scales appropriately and does not cause data issues between the two systems. We'll look at some of these considerations now.

Key considerations

When looking to integrate two separate systems, it is important that several key considerations are discussed, and that decisions and designs that are made are documented to assist in the future. Without fully reviewing the topics we will discuss in this section, you run the risk of causing synchronization issues and data discrepancies between the two systems, which will become increasingly more difficult to unpick. Let's review some of the key considerations, one at a time.

Data mastering

When working with two independent systems, it is important to decide which system is the master of which sets of data. For organizations working in a jurisdiction covered by regulations such as the GDPR, it is a legal requirement for you to ensure that you keep personal data accurate and up to date. We discussed this in *Chapter 3 – Design and Build: The Core Sales Process*.

As an example, if we have an integration between Sales Cloud and a finance solution, we would expect that Sales Cloud is the master of all account, contact, and sales data, with this data then feeding into the finance system to provide data for invoicing. The finance system would be the master of the financial data, such as invoices, credit notes, and payments, which may then feed back into Salesforce to provide contextual information for a salesperson.

Sometimes, the data will be mastered by different systems in its life cycle. For example, contact data will be mastered by an eCommerce system until a purchase is made, at which point it enters the CRM system and is mastered within Sales Cloud. Care and attention must then be paid to how the data will be updated in each system – for example, if a customer wishes to change their billing address, where that update is sent, and how it propagates to other solutions.

Once a robust master data management plan is put in place, it is much easier for you to feel confident that no data is being leaked between platforms, as well as making it simpler to enforce strict access controls to data based on the owning system.

The following are some of the key steps we can take:

- Document what data points are sent from each system to the other system

- Determine which system owns the master copy of the data and how that will be propagated to the other system(s)

- Determine where there are handovers in ownership of the data throughout its life cycle and how that handover is managed

Key/reference management

All systems that utilize a database will store records with a unique identifier or reference, which in database terminology is called a primary key. Each system involved in the integration must have a way of referencing the matching data in the other system(s) to keep the data synchronized correctly.

Within Salesforce, it is a best practice to store identifiers from other systems in a custom field that has been marked as an External ID. This will enable indexing using this field to improve performance in querying this data, as well as enabling features such as upserting using the key.

The following are some of the key steps we can take:

- Identify reference keys from each system and where they should be stored

- Validate whether the keys have a uniqueness requirement between systems

When you are planning your integration remember to create External ID fields to capture keys.

Security

Historically, on-premises integrations were easier to manage as you could limit access to only those systems within the organization's network. With most systems now in the cloud, you must maintain the correct level of security when integrating different systems.

Firstly, integrations (wherever possible) should not be run under an individual's user account but under a restricted integration account while following the principle of least privilege. The integration account should not have administrator-level access and should be restricted to only perform the functions needed – for example, creating and updating records of a particular object, with field-level security enforced appropriately. Salesforce provides five free integration user licenses for this purpose and they should be utilized with the minimal additional permissions applied via permission sets. Unfortunately, it is not usually possible to use this license type for integrations via an AppExchange connector. It should be used for integrations via the API.

Once you have correctly provisioned and set up the user to run the integration, you should review how the necessary credentials are going to be utilized. Ideally, you want a secure way to authorize that doesn't mean sharing username and password details such as OAuth. This enables you to authorize as the integration user, generating a token that can be used and refreshed on the user's behalf. If the integration can only authenticate via a username and password, these should be stored securely and encrypted at rest. If performing an outbound integration from Salesforce, the Named Credentials feature is ideal for this purpose. Care should be taken to be aware of security policies for integration users utilizing a username and password as any password refresh requirements (for example, changing password every 30 days) can impact integrations and cause unnecessary downtime.

> **OAuth**
>
> OAuth is an open-standard authorization protocol or framework that allows third-party services to exchange web resources on behalf of a user, without revealing the user's passwords. It enables users to grant a website or application access to their information on another website but without giving them the passwords, using tokens instead of actual credentials, which increases security and convenience.

Finally, all data should be transferred via HTTPS and therefore encrypted in transit so that it is secure from eavesdroppers. Where possible, look to restrict possible IP ranges for integrations to increase security. If you're utilizing a middleware solution such as Zapier or MuleSoft, you should review if any data is stored on the middleware, for how long, if it is encrypted, and where it is located.

> **Hypertext Transfer Protocol Secure (HTTPS)**
>
> HTTPS is the secure version of HTTP, the protocol over which data is sent between your browser and the website that you are connected to. It uses SSL/TLS encryption to protect the data transmitted, ensuring that the data exchanged between the user and site is secure from eavesdropping and tampering.

The following are some of the key steps we can take:

- Identify and configure a separate integration user using the principle of least privilege to determine access rights and permissions

- Review authentication and authorization options for the integrating systems. Salesforce provides guidance on who should do this to access the Salesforce platform.

- Ensure any passwords are strong and stored securely

- Verify any data that is stored on middleware is encrypted at rest

- Verify that all data is encrypted in transit

The movement toward predominantly cloud-based systems means that security is a fundamental consideration. It is important to ensure that an integration doesn't introduce security vulnerabilities. If you don't have the knowledge and skills internally to ensure this, you should consider engaging an external supplier.

Data volumes

A side effect of integrating two solutions is that you can end up dramatically increasing the data stored in each system through duplication. Care should be taken to project the likely data volumes and storage usage, particularly in Salesforce, where additional data storage can be costly.

Equally, as the solution grows and a greater number of transactions between the systems occurs, the volume of requests will also grow and may surpass governor and feature limits. Again, analysis should be undertaken to map out the data flows and volumes to ensure compliance with org limits.

The following are some of the key steps we can take:

- Calculate and project data volume and usage alongside available storage

- Validate that the integration will not lead to governor limits being exceeded

Uni-Directional vs Bi-Directional

Integrations can either be uni-directional (one way), where a change or action in System A causes some data to be sent to System B, or bi-directional (two ways), where data changes in either System A or System B will cause data to be sent to the other system. You must map out and understand whether or not data is flowing uni-directionally or bi-directionally early in the integration planning as you will need to ensure that processes within each system align so as not to cause recursive updates or data corruption as data falls out of sync.

In general, it is simpler (and safer) to have a uni-directional integration as there is a far reduced risk of data falling out of sync or there being conflicts to resolve. That said, bi-directionality is perfectly feasible is properly planned and structured. It would always be advisable to start with a uni-directional flow and then decide if the reverse direction is needed.

The following are the key steps we can take:

- Determine if the integration needs to be uni or bi-directional
- Map out your data flows between the systems
- Map out and plan for errors, loss of connection, data corruption, and conflicts to ensure robust practices and plans are put in place from day one.

Transformation and mapping

When transferring data from one system to another, there will inevitably be some form of transformation and mapping. It is important that this transformation and mapping is well understood and documented, as well as, wherever possible, being repeatable with no side effects on the data (for example, changing the value of the data itself).

Having a clear understanding and thorough documentation of the mapping and transformation data undergoes within the integration can make it much easier to debug any issues with the integration, as well as provide you with a clear and easy way to match data through the pipeline and test.

It should be noted that transformations can also include between data formats – for example, from CSV to JSON – and in these instances, it should be mapped and thoroughly tested as to the robustness of the transformation, especially when dealing with special characters, date strings, and null values.

The following key steps can be taken:

- Identify any mapping and transformation that is required on the data
- Document all mapping and transformation for use in development and testing
- Verify any data format changes around special characters, null values, and date strings

Now that we have reviewed several of the key considerations and steps that should be taken when defining and planning integration, we will consider who you should involve in the Sales Cloud implementation.

Who should be involved?

If a prebuilt connector is not available, then a more bespoke solution will be required. If this is the case, the idea is to get guidance from someone or a team of people who have experience designing and building integrations. Your first step should be to identify if there is someone in your organization who is responsible for how all your business systems connect. This is part of the role of an **Enterprise Architect**. The person in your organization may or may not have this specific title. If any of your business systems are already connected you likely have someone with this responsibility.

In organizations that have a lot of business systems, some strategic decisions have likely been made on how to approach connecting them. This might be documented as architectural principles. An example of a decision that might have been made is that an integration middleware solution will be used to connect business applications where a native connector is not available. If this is the case, the organization is likely to have gone through a middleware selector process and have people internally with the skills to manage and maintain the integrations. If you have requirements that expand beyond the Salesforce platform, you must identify additional business stakeholders that may need to be involved, such as an enterprise architect. If you do not do this at the start of your implementation, you may experience delays once they become aware of what is happening and have questions and requirements of their own.

If you don't have anyone in your organization who has knowledge and experience in implementing integrations, you should consider seeking guidance from people who have – in particular, people who have experience integrating with the Salesforce core platform since Salesforce has a range of integration tools. You can find individuals or Salesforce partners either via your Salesforce Account Executive or from a listing on the AppExchange' there's a filter for **Multi-Cloud Integration**. When selecting an external provider, you will want to identify people with the appropriate skills and experience. Experience is always the most important factor, but Salesforce does have a few certifications that people can take to validate they know how to integrate with the Salesforce platform. These are the Salesforce Integration Architect certification and the Salesforce Certified Technical Architect. The first means the person had provided their knowledge via a proctored exam. The latter requires the person to have passed the Integration Architect certification, along with X other Architect certifications testing a range of knowledge. It also means that they have to design and present a multi-cloud to a review board, which challenges the decisions made. This is the hardest certification to achieve in the ecosystem. There are only in the region of 400 of these certified professionals worldwide.

Salesforce certifications

Salesforce has a range of certifications that people can achieve to illustrate that they have a specific level of knowledge on an aspect of Salesforce. A full list of certifications can be found on the `trailhead.salesforce.com` site, in the **Credential** section. Here, you will find various study guides and links to training materials and courses. You can also verify that a person has attained the certifications they have claimed to by entering their name or email address. You should also be able to see their certification on their Trailhead profile page.

So far, we have learned why you might want to integrate other systems with Sales Cloud, as well as the types of systems that are commonly integrated with Sales Cloud. Finally, we will look at how you might start determining if and how you might integrate a business integration with Salesforce.

Where to start?

Salesforce integration is a big topic that we have only covered at a high level here. There is a lot to consider and a lot of options, so it can be a bit unclear how to start. For a Sales Cloud implementation, the most important steps are identifying if an integration is required, the extent of integration that is required, the overarching approach – that is, pre-built connector versus bespoke solution – and who will be required to deliver the solution.

Just like other aspects of the implementation, getting started is about gathering key information and making key decisions. *Figure 13.2* shows a decision tree that you can use to determine how you are going to proceed with your integration requirements:

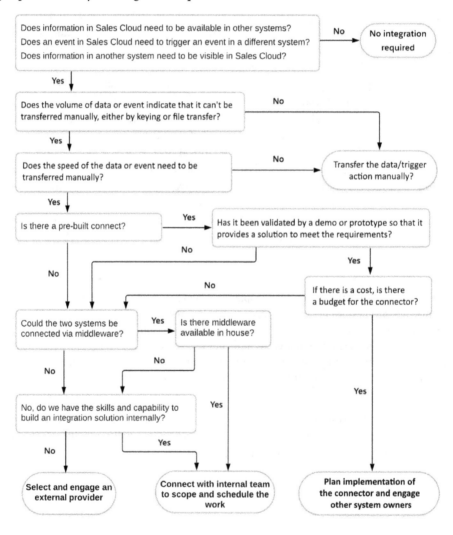

Figure 13.2 – An overview of your integration decision tree

As shown in *Figure 13.2*, there are several considerations to even get to an integration implementation approach. To view *Figure 13.2* in greater detail, you can visit this link: `https://packt.link/gbp/9781804619643`.

If you already have people in your organization who are experienced with integration, they will be able to accelerate you through this process by both providing insight and possibly reducing the options available as they are not in line with adopted architectural principles. Once you have engaged the right people to help you, either in your implementation team, within your organization, or from an external provider, you will be able to get into detailed planning and delivery.

Now that we have learned about integrating with Sales Cloud, you can make decisions about how to approach your integration implementation. Next, we'll summarize what we've learned in this chapter.

Summary

In this chapter, you learned how to extend and enhance your Sales Cloud implementation through various integrations with different solutions, both on and off the platform.

We began by covering the benefits of integrating Sales Cloud with other systems before looking at some common integrations with Sales Cloud that can enhance and extend its functionality to deliver greater value and return on investment to the business. Implementing Sales Cloud as a CRM for your organization is a key and important first step, but connecting different business processes and functions into a single solution is where the greatest benefits can be obtained. With the examples we have seen, you can easily have leads captured and generated from external systems, at which point they're managed and worked through the sales cycles in Sales Cloud, with documentation generated from Sales Cloud data and a contract sent to be signed when the deal is won. This can seamlessly create invoices and other billing data for your finance team, removing manual work and allowing your organization to sell more, more efficiently.

Next, we looked at the different types of system integrations on the platform and how you can integrate Salesforce with other systems. We then looked at several key considerations you should review before undertaking any integration to ensure that you do not lose or corrupt data within your systems or have unintended side effects.

Finally, we stepped through how you get started as integration is a big and complex topic with many options. But once you work through a basic set of questions, identify an overall approach, and know who to engage with, you can start to develop a plan.

Further reading

External Services

- *Trailhead: External Services:*

   `https://trailhead.salesforce.com/content/learn/modules/external-services`

Architects.salesforce.com – Decision Guides

- *Data Integration*:

  `https://architect.salesforce.com/decision-guides/data-integration`

- *Event-Driven Architecture*:

  `https://architect.salesforce.com/decision-guides/event-driven`

Developer.salesforce.com

- *Integration Patterns Overview*:

  `https://developer.salesforce.com/docs/atlas.en-us.integration_patterns_and_practices.meta/integration_patterns_and_practices/integ_pat_intro_overview.htm`

Trailhead

- *Trail: Explore Integration Patterns and Practices*:

  `https://trailhead.salesforce.com/content/learn/trails/explore-integration-patterns-and-practices`

Salesforce Integration Architect Certification

- *Salesforce Integration Architect Overview*:

  `https://trailhead.salesforce.com/en/credentials/integrationarchitect`

- *Architect Journey: Integration Architecture*:

  `https://trailhead.salesforce.com/users/strailhead/trailmixes/architect-integration-architecture`

Salesforce to Salesforce

- *Help: Salesforce to Salesforce*: `https://help.salesforce.com/s/articleView?id=sf.business_network_intro.htm&type=5`

Finding an external provider

- *Consultants on the AppExchange*:

  `https://appexchange.salesforce.com/consulting`

14

Extending with the AppExchange

You have been able to meet the majority of your requirements with the Sales Cloud out-of-the-box functionality and your solution is looking in good shape but there is a group of requirements that just don't have a good fit for the standard functionality. You need to decide whether to buy or build and you want to know what your options are.

In this chapter, we will look at **Salesforce AppExchange**, your go-to place to understand what pre-built solutions are available. This is Salesforce's marketplace for applications, components, flows, and more, which **independent software vendors (ISVs)** and partners have published to allow you to enhance your Salesforce solution.

We will cover the following topics:

- What is the AppExchange?
- Getting the most from AppExchange
- Common types of applications to enhance your implementation

Supporting tools and information

Whilst AppExchange itself is a public website, to install any applications, you will need a Trailblazer account that you have connected your Org to. Your Trailblazer account is used for logging into the following Salesforce sites:

- AppExchange
- Commerce Cloud Developer Center
- Events
- IdeaExchange

- Salesforce Help

- Trailblazer Community

- Trailhead

- Salesforce+

- Salesforce.com

- Partner Community

You can sign up for a Trailblazer account at `https://digital.salesforce.com/signup` and use your Salesforce login credentials as the basis of the account. More information about the Trailblazer account, the benefits of the account, and how to sign up can be found in the following Salesforce help article: `https://help.salesforce.com/s/articleView?id=sf.get_started_with_trailblazer_id.htm&type=5`. If you type in the URL for AppExchange, you will be immediately prompted to log in with a Trailblazer account. However, if you search for an app including the term "AppExchange," you can browse the content without having to log in.

What is the AppExchange?

AppExchange is Salesforce's enterprise application marketplace, designed to allow customers and implementation teams to discover pre-built applications, components, and templates to help deliver a much quicker ROI for your implementation. You can find AppExchange at `https://appexchange.salesforce.com`.

AppExchange was launched in 2005 to allow ISVs to build and sell applications to Salesforce customers, providing them with pre-built solutions that Salesforce themselves would not be building and delivering on the platform. Many of the earliest applications were delivered to supplement the standard Sales Cloud functionality and enhance business integration. Over time, AppExchange has grown alongside Salesforce to include both applications that enhance and extend the Salesforce product suite and those that aren't related to the standard Salesforce applications at all.

AppExchange has expanded from its original structure of being an application marketplace to the place for all ways of extending the platform. It matches the changes in technology and acquisitions by Salesforce by offering a place to find professional services, pre-built functionality, and apps. Let us briefly look at the different types of solutions you can find on AppExchange.

Applications

The first and most obvious type of solution on AppExchange is the apps. Apps are made by ISVs and **original equipment manufacturer** (**OEM**) partners and are listed on AppExchange for Salesforce customers to purchase and utilize in their Org. Some apps will require you to have specific Salesforce licenses or functionality to work with their solution or may not work with certain editions of Salesforce (most typically, Professional Edition and below).

Apps can be thought of broadly as fitting into one of the following three categories:

- **Apps that enhance a Salesforce product**: These include a sales commission calculation tool for Sales Cloud or a telephony integration for Service Cloud

- **Apps for use across the Salesforce platform**: These include an SMS messaging tool or form builder

- **Apps that utilize the Salesforce infrastructure**: Specifically, ones that do not require the customer to be an existing Salesforce customer, for example, an accounting or human resources application

Apps are sold either on an Org-wide or per-user license basis. In the former, you pay a single license fee for the application and utilize it as much as you wish. In the latter, you must determine how many users need access to the functionality and then purchase the requisite number of licenses.

Some applications are released for free on AppExchange, most notably those from Salesforce Labs. Salesforce Labs apps are free applications built and utilized by the team internally at Salesforce and released to assist customers and implementation teams. We have mentioned the Agile Accelerator app from the Salesforce Labs team multiple times in this book as an example. We will explore some of the most relevant Salesforce Labs in the section, *Salesforce Labs Solutions*.

Bolt Solutions

Bolt Solutions are pre-built templates for **Experience Cloud** that enable organizations to have a pre-configured experience that they can customize, reducing the overall time to deliver, and providing a best-in-breed solution based on the provider's knowledge and experience in the industry or sector.

Salesforce Experience Cloud is a solution that enables organizations to collaborate with external parties through a web portal that can allow access to data held within the company's Org. The most common use cases for experience solutions are customer support portals and knowledge bases, partner sales engagement portals, and employee hubs. Though, I have seen experiences in a wide variety of industries and use cases.

Flow Solutions

Flow Solutions are pre-built and configured Flows and Flow templates to help you achieve a specific process or function within your organization. They are commonly either small processes and templates for activities such as creating multiple records quickly and efficiently or provisioning Experience Cloud users, or enhancements to other applications for common use cases such as document generation tools or feedback and survey applications.

The **Flow Solutions** section of AppExchange is dominated by Salesforce Labs solutions that provide several utilities to enhance an administrator's daily tasks. I expect to see more solutions of this type added, including more paid solutions, as the more recent purchases from Salesforce are integrated further into the core platform. We will look a lot more at some of the Salesforce Lab Flow Solutions that might be relevant for your implementation in a later section, Salesforce Labs Solutions.

Lightning Data solutions

Lightning Data solutions provide pre-built connectors to standard data sources and platforms to enable organizations to enhance the data within their environment. At the time of writing, only a handful of solutions are available, and it is becoming more prevalent to work with other options for integrating data into the platform as discussed in *Chapter 13 – Common System Integrations*.

Components

In 2014, Salesforce announced a redesign of the entire user interface for the platform called **Salesforce Lightning**. Salesforce Lightning takes a modern, component-centric approach to building and delivering applications on the platform, replacing the previous legacy page-centric model.

As part of this, developers and partners can build and release pre-built components for administrators and consultants to use in building out their applications on the platform. Some common examples are components for charting, visualizing data hierarchies, or managing related records and data.

Consultants

Although not offering pre-built solutions, AppExchange also offers a directory of Salesforce Partners that offer consulting services, **System Integrators** (**SI**). In the course of this book, we have referenced points where there are different considerations if the implementation work is being carried out by an external supplier. If you don't have in-house Salesforce knowledge or need additional capacity to deliver your solution, AppExchange is where you can find people who can help. All the companies listed are official Salesforce Partners, which means they met the criteria for the Salesforce program and benefit from Salesforce-run enablement.

This covers the types of solutions that you can find on AppExchange and some of the common use cases. The next step is discovering what apps are available and matching them to your requirements. We learn how to do this in the next section.

Getting the most from AppExchange

In this section, we learn about the different ways to identify apps, analyze your requirements to understand what is important, and select and then install apps from AppExchange. We start by searching the site itself.

Searching the AppExchange

When you begin navigating the AppExchange, you will be presented a list of solution cards as shown in the following image.

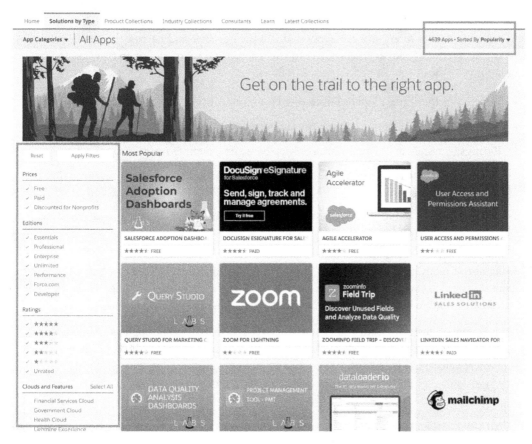

Figure 14.1 – AppExchange

In the top right, which is highlighted, you can see that the default ordering for applications is by popularity, that is, the number of installs. You can choose to change this to any of the following:

- **Popularity**
- **Rating**
- **Release Date**
- **Name**
- **Provider**

Doing so will update the list of items you will be presented and how they are organized. On the left of the screen is a set of filters you can apply that will further filter and narrow the results for you. The available filters are grouped to allow you to select a granular set of criteria to focus on the right solution for you. The categories of filters are as follows:

- **Prices**: Whether **Free**, **Paid**, or **Discounted for Nonprofits**
- **Editions**: Which Salesforce editions are supported
- **Ratings**: A system of 0-5 stars rating the app based on customer reviews
- **Cloud and Features**: Particular Salesforce clouds (i.e., solutions) or features that the solution supports
- **Other Filters**: Whether the application is native, is part of the Pledge 1% program, and so on.
- **Languages**: Which languages the application supports

Selecting one or many of these filters and then pressing **Apply Filters** will narrow down the list of solutions displayed to you. Additionally, you can choose to search across AppExchange using keywords to describe the solution or utilize some of the pre-defined categories provided by Salesforce.

Clicking on any single listing card will enable you to see the details of the application including its features, an overview, demo videos, details of the application, reviews, and links to the provider's website where you can find more information.

> **Tip**
>
> When you consider the rating, don't just look at the overall score; read at least some of the reviews. Check when the reviews were left – if there haven't been any reviews for a while there might not have been any updates. The reviews can be a great way of finding out whether people have problems setting up the app or whether any expected features missing. If it is a paid app with support, you would expect to see people from the ISV respond to reviews, particularly ones that ask questions.

With this understanding of how to navigate AppExchange, we can now discuss the power of AppExchange for a customer and how to best work with AppExchange solutions.

Discovering apps from the Demo Jam

A great way to learn about apps on AppExchange is via the **Demo Jam**. A Demo Jam is an event where app providers compete against each other and provide three-minute demos of their solution to win a Demo Jam trophy. This is a great, time-efficient way to understand the capability of the apps available. The Demo Jam has a strict set of rules: it is a live demo only, it can be no more than three minutes, and it is voted for by the audience. All this means the demos are really well rehearsed and focused on showing as much of the app as possible.

These events happen monthly online, hosted by AppExchange, or in person at Salesforce events or Salesforce community-hosted conferences. You can find more information about Salesforce Community Conferences in the *Further reading* section. Many of these events are recorded and available to view on AppExchange YouTube (`https://www.youtube.com/@AppExchangeTV`). The events hosted by AppExchange usually have a theme, allowing you to find sessions that have the types of apps that are relevant to you. The AppExchange YouTube channel also has testimonials from customers and video summaries of many of the Salesforce Labs apps, so it is a great place to learn about the capability of AppExchange.

The Power of AppExchange

We have seen that AppExchange offers us a variety of different solution types that we can incorporate into our system, which enable us to both deliver more and deliver faster. It is this underlying ability that is the basis of the power of AppExchange.

Firstly, when you are capturing requirements for your system, you should look to map these requirements to the different capabilities of Sales Cloud and see where there are gaps between what is required and what is possible through basic configuration and customization.

At this point, you have three options to deal with these requirement gaps:

- Discuss whether these requirements are truly needed or not. If not, then it may be best to remove them from the scope and discuss them later.

- Custom-build a solution to meet these requirements from scratch using the declarative and/ or programmatic development tools for the platform.

- Look to see if there is a possible solution on AppExchange to meet these requirements and evaluate whether it should be utilized.

It is always advised to undertake the first option from the preceding list and verify the importance of the requirements where there are gaps. Often, "wish list" items will make it onto the requirements list and can derail a project if they are not carefully considered and discussed. It is common on larger projects to rank requirements using the **MoSCoW rating system**:

- **Must**: Key requirements for the solution

- **Should**: Important features that would hamper usage and adoption if not delivered

- **Could**: Features that could improve adoption and processes but are not key

- **Would**: Requirements that the customer would like to have but are not currently important

Once it is determined that the requirement is needed, then you should review AppExchange to see whether a solution exists that meets this requirement, particularly in instances of larger feature sets.

Solutions released on the AppExchange must go through a security review process in which Salesforce verifies that the application has followed the best practices and principles for development on the platform and that the application does not contain any security vulnerabilities. This is one of the key benefits of a solution from AppExchange versus a custom-built solution, which is not likely to be held to the same level or rigor.

AppExchange providers also offer ongoing updates and support as part of their agreement, ensuring that you can continue to benefit from the latest improvements and updates to the solution. You will typically find as well that AppExchange solutions will have extensive features that you may not have considered, which you can make use of in the future, further enhancing your organization's productivity and ability to deliver.

If you are working with an external provider, they will be well-placed to assist you in providing recommendations for specific applications and solutions based on your needs and their experiences. Many solution providers will also be able to recommend other partners or solutions that interoperate well together to help improve the time to deliver.

It is easy to see that AppExchange offers many benefits for customers and implementation teams, so, let us now look at how you would implement a solution purchased from AppExchange.

Installing an AppExchange solution

There are two primary ways a solution can be installed from AppExchange. Either by purchase and install via the AppExchange checkout process, or through a package link provided by the ISV partner.

> **Salesforce checkout versus vendor invoicing**
>
> ISV partners can choose to bill customers for paid solutions through either the Salesforce Checkout or via what is known as the **Channel Order Application (COA)**. Salesforce Checkout allows a customer to pay using their credit card through AppExchange and requires no involvement from the partner. The COA route is used when partners wish to manage their invoicing and additional steps may be involved in setting up the application. In either scenario, the implementation process and practices discussed here still apply, only the initial steps change. In the rest of this section, we will assume the Salesforce Checkout process is used, as a simplified version of this is utilized by free applications like the examples shown.

To install an application from AppExchange, visit the app's listing and press the **Get It Now** button. To provide a complete illustration, we will install the free Salesforce Adoption Dashboards app from the Salesforce Labs team. *Figure 14.2* shows the standard format of a listing page with the **Get It Now** button.

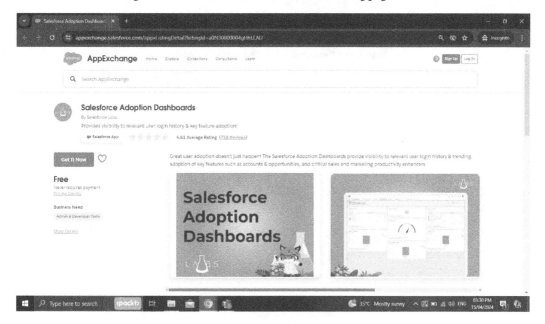

Figure 14.2 – An AppExchange app listing

You will then be prompted to log in with your Trailblazer account, and then you will be asked to choose an environment to install the application in, as shown in the following image.

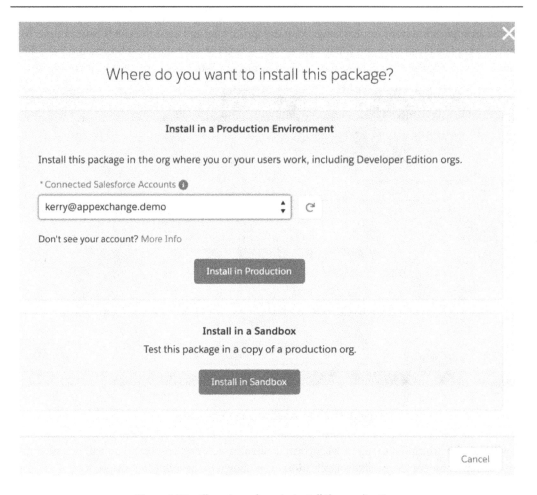

Figure 14.3 – Choosing where to install the application

It is a best practice to always install the application into a Sandbox first as you can test the application's functionality and verify that it meets your requirements. Setting up an app from AppExchange is no different to performing any other development with Salesforce and you should avoid installing directly into Production wherever possible.

Once you have selected the environment, you will be redirected to authenticate and accept the relevant terms of service for the application as shown in *Figure 14.4*.

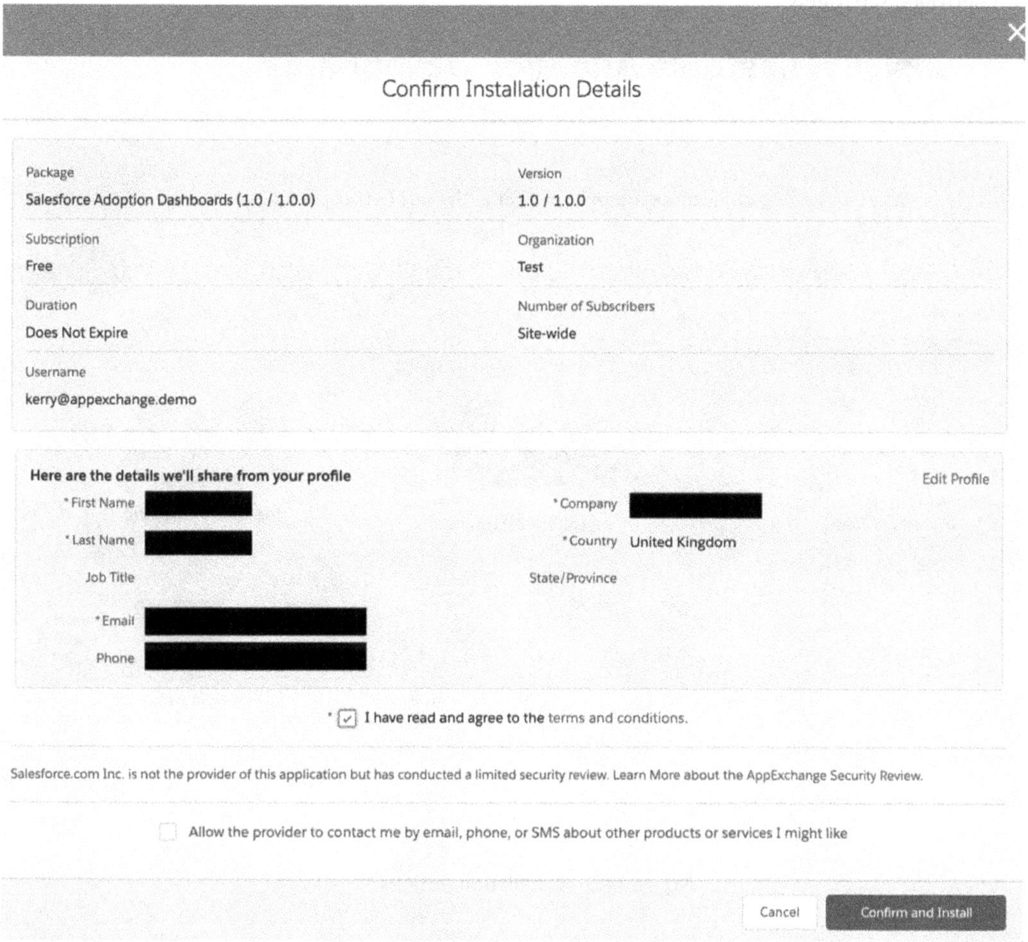

Figure 14.4 – Confirming installation details

You will then be asked who you would like to install the application for, as shown in *Figure 14.5*. This screen is a legacy implementation for control, and all options will have the same effect as licensing is now controlled separately.

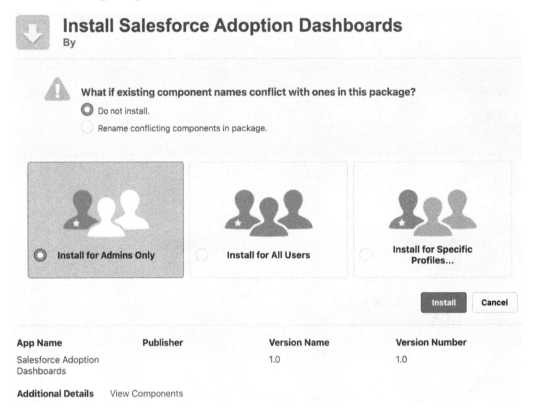

Figure 14.5 – Installation options

Once you press the install button, the application will begin installing into your Org. This process can take anywhere from a few seconds to around an hour depending on the application's size and complexity. If the installation is taking more than a few minutes, you will be notified via email when the installation is complete.

At this point, you can begin to configure the application for your needs and requirements. Depending on the size of the application, the ISV may have its own implementation team to help implement or suggest a partner to assist. This is particularly true in larger implementations of solutions such as a finance system or **enterprise resource planning** (**ERP**) solution. In these situations, you should ensure that roles and responsibilities are clearly defined with the handover between the implementation teams well understood and structured.

We have now seen the process of how to install an application into our Org, ready for implementation, and discussed when you may need to work with other partners to support this implementation. We will now finish the chapter by discussing some of the common application types you may wish to review to enhance your Sales Cloud implementation.

Common types of applications to enhance your implementation

In this section, we will list out and describe at a high level some of the more common application types that you may want to consider to enhance your Sales Cloud implementation. This list is not meant to be exhaustive, but it will help you think about additional ways you can deliver requirements for your sales team's Sales Cloud solution. Let's review the decisions and discussion points you should be aware of when evaluating solutions.

Salesforce Labs solutions

As mentioned earlier in the chapter, there are a number of solutions that are created by Salesforce Labs. These are free, so it is a good place to start, however, it is also worth remembering that these don't benefit from the level of support you get with paid apps.

The following are some of the apps that were available at the time of writing. A link to a summary video on YouTube has been included with each.

- **Task Follow-Up Rules**: This gives business Users the ability to set rules to automatically create follow-up tasks. See `https://youtu.be/w62UZrIfZdg?si=_uEkx7jFXNgfqoNz`.

- **Time Warp**: This is a horizontal timeline component that can be added to the page layout of different Objects. As an admin, you can decide what records you want to display on the timeline. See `https://youtu.be/D2k26qaKztk?si=4MvAo_oZXxVBr8rB`.

- **Multi-Factor Authenticator Dashboard**: This allows you to monitor and audit multi-factor authentication adoption in your Org. See `https://youtu.be/OahdDjwIAw0?si=HO04-B0_ysCRfcLU`.

- **Consent Capture**: This Flow template works with the standard consent Objects. The template allows you to see and set up Consent records from the Lead and Contact records. See `https://www.youtube.com/watch?v=MSfYNeSO0lO`.

- **Lead Scoring Process**: This allows the creation of rules to define a lead score based on Lead and Campaign Member data. See `https://appexchange.salesforce.com/appxListingDetail?listingId=a0N300000024tT3EAI`.

Consider these apps are a starting point or a pact for inspiration, particularly if you don't have any specific budget or you are looking for a stepping stone to justify a budget for a solution. You should thoroughly review the functionality and always test it in a Sandbox before deciding if it should be part of your solution. Be aware that these are not maintained in the same way as paid apps and it is possible they may be impacted by platform releases. It is likely that there is a more functionally rich paid app however this offers an option for those who don't have a budget.

Document creation

As part of your sales cycle, particularly in B2B organizations dealing with larger customers, you will need to generate many documents, such as quotes and contracts. A document creation or document generation solution can help you generate these documents in a consistent and controlled manner at scale, using your Salesforce data as the source of truth.

When considering which solution is right for your needs, it's important to think about the volume of documentation you typically create, the format you need it in, how you wish to distribute the document, and how much of the document is dynamic based upon data versus static standard text. Having a clear understanding of these needs will help you to choose a solution that enables your sales team to focus on selling whilst maintaining a consistent and clear structure and format for all your documentation. Beware that depending on the capability of the tool, you might need to make changes to your data model, for example, make data available on different Objects. You will want to make sure you are very clear on what data you need to merge in, so you can confirm this is possible during the vendor assessment process.

Digital signatures

Once a customer has agreed to a purchase, they will often need to sign a contract, and this is more commonly done digitally now than using what is referred to as a "wet signature."

There are a variety of e-signature solutions on AppExchange that enable you to send contracts to customers for signature straight from Salesforce, utilizing the underlying automation. Many solutions can also track information such as whether the contract has been opened and how long it has been viewed, as well as allowing for reminders to the signatory to ensure documents are not forgotten about. Some also allow you to capture data and write it directly into Salesforce Objects, an example being capturing a PO number or other data required to create an invoice.

Accounting

Connecting your finance and sales systems to make your invoicing and financial management simple is a common requirement for businesses and helps alleviate the need for manual handover between the sales and finance teams. This both saves significant time and reduces human error.

There are several native finance applications on Salesforce, as well as solutions that can integrate Salesforce with your existing accounting platform, enabling users to collaborate more effectively to ensure bills are paid on time. A common example is allowing the account executive for an account to be able to see and be notified of overdue invoices so that they can proactively engage with the customer to resolve issues using a pre-existing relationship.

Marketing

As discussed in *Chapter 4 – Design and Build: The Lead Generation Process*, the sales team will need leads to pursue and convert into opportunities and closed businesses for the organization to succeed. Marketing applications can work hand in hand with Sales Cloud to connect the sales and marketing teams and ensure that you have a single source of truth and data platform for all your marketing data that is then handed to sales as qualified leads.

Some example solutions might include integrations with social media, email campaign tools, SMS messaging and marketing tools, or data enrichment tools.

These are all common types of applications you may want to consider to enhance your Sales Cloud implementation and deliver greater value to the organization by bringing disparate systems and data sets together. Let us review what we have covered in this chapter.

Summary

We began this chapter by discussing what AppExchange is and the types of solutions you could find on AppExchange. We then looked at how you can search and navigate AppExchange, adding filters and narrowing down the results to the right solution for you.

Following this, we discussed why AppExchange is so powerful for customers and consultants and how the Salesforce Security Review process ensures that you are getting a well-structured solution that can help you grow and scale.

We then looked at the process and steps involved in installing a solution from AppExchange and when an external party may become involved. We then finished the chapter with an overview of some of the most common types of applications you may want to install in your Org to enhance your Sales Cloud implementation.

Further reading

AppExchange

- *App List:*

  `https://appexchange.salesforce.com/learn?contentType=app-listicle`

Salesforce Community Conferences

- *Trailhead: Salesforce Community Groups:*

  `https://trailhead.salesforce.com/content/learn/modules/`
  `trailblazer-community-basics/discover-community-conferences`

- *Community Conference Timetable:*

  `https://trailhead.salesforce.com/community/conferences`

Index

packtpub.com

Subscribe to our online digital library for full access to over 7,000 books and videos, as well as industry leading tools to help you plan your personal development and advance your career. For more information, please visit our website.

Why subscribe?

- Spend less time learning and more time coding with practical eBooks and Videos from over 4,000 industry professionals

- Improve your learning with Skill Plans built especially for you

- Get a free eBook or video every month

- Fully searchable for easy access to vital information

- Copy and paste, print, and bookmark content

Did you know that Packt offers eBook versions of every book published, with PDF and ePub files available? You can upgrade to the eBook version at packtpub.com and as a print book customer, you are entitled to a discount on the eBook copy. Get in touch with us at customercare@packtpub.com for more details.

At www.packtpub.com, you can also read a collection of free technical articles, sign up for a range of free newsletters, and receive exclusive discounts and offers on Packt books and eBooks.

Other Books You May Enjoy

If you enjoyed this book, you may be interested in these other books by Packt:

ChatGPT for Accelerating Salesforce Development

Andy Forbes, Philip Safir, Joseph Kubon, Francisco Fálder

ISBN: 978-1-83508-407-6

- Masterfully craft detailed and engaging user stories tailored for Salesforce projects
- Leverage ChatGPT to design cutting-edge features within the Salesforce ecosystem, transforming ideas into functional and intuitive solutions
- Explore the integration of ChatGPT for configuring Salesforce environments
- Write Salesforce flows with ChatGPT, enhancing workflow automation and efficiency
- Develop custom LWCs with ChatGPT's assistance
- Discover effective testing techniques using ChatGPT for optimized performance and reliability

Salesforce End-to-End Implementation Handbook

Kristian Margaryan Jørgensen

ISBN: 978-1-80461-322-1

- Discover the critical activities in Salesforce implementation
- Address common issues faced in implementing Salesforce
- Explore appropriate delivery methodology
- Understand the importance of a change management strategy
- Govern Salesforce implementation through all its phases
- Gain insights on key activities in the continuous improvement phase
- Leverage customer 360 for analytics, AI and automation

Packt is searching for authors like you

If you're interested in becoming an author for Packt, please visit `authors.packtpub.com` and apply today. We have worked with thousands of developers and tech professionals, just like you, to help them share their insight with the global tech community. You can make a general application, apply for a specific hot topic that we are recruiting an author for, or submit your own idea.

Share Your Thoughts

Now you've finished *Salesforce Sales Cloud - An Implementation Handbook*, we'd love to hear your thoughts! Scan the QR code below to go straight to the Amazon review page for this book and share your feedback or leave a review on the site that you purchased it from.

https://packt.link/r/1-804-61964-7

Your review is important to us and the tech community and will help us make sure we're delivering excellent quality content.

Download a free PDF copy of this book

Thanks for purchasing this book!

Do you like to read on the go but are unable to carry your print books everywhere?

Is your eBook purchase not compatible with the device of your choice?

Don't worry, now with every Packt book you get a DRM-free PDF version of that book at no cost.

Read anywhere, any place, on any device. Search, copy, and paste code from your favorite technical books directly into your application.

The perks don't stop there, you can get exclusive access to discounts, newsletters, and great free content in your inbox daily

Follow these simple steps to get the benefits:

1. Scan the QR code or visit the link below

https://packt.link/free-ebook/9781804619643

2. Submit your proof of purchase
3. That's it! We'll send your free PDF and other benefits to your email directly

www.ingramcontent.com/pod-product-compliance
Lightning Source LLC
Chambersburg PA
CBHW080614060326
40690CB00021B/4693